Samantha's Diary

A Hotwife's First Erotic Adventure

D.Z. Morgan

HOUSE OF EROTICA

Published in 2023 by
House of Erotica
houseoferotica.uk

Contents

Samantha's Diary

1: The Setup

James

Dear reader,

My name is James, and this is a story about my wife, our relationship, and an erotic adventure that changed our lives forever. In the following chapters, you'll read the virtual diary of my wife, Samantha, as she records the various steps of her sexual journey. Each entry was written as an email to me to keep me informed as I allowed her – even encouraged her – to explore her sexual desires during a week we spent apart. Through her narratives, she not only discusses the intimate details of her extra-marital affairs, but she also shares her inner thoughts and feelings. I add a bit of my own writing along the way to disclose my reactions to her exploits, as well as to provide some context for what you will be reading.

Samantha and I met and began dating when we were both 18 years old. We were married when we were 22 years old. The story of her diary began when we were 26, and since we were virgins when we met, I was the only person she'd ever slept with and vice-versa. For the bulk of our relationship, the thought had never crossed my mind about Samantha being intimate with anyone else. Why would it? Samantha and I loved each other very much, and we both felt sexually fulfilled. We were young, fit, and full of life. We had sex regularly, more days than not, and often more than once a day. There was nothing missing in our sex life, or at least that's how it began.

You're probably wondering what we look like. Samantha is a slender natural blonde with stunning blue eyes and the sweetest dimples when she smiles. She has a small, slightly upturned nose that shows light freckles when she's been in the sun. Her lips are full, symmetrical, and perfect. She has the slender physique, limber arms, and the long, toned legs of a dancer. A healthy regimen of long-distance running and dance has kept her body in fantastic shape. At 26, she is just as much the perky, energetic young beauty she was when I met her in our teenage years. Although she is naturally fair-skinned, she develops a beautiful tan in the summertime from her time spent outdoors, often in a bikini to help reduce her tan lines. I like to tease her about how sexy her tan lines are to me – when I see the contrast between her sun-kissed skin and the lighter skin of her breasts and her backside, I know that I'm seeing parts of her no other man – or at least, very few – ever get to see. And although she rolls her eyes when I mention this, I know the compliment is well-received.

On to some of Samantha's, ahem, finer features. Scanning up from her legs, you would find the most wonderful, lifted, bubble of a butt framed by her narrow hips. She has a cute, conspicuous freckle on her left butt cheek that I sometimes like to kiss. Her breasts are natural C-cups – slightly more breast than I can hold in each hand. Her silver-dollar nipples are light in color; although they tend not to stand very erect, they are well-matched and quite sensitive to the touch. Her vagina is small, tight, and symmetrical. She keeps her bikini area waxed throughout the year, for my viewing pleasure. The outer lips of her labia rest gently together, concealing her inner lips entirely within. Upon spreading her lips apart, her small, delicate clitoris is revealed. It goes without saying, but this is also rather sensitive to the touch.

I've also asked Samantha to provide a description of me. I think it's rather generous, but here it is:

> James has olive skin and dark, wavy hair. He usually has a well-kept beard or sometimes facial stubble. His hazel eyes are deep-set, soft, and caring. His nose is balanced, and his chin and jawline are firm but not protruding. He has thick, expressive eyebrows that I know he sometimes trims.
>
> He's around average or slightly below-average height, about the same as me, but I find that he's the perfect height to cuddle at night and to kiss while standing face-to-face. He works out every day, so of course he has great muscle definition. He has the coveted inverted-triangle build, wider at the shoulders and narrower at the hips. He has well-defined back muscles like a swimmer, and his arms stand out in a tank top. His pecs are built from working the bench press, but they still are soft enough to lay my head upon. He's a runner, so his legs are strong, and his butt is round and firm – at times I'm a little jealous! It certainly does the job of keeping his pants upright, and when he wears jeans or slacks, the material tends to grip him tightly. Despite all this, he worries he's getting a "dad bod," so I tease that he has the fittest "dad bod" in the world. The "dad bod" joke comes from James's tendency to eat whatever horrible food he wants – or that I let him, I should

say. If I'm the one baking cookies, he's the one eating them. Because of his eating habits, he doesn't exactly have 6-pack abs, but he doesn't have a beer gut either. I tell him that his main issue is his posture, as when he stands up straight and tightens his abs, he could pass as a fitness model.

Because James asked me to, I will describe his penis. Per our measurements, it is about 3.5 inches flaccid (barring when it's cold, he says) and 6.5 inches erect. From what we've read on the internet, his thickness is a bit above average but not overwhelmingly so. His dick points straight out when erect, is a uniform color that matches his skin tone, and does not have any odd bumps or blemishes. He is circumcised, and the head is proportional to the shaft. He keeps his pubic hair trimmed but not shaven, per my request. His testicles are normal-sized and very sensitive – any testicle play and he squirms, so usually we avoid that unless I'm mad at him for something (and then it's on!). Overall, I'm very pleased with his penis and wouldn't change a thing about it, or anything else about James. He's confided to me that he wishes it were bigger, but I get the sense that most men feel that way a little.

Hopefully these descriptions give you an adequate picture. I hope you see us as appealing, as the upcoming stories feature us – especially Samantha – in rather raunchy positions. Alternatively, I encourage you to visualize us however you like, in whatever way you find attractive. Bear in mind that to me, Samantha is a perfect physical specimen, a person as beautiful on the outside as she is within, who I feel blessed to be with every day. Samantha says she feels the same way about me – that given the chance, she would change nothing about me. My hope is to give each reader at least a glimpse of that experience in your own imagination, with imagery from your own inner world. To that end, please indulge me in a brief mental exercise.

Take a moment now to visualize the "Samantha" and "James" you'd like to imagine. Perhaps you enjoyed the descriptions I've given, or perhaps you'd prefer your own fantasy couple. Perhaps you'd like to imagine *yourself* as one the characters, whoever you relate to best. Maybe the other character looks like your spouse, your hairdresser, the person you have a crush on at work, your favorite celebrity, or "the one that got away." We could look like people of your own mental creation. Imagine me as a woman, if you prefer – the choice is yours. I would ask that you close your eyes for a moment and envision the characters' bodies, what they look like in clothes, and what they look like when they're not wearing clothes. Think of their faces – what they look like when they smile, when they're sad, when they're angry or perplexed. Imagine the features of their hair, or lack thereof – and their body hair, or lack thereof. Do you have specific images in mind? Good. Now we can proceed.

***

Let me set the stage for how my wife's erotic adventure came to pass. One evening after a session of lovemaking, we laid together in bed reflecting on one of our mutual friends, Todd, who had always seemed to have problems in his dating life. He was our age, and although he was attractive and often had dates, he rarely spent time with a woman for more than a few weeks. We were discussing how Todd recently went on some dates with Samantha's friend, Jenny, but that the fling had ended in less than a month. In my naivety, I remarked that Todd must be lonely and was probably feeling desperate for sex.

"Hmm, I don't think so," Samantha said. "Not from what I've heard."

"What do you mean?" I asked.

"Well, Todd and Jenny can have sex without being in a relationship."

"True." Her certainty made me curious. "Wait, do you have inside information on this?"

"Maybe. Jenny and I are good friends, and we girls do talk about these things, you know."

"Actually, I don't. I knew that *some* girls talked about that stuff. I didn't know *you* did."

"Not with just anyone," Samantha assured me. "But Jenny and I have been friends for years. She likes talking about her love life, whether she's bragging or complaining or whatever."

"And was she bragging about Todd, or complaining?" I added a nervous laugh, as I felt a bit intrusive for asking.

"A little of both," she said. She sounded playful.

"Oh, never mind," I said, as my rational mind won over. Todd was a good friend. "I don't think I want to know."

"Suit yourself." She turned away and pulled the comforter up around her shoulders.

I sat in silence for a moment, thinking. "Sam," I said finally. "Do you tell Jenny about *us* in that way?"

Samantha looked towards me. "You and me? No, I don't."

"Well, why not?"

"You're my husband, James. You're different. Jenny, she just tells me about guys she's hooking up with. It's funny gossip, but nothing serious."

"Oh, ok. That makes sense." I was quiet again for a moment. "But if you *did* tell her about our sex life, what would you say?"

Samantha rolled over toward me and placed her arm on my chest, bringing her head nearer to my ear. Softly, she said, "I'd say that my husband rocks my world in bed every night. With his firm, strong body. And his big, hard dick."

I felt my cock awaken under the covers. It was funny to hear my wife talk to me like this. I knew most of what she was saying was true, as we did have a fabulous sex life and had given each other many earth-shattering orgasms over the years. But I also felt a bit strange when she complimented my dick, knowing that from what I've seen and read about online, my penis was fairly close to average. Also, because my wife was a virgin when we met, I knew she didn't have much to compare to in real life. Nonetheless, knowing Samantha loved me and wanted me to feel good about myself warmed me inside.

"Hmm," I moaned, as my hand reached down to stimulate my restless cock. An idea came to me. I thought about how her friends, like Jenny, probably told her stories about various sexual partners who had different physical qualities than me, different moves in bed, maybe even some interesting kinks. I wondered what Samantha thought of those stories, given her limited personal experience, and without thinking, I started a line of conversation to explore that idea. I didn't yet know it, but I was opening a Pandora's Box of sorts.

"I'm glad you think my dick is big," I said in an appreciative tone, trying to conceal my intention. "Good thing for me, it's the only dick you've ever seen in person." I waited, my hand slowly stroking my growing cock, and I sensed Samantha pause.

"I wouldn't quite say that," she finally answered. "But close."

I stopped what I was doing. I was initially going to ask her what kinds of stories she'd heard from her friends that made her curious, but now I'd stumbled upon something else entirely. "Wait, you told me I'm the only man you've ever slept with. When were you with someone else?"

"Well, of course I wasn't *with* anyone else." There was a hint of defensiveness in her voice. "I'm just saying I may have seen a dick or two in person before, that's all."

"A dick *or two*?" I had abandoned touching my penis, but for some reason it kept getting hard. "Samantha – I'm intrigued. Would you mind telling me about this?"

"Oh my God, it's no big deal, please. Trust me, I've never been with anyone else, and I'd never cheat on you."

"I trust you," I said. "Truly. But I have to admit – you've got me curious. I want to know what you've experienced."

"Really? There's not much to tell."

"Please," I said. "I love you. You're sexy, and your body drives me crazy. I'm sure it drives other men crazy, too. I think it would be kind of hot to hear about your stories, of other men you've turned on in the past. I'm sure they'd be interesting, and – it's hard to explain, but it's kind of turning me on."

"It is?" she asked. She sounded surprised. "It's honestly nothing to talk about, but since you're curious, I guess I can indulge you."

I settled back down in the bed, placing my hand on my swollen cock, prepared to listen.

"Ok," she said, "the first time wasn't long before I met you. Remember how I briefly had a boyfriend before you? My first boyfriend ever?"

"Tommy-boy?" Tom, whom Samantha referred to as Tommy-boy for some reason which made me faintly jealous, was a football player at our high school. He was an offensive lineman, tall, sturdy, and somewhat overweight. He mostly rode the bench on the team and was known as a "gentle giant" at our school. When I first learned Samantha had dated him, I was surprised, as she seemed so much better-looking than him. Samantha was a late bloomer in high school, which protected her from the superficial "popular" crowd. I'm sure it was the only reason I had a chance with her, as she always valued personality over looks. Anyhow, I went on, "Didn't you only date him for a couple of weeks?"

"I did. We were both very timid, I was surprised when it happened. I think we only kissed maybe two or three times."

"But at some point you saw his dick?" My tone of shock was meant to mask my excitement.

"Yes. Well, more like I felt it. We were in the pool at his parents' house. Everyone else had gone inside and it was getting dark when he grabbed me and started kissing me. I remember his hands moved down to my ass, and it felt surreal, as it was the first time a guy had ever touched me that way." I imagined Samantha as a cute, vibrant 18-year-old, wearing her small, black-and-white striped bikini in a pool with that big oaf, Tom. I saw his hands sliding down and touching her backside, first over the cloth of her bikini bottoms and then finding the flesh of her lovely ass that the bottoms didn't quite cover. In that moment, I felt both like Tom and myself, taking the place of Tom in Sam's memory while feeling aroused and deeply jealous.

"And then?" I urged her forward with her story while my hand picked up speed on my cock. She could clearly tell I was aroused by this, although she was likely confused about why. Nevertheless, she continued in her sexy, low voice.

"As he squeezed my ass, he pulled me closer to him, closer to his body. At first, I felt my stomach press against his belly. But as he pulled me tighter into him, I could feel his hard cock poking me in the abdomen. It was my first time feeling a penis."

My eyes closed tight, and I was engrossed in the imagery she cast in my mind. "Did you know at that point? Did you know right away that you were feeling his penis?"

"I did. It was pretty obvious."

My stomach lurched. Something about the way she said that made me feel even more jealous, but also more aroused. "It was obvious, huh? You mean, it was really big?"

Samantha laughed. "Oh my God, no. I meant it was obvious because of what we were doing. Looking back, I actually think it was probably pretty small."

"Oh." I laughed nervously again, both relieved and a little let down. "You mean you could tell?"

"Well, as we were kissing, he eventually untied his swimming shorts and maneuvered my hand toward his cock. I remember feeling it in my hand, thinking about how I was actually holding a boy's hard cock, a cock that I had made hard myself. I didn't know what to expect, but like I said, I think it was kind of small. I think my hand covered most of its length, and it didn't feel all that thick either. It was very hard though, I was a little surprised."

"What did you think about it? Did you know at the time that it was small?"

"I don't think I knew. The whole situation was new to me, and I had no real comparison back then. I wasn't really judging his cock, just thinking about the fact that I was holding it, that it felt so hard, and that it was me who had made it that way. I liked the feeling, it was sort of – empowering."

"That makes sense," I said. I tried to put myself in her shoes, considering how a young woman would feel when touching a man's hard cock for the first time. Empowering – that made sense. "And what happened next?"

"Well, I don't think I was holding his cock for much more than a minute before his mom came outside and called for us to come in. She couldn't see what were doing, so we felt like we got away with it."

"I see," I said. I was still imagining the scene.

"You know," she went on. "I didn't know his dick was small until the first time I was with you." She looked up into my eyes. "When I first pulled your cock out, I was so impressed." She reached for my erection under the covers, and I relinquished control. She massaged me gently as she continued. "Tom was a big guy, so I assumed his penis was proportional. But when I saw yours, I was like, 'Damn.' It made me forget about *his* in a second."

"Thanks, babe. I'm glad I make you happy." My mind briefly flashed to the first time I revealed my manhood to her, the first time any girl had seen my penis, her reaction of telling me it was "so big," and how that comment had filled me with joy. But the memory was fleeting, and that's a story for another time. I closed my eyes and let her stroke me for a few more seconds, waiting to hear if she'd say any more. Eventually, I broke the silence.

"Was that it?" I asked. "Did anything like that ever happen with Tom again?"

"No," she replied, letting go of my dick. "We broke up pretty soon after that. It didn't have anything to do with what happened in the pool," she added quickly. "I just wasn't that into him. He seemed a little too immature for me – too boyish."

I brushed the imagery away. The excitement of the story had ended, but my penis was still hard, and I hadn't finished. I felt a little too tired for more intercourse, but I wondered if I could still get information that would help me achieve an orgasm.

"Samantha," I said gently.

"Hmm?" she asked absently, clearly starting to drift.

"You know, you said you've seen *two* other penises before."

"I did? Yeah, I guess I said that."

The idea of a second story intrigued me even more. I had forgotten about her first boyfriend Tom because he was such a minor detail in her life. But I knew for a fact that she hadn't dated anyone else but Tom and me. What was this second story she had in mind? When did this happen?

"Care to tell me about it?"

"Maybe," she said, clearly hesitant. "Promise not to get mad?"

Another unexpected turn. Had she done something wrong? She already said she hadn't cheated on me. I felt panicked chills run through my body, but I needed her to go on. "I can't make that promise," I said, "But I think I need to know."

"I didn't cheat on you," she assured me again. "Trust me, nothing like that happened."

"Ok. Thanks for telling me. But I'm still dying to know – what *did* happen?"

She went on. "It was back in college. Remember when my dance team went out of state to the team competition one summer? The one where we made it to the semi-finals?"

"Of course," I said. I hadn't traveled with her that occasion, as I was working a summer job at the time to earn some money. "So what happened?"

"Well, at the same time as the dance competition, there was a basketball clinic taking place at the university. Both the basketball players and the dancers were housed in dormitories that were vacant during the summer term."

"Ok." I was eager for her to continue. "Go on."

"One night, a group of us girls met in one of the dorm rooms with a few of the basketball players. I never told you because we did some drinking that night, and I know you were nervous about me drinking when you weren't around."

"I remember. I don't mind the drinking. What happened at the party?"

"We started playing some drinking games – King's cup, flip cup, fuck the dealer, normal college stuff, you know? And I could tell one of the basketball players was eyeing me all night, giving me 'the look.' He was tall, of course, over 6 foot. He was reasonably handsome, dark features—"

"Ok, ok," I said, slightly annoyed that she had used the word *handsome*. "So what, he whipped his penis out at the party or something?" I wanted her to move forward, and my jealousy started to come out in my tone.

"No," she said. "But with all the drinking going on and my low tolerance for alcohol at the time, I started to feel drunk pretty fast, and then a little sick. I asked one of the girls to walk me back to our dorm, but she said no. I wasn't sure I could find my way across campus on my own, so of course, this guy who was eyeing me offered to walk me back."

"How chivalrous," I said, taking offense. I could imagine what was on his mind.

"I remember walking back across the campus," she went on, "trying desperately to drop hints that I had a boyfriend whom I was crazy about. But he kept changing the topic, commenting on how nice the air felt that night, how pretty I looked in the moonlight. I remember he was wearing a loose tank top that showed his long, toned arms, and he had on basketball shorts that didn't quite contain his junk very well – I'm pretty sure he wasn't wearing any underwear."

"Really?" I tried to soften my tone, not wanting to discourage Samantha from telling me all the details. "Were you looking?"

"I guess a little. I mean, I think he was trying to make it obvious, he kept pulling his shorts up in a way that showed the outline of his penis."

"And? What did you think?"

"Honestly, I was trying to ignore it. Again, I just wanted to get home and kept trying to talk about you. Eventually, we arrived at my door. When we got there, I tried to take the keycard out of my purse, but I fumbled and dropped it. He picked it up before I could reach it, and he used it to open the door and let himself inside."

"That creep!" I said, feeling defensive of my wife.

"I was taken aback," she said, "but he was so casual about it. He said, 'Let me just make sure you can get yourself in bed. Then I'll leave.'"

"Wait," I said. The image wasn't quite complete in my mind. "What were you wearing?"

"Dance shorts," she said. "And a t-shirt." I knew of the shorts she was talking about. They were short, tight, and left little to the imagination. "I was basically already in my pajamas. But I was feeling nauseous, so I went straight into the bathroom. He stayed in the bedroom while I splashed some water on my face and attempted to sober up. I nearly got sick and hardly remembered he was in there. But when I left the bathroom, there he was, just lying on my bed. Naked."

"Completely naked?!" I asked. "That must have been horrifying for you!"

"It kind of was," she admitted. "His dick was already erect even, and he was leaning back on the bed, presenting it to me as if he were proud of it."

"So, what did you think? Did he have something to be proud of?"

"He did. I mean, if you're into that sort of thing."

"So, it was big?"

"Yes. It may in part have been the angle, but it looked pretty huge. He held one hand around the base of it by his balls, and I'm betting he could fit two more hands around the shaft before getting to the head." I heard a tone of awe in her voice.

"Did – did you like it?"

"Hell, no!" she answered. "I was drunk as hell and wanted him to get the heck out so I could sleep! I already told that dumb asshole that I wasn't interested and had a boyfriend, but I guess he didn't take no for an answer. Well, anyway, his little stunt sobered me up pretty quick. I grabbed a hairbrush from the desk and chucked it at him, screaming at him to get out. He jumped up, grabbed his clothes and struggled to pull his shorts up over his erection, shouting, 'I'm sorry, I'm sorry!' The only reason I didn't freak out more is because of how sorry he seemed and how quickly he left. I suppose a person could feel traumatized by the experience, but I was just glad it was over. I went instantly to sleep, woke up hung over the next morning, and moved on with my life. It really meant nothing to me, but looking back, I guess I should have told you."

I appreciated her assurances. I actually thought that she was right not to tell me, because in the heat of the moment, I'm sure I would have freaked out and called the police. The whole aftermath may have then made the situation even more traumatizing, whereas Samantha had preferred to just put it behind her.

"So, what do you think?" she asked. "Are you mad? Disturbed?"

I reflected. My erection was gone, totally ruined by my outrage about the guy's behavior. It was curious that her first story made me so aroused, but this one just made me shocked and upset. "Disturbed? I'm disturbed about *him*. I'm glad you were okay and that it didn't traumatize you. But did you think about it much after the fact?"

"Not really. It felt a lot better to just pretend it didn't happen."

"That makes sense. But I wonder – clearly his cock was bigger than Tom's. I assume it was bigger than mine too." There was that pit in my stomach again, the mix of arousal and jealousy.

"Well, yes," she said. "But of course, that didn't matter to me."

"I know, I know," I assured her. "But it was the biggest cock you had ever seen. Didn't it make you a little curious?"

"Like curious how?" she asked suspiciously.

"Like, curious what it would feel like. Inside of you. I mean, some women swear that big cocks are better, that they feel better, or are more intense."

"What women?" she challenged.

"Internet women," I said sheepishly. "Like, women in forums on the Internet. Or women in movies or on TV, alluding to the glory of a giant cock. Don't tell me your girlfriends haven't bragged about a guy with a big penis."

"Okay, I won't lie. I may have heard that before."

"And haven't you been curious about it?"

"Not really, I'm satisfied with what I have. I've only ever wanted *you*, I've never needed anything else."

"I'm touched, honey, truly." I made sure to look her in the eyes. "I love you, and I know you'd never want to cheat on me."

"Of course not."

"But I guess what I'm asking is – haven't you ever wondered? Haven't you heard another woman talking about it, or seen it in porn, or thought back to that basketball player and had a moment of curiosity?"

She paused. "Fine," she said finally. "I guess as a passing thought, but nothing serious."

"Thank you," I said.

"For what?" she asked.

"For being honest with me. I asked you a sensitive question, and you were honest with me. I appreciate it."

"Okay," she said. "You're welcome. But really, it's getting late, and those are all the stories I have. Can we go to sleep, babe?"

"Of course," I said. "I love you."

"I love you too." And as I felt her drift off to sleep, I imagined her in the dormitory with the basketball player. Instead of chasing him out, she approaches him timidly, reaching for his giant cock and then stroking it with gently with her hand. The fantasy continues until Samantha is straddling his dick, the obscene length of it unable to push fully into her womanhood, his shaft and balls protruding from beneath her beautiful, moonlit ass. She rides him to a stunning climax, nearly screaming in unbridled pleasure. Caressing myself in bed, I reach a climax of my own, coming intensely into a wad of tissues and tossing it in the trash before falling straight to sleep.

***

After that night, I backed off from requesting more erotic stories. For one thing, I knew that Samantha didn't have more stories to tell. For another, I didn't want her to worry that I was obsessing about her fantasies and her past sex life. But the idea hadn't left my mind – for the first time, I had imagined my wife with another man, and something about it transfixed me.

A few weeks after our night of storytelling, I came home from work to find Samantha leaning over the counter in the kitchen, reading a magazine. She was wearing tight yoga pants and a tank top, and her back was toward me as I approached. I came up behind her, wrapped my arms around her waist, and began to bump my crotch playfully into her protruding behind.

"Hey, babe," she said without looking. "How was your day?"

"Good," I replied. I felt the perfect curvature of her ass against my crotch. I moved my hips front to back in a teasing, humping motion.

"You're in a fun mood," she said. "Are you trying to distract me from my reading?"

"Depends. Is it working?"

"A little," she answered. "But you're gonna have to be a bit bigger down there to entice me."

I knew that my wife had meant to imply an erection, but her choice of the word "bigger" had triggered something within me. "Oh," I said, keeping my tone playful and non-defensive. "You wish your husband was *bigger*, huh?"

"Ugh, you knew what I meant." But simply planting the idea in her mind had gotten me excited. My penis did start to grow bigger, and harder against her ass. I continued to grind on her, and soon my erection became too uncomfortable for my jeans. I turned my wife around and started kissing her as my hands went down to my waistline and started working on my belt. I pulled my erection free from my open pants, and she eagerly reached for it and gripped it in her hands as we continued to kiss. I pushed my pants and underwear down around my ankles, and then worked my hands around Samantha's lower back and down inside her yoga pants, feeling the soft skin and firm muscles of her lovely ass. Before long, with my tongue still darting in and out of her mouth, I pulled down her yoga pants and thong.

"James," she said, sounding astonished yet pleased. "You must have missed me today."

"I miss you constantly," I replied, somewhat lamely; the blood to my penis must have shut off my brain. I turned her around again with some force so she would lean over the counter, I kicked off my jeans from around my ankles, and I crouched to the floor so that my face was just under her backside. Her pants around her own ankles had kept her legs held mostly together, and I spread her ass cheeks and pushed them up gently to allow a direct view of her anus and her slowly opening flower. I could tell her juices were already flowing from the force of my sexual advance, but I nonetheless ran my tongue across the opening of her pussy to ensure she was pleasured and damp. She moaned and cooed softly as I did so, at first jumping a bit from the startle response that the sensation produced. I could taste the familiar, sweet flavor of her womanhood as I ran my tongue along her slit a few times, pausing each time to flick the end of my tongue against her tiny, sensitive clit.

I no longer could resist. Standing up, I took my rock-hard cock and started to massage the head and the shaft along the opening of her pussy, copying the previous motion of my tongue. In doing so, I allowed Samantha's natural wetness to lubricate my cock, which slid smoother along her folds as it grew moist. After a few tantalizing strokes, I pushed my head slowly into her opening. With her legs still closed as they were, her pussy felt even tighter than normal, and I had to work my cock in and out for several repetitions before the shaft went entirely in.

"Mmm," Samantha moaned as my full length pushed inside her. All the sensations, the warmth, the tightness, the slickness of her pussy, it all felt irresistible on the bare skin of my cock. For some reason, I began to imagine my cock was bigger than normal, thick to the point that it stretched and strained the walls of her pussy. I imagined Samantha experiencing the same thing, feeling stretched and overwhelmed by a cock much bigger than she was used to. Before long, the fantasy evolved into her being fucked by someone else's cock, not only thicker, but longer, and going deeper than my own cock could reach. Then I thought of Samantha taking my own dick, and I thought of her wishing I was fucking her harder and deeper like a larger man could. It compelled me to increase my speed and pressure as I fucked her harder, desperately trying to compete with a mystery man's performance. In what must have been less than five minutes of penetration, I achieved an orgasm I was unable to avert. I groaned from the exertion, and I could tell that Samantha had reached an orgasm of her own, as she was breathing hard, and I could feel the muscles of her vagina squeeze and contract against my throbbing cock. When my orgasm had finished, I kept the length of my shaft still buried in my wife's vagina as we struggled to catch our breath. I leaned forward and hugged her from behind, gently cupping her breasts through her tank top and kissing her at the base of the neck. I slowly withdrew my sword from its proverbial sheath, and then stepped away to allow Samantha to remove the yoga pants that were still around her ankles.

"Wow," she remarked. "That was intense."

"I know," I said.

"What came over you? Not that I'm complaining." It had been a while since we had had sex so spontaneously, and in the kitchen no less.

"I don't know," I replied, although a part of me knew. "Let's catch our breath and wash off. I think I have something to tell you."

"Okay," she replied, and I felt her eyes follow me as I left the room.

∗∗∗

Twenty minutes later, we had finished showering and were in our bedroom, lying on our bed with our towels still wrapped around our bodies. Samantha traced her fingers through the hair on my chest, avoiding eye contact. "So, what did you have to tell me?"

"It's not a big deal," I said. "Just something kind of sexy that's been on my mind a bit lately."

"Tell me." She looked up and eyed me carefully.

"I've been thinking about that night a few weeks ago when you told some stories about your past. Something about that night stuck with me."

"What was it?"

"I'm not sure," I said. "I've been trying to figure it out myself. Until that night, I had never even thought about you with another man. But somehow, just the notion is kind of – I guess – intriguing to me."

Samantha furrowed her brow. "What about it is intriguing?"

"That's what I'm struggling to understand. Maybe it's just a new way of fantasizing about you. If we hadn't met in high school and fallen in love, I'm sure your college days would have gone a lot different. I'm sure every guy in school would've wanted to date you."

"Okay," she said. "Things would have gone differently. So?"

"I'm just thinking aloud," I said. "I guess it's funny to think about all of the different situations you would've been in. The different experiences you would've had. The different guys you would've dated."

"You mean the different guys I would've *slept* with?"

"Yeah, well, that too."

"James," Samantha said seriously. "I don't regret falling in love with you while we were young. I don't have any wild dreams of being with a bunch of other guys. I'm completely happy being only with you."

"I know," I said. "It's silly. And I don't think I have any *true* jealousies. Like, I'm not worried some hot stud with a bigger dick is going to come steal you away from me or anything."

Samantha laughed. "Still curious about the size thing, huh?"

"I guess that's part of it," I confessed. "But apart from being jealous, the idea of you being with another man makes me feel turned on for some reason."

Samantha seemed shocked. "Really? Wait, is that why you came so hard earlier? Were you thinking about – something like that?"

"Sort of," I said. I explained to her about her use of the word "bigger," my fantasy that my cock was extra thick, and even thinking about Samantha with other men. "It's confusing," I said. "I don't understand why it turns me on, it just does."

"Alright," Samantha said. "Well, what does this mean?"

"I'm not sure," I answered. "Maybe it's something we can keep talking about to figure out? Maybe it's something to explore?"

Samantha considered this. "Like – you want me to be with someone else?"

"No, I don't think so," I said quickly. "Definitely not now, at least. I don't know." We paused for a moment, both unsure of what to say. "Hey, Sam," I began timidly. "Mind if I ask you something?"

"Sure."

"After that night you told me those stories from your past – did you think about those things at all after?"

"Not really." After a short pause, she said, "Well, maybe there was one thing."

I held my breath, awaiting her response. For context – my job requires me to leave town approximately one weekend per month. Samantha and I have an agreement that we're allowed to watch pornography during our time apart. Samantha explained that when she last accessed porn, she thought about what she was seeing a little differently. She went on.

"I usually watch lesbian porn or porn focused on the woman," she said. "I tend to notice her eyes, her body, her facial expressions. This last weekend I watched heterosexual porn, and I guess more than usual, I watched the man's dick."

"Really?" I was curious but unsure what to ask.

"Yeah," she went on, "I was drawn to the man's size and thought about what his dick might feel like. Like if it was inside of me." She suddenly stopped and turned to me, a sheepish look on her face. I could tell she was concerned for my reaction, like perhaps her words had hurt me.

"That's kind of hot, actually," I said. "I'm surprised you don't usually think of porn that way."

"I don't," she said. She ventured to go on. "In fact, it did make me think back to that basketball player I met in college. And for the first time, I guess I was a little bit curious. Not like I'd want to act on it, but just in a passive, fantasy sort of way. Like, just wondering about it."

"I get that. That's pretty much how I feel when I watch porn, to be honest. I've only ever been with you, so porn lets me explore fantasies of people I'd never be with. But I wouldn't even want that in real life. In real life I have you, and I don't need anyone else."

"Then we feel the same way," Samantha concluded.

"Kind of," I said. "We both fantasize about other people, but neither of us has an urge to actually be with anyone else." Lying back on the bed, I looked up at the ceiling, unsure if I could say my next thoughts directly to Samantha's face. "In a way it's different, though. If you thought of me with another woman, I assume the idea would be devastating and turn you off. But to me, the idea of you wanting another man, fantasizing about another man, and even being with another man would turn me on."

"I guess we are different that way. Does that bother you?"

"Not at all. Does it bother you?"

"I don't think so. But like I said, I'm not really sure what to do about it. Like, we discovered you have this turn-on, but I don't know what we should do."

"Maybe we shouldn't do anything," I said. "Maybe it's just a crazy idea, a phase that will pass. Soon enough, I'm sure the idea will start to freak me out."

"Maybe," Samantha said. "I guess we'll find out."

***

A few more months passed. In some ways I was right, a majority of the time I didn't have any thoughts at all of Samantha being with another man. However, when I'd return from my work trips, I'd be curious about the porn Samantha had been watching and how she'd experienced it. I'd ask her what she watched, what the actors looked like, and what she paid attention to. To my surprise, her interest continued to gravitate more toward the male talent than ever. She even confessed once that she had searched for the term "huge cock," just out of curiosity, she insisted. She said that those scenes were too intense and hardcore to her liking, but she did admit to being shocked and impressed at the male actors' erections. She empathized with the women, however: "That shit has to hurt," I recall her saying. "Like giving birth in reverse."

Apart from these short conversations about porn, our relationship was as normal and thriving as ever. We continued to have sex almost every day, and I hardly ever thought of her with other men. Meanwhile, we were having conversations about our careers and the idea of having children. I had recently gotten a promotion at work, and I used my increase in salary to save for a nice vacation south of the border in Cancun, Mexico. We booked our plane tickets and purchased a room at an all-inclusive, adults-only resort on the Mayan Riviera in the spring. As our tropical getaway approached, Samantha and I grew more and more excited to enjoy our trip together. I even took her shopping for new swimsuits, and I bought her some scandalous-looking items that I was sure would turn some heads at the beach. Things were going exactly as planned, until one night, less than two weeks before our expected travel date, I got an email from work.

"You're kidding me," I groaned, reading my email from my phone one evening while we hung out on the couch. "Our biggest client will be visiting from out of the country and is insisting on meeting with me. Right in the middle of our trip!"

"What?!" Samantha exclaimed. "Tell them no!"

"I want to," I said, "but I'm not sure I can. They're honestly our biggest account, and my work with them was a major reason for getting my promotion. They want me to personally tour them around our facilities, so I can't just video in."

We rushed to the computer to try to revise our travel itinerary. We learned that our plane tickets were non-refundable but were transferable – we could change them to another date, or even to another name. But the resort, which we had gotten a pretty good price on, was already holding a large deposit over our heads that we couldn't get back.

I sighed. "You should go without me. You can take a friend."

"What? No!" Samantha said. "No way. I only want to go with you."

"Well, you're not going with me," I lamented. "At least not this spring."

Samantha hugged her knees to her chest and pouted. It was disappointing to say the least. I imagined all the fun we could have had together, drinking cocktails on the beach, snorkeling in romantic coves, having sex in new and exotic places. That's when an idea hit me.

"Samantha, I have a suggestion. I want you to go on this trip if you're able to find a friend to go with you." Samantha was about to protest, but I cut her off. "Now hear me out. I'd like you to go on the trip, and I'd like you to go as if you were single."

"I beg your pardon?" she asked. She looked dumbfounded and distressed.

"Think about it," I said. "Those crazy fantasies I have, thinking of you having fun with other men, dating around, enjoying their attention—"

She caught on. "You want me to actually live out your fantasies? And flirt with other men?"

"Yeah," I replied. "Flirt with them, and maybe even more. If I give you permission, it isn't cheating. We'd come up with some parameters, some boundaries we'd agree on. And in return, I'd like you to tell me everything that happens on your trip. In detail."

"I don't know," Samantha said. "The fantasies were one thing, but I can't see myself doing this in real life. What if it backfires? What if one of us ends up really hurt?"

"*I* won't be hurt," I assured her. "As long as you follow the rules." She gave me a skeptical look but said nothing. "I think it could be fun," I went on. "I know it will be fun for me – I'll hear all about it. And about how sexy my wife is to all kinds of strange men. Your pleasure will be my pleasure," I insisted. I tried to sound playful, as I got up and moved toward Samantha, wrapping her shoulders in an embrace. She leaned in toward me.

"Give me some time to process this," she said. "I'll think about it."

"That's all I ask." I kissed her on the cheek. And despite the sting of not joining her on our trip, deep inside I was more excited than ever.

***

The next morning was a Saturday, and I'd slept in more than usual. It was nearly 10 a.m. when I rolled out of bed, and when I got to the kitchen, Samantha was making pancakes.

"Good morning," she greeted me, eyes still down in the pan. "I talked to Jenny. She said she can go."

My mind erupted in shock and excitement. Not only had Samantha agreed, but it had only taken one night to convince her, *and* she had already asked a friend! Could she be as excited about this idea as me?

"Great," I stammered. "What did you tell her?"

Again, not looking up, she said, "Oh, I told her about your meeting, how important your work function was, but also about how amazing the resort photos looked online. I sent her the link, and she's totally stoked."

"I see," I said. In some ways, Jenny was an ideal companion for this trip. Her family was from Puerto Rico, and not only did she speak Spanish, but she was a total flirt, which would help Samantha get in the groove.

"By the way," Samantha added, quickly glancing up at me and then away. "I hope you don't mind, but I told her she'd only have to pay for half of the room, and we'd cover the plane ticket. Since the trip's short notice. Is that okay?"

"Yeah, perfect," I said. I hadn't even thought about whether we'd ask her to pay. Our finances had looked good lately, and I wasn't even worried. "Did you tell her about – about the stuff from last night?" I couldn't quite say it aloud.

"About that," Samantha began. She looked at me fully now and her eyes looked serious, almost concerned. "Are you sure that's what you want?"

I took a breath. My balls were screaming, *YES,* but in my mind, I had a whisper of doubt about how things might unfold. I decided to side with the screaming. With measured restraint, I answered, "I still feel good about that, yes. As long as you do."

"I admit it sounds fun. Scary, risky even, but fun. And we'd have to figure out our rules before I agree."

So that morning, as we ate our pancakes, we devised the following rules:

1. Only do something if it feels entirely safe.

2. Only do things you want to do. Don't do anything just to please James.

3. Always let Jenny know where you are and who you're with. Always.

4. Do not form attachments. Do not have an encounter with someone on multiple days.

5. If you decide to have intercourse with another man, he must wear a condom.

6. You will send a daily email update to James. Apart from a general update on the trip, it will include a detailed account of any flirtatious or sexual encounters that may occur. Leave no details out. There should be no secrets.

7. Write what you truly feel: the sensations, good and bad; the emotions, positive or otherwise. Write the truth, not just want you think James wants to hear!

And that was it. We read the list through a few times and agreed that it was a sound plan. Although she would email me daily, we agreed that she'd get no response from me, as I didn't want my input to influence her behavior. The exceptions, of course, would be in case of an emergency or if I got cold feet about our plan. In addition, I assured Samantha that if nothing ended up happening or if she realized she didn't feel comfortable, she could abandon the idea and simply enjoy a fun, relaxing vacation with her friend.

When their departure date finally arrived, I drove Samantha and Jenny to the airport and pulled over in the drop-off zone. We exited the vehicle, and I pulled their luggage out of my trunk. With tears in her eyes, Samantha kissed me goodbye and handed me her wedding band to hold on to – she wasn't going to wear it on the trip, and it was safer leaving it with me. The symbolism wasn't lost on us, as we held each other tightly for a final embrace.

"I love you," she whispered in my ear.

"I know." The Star Wars reference was our little joke, and I think the familiarity gave her comfort as she gave me a final squeeze.

"I'm not sure if I can do this," she said.

"It's okay." Holding her by the shoulders, I looked in her eyes. In my best Yoda impression, I began, "Do or do not," then shifted to my own voice to say, "I will love you just the same."

A moment later, as I watched her and Jenny roll their luggage into the airport and out of sight, I found myself filled with hope but devoid of expectation.

2: Arrival and the Hot Tub

Samantha

Saturday, May 11, 2019; 11:06 p.m.

Dear James,

Greetings from the beautiful beaches of the Mayan Riviera – we made it! As per your request, this is my first entry into my digital diary to keep you updated on our exciting adventures. For each entry, I will set the scene with the basics of our trip, and then I'll proceed with a description of any (cough cough) extracurricular activities you're permitting me to engage in. Not to say there were any to report on this first day – or were there?

To begin, it was a *long* day of travel. After you dropped Jenny and me off at the airport, we cleared customs, made it to our terminal, grabbed some cups of coffee at Starbucks, and waited for our plane. Ho hum, nothing too exciting so far. We boarded our plane for an on-time departure, settled in to a fairly full flight to Cancun, and away we went.

Jenny is a total riot. After we took our seats on the plane, me in the window seat and Jenny in the middle, Jenny plopped her bulky, fur-lined jacket right into the aisle seat next to her. "What?" she said, "Planes are fucking cold!" I'd wondered why she was carrying that thing around in the airport. The jacket won't do her much good here in Mexico, but it sure kept other people from taking the seat! Anyway, the privacy turned out to be really convenient. I'd briefed Jenny on the details of our – situation – before we left, but she was definitely still curious.

"So show the rules to me again," Jenny requested once our plane was in the sky.

"Okay." I pulled up the Notepad app on my phone and let her reread the rules.

"I can't believe James is letting you do all that." She grinned in amused disbelief. "You finally get to experience life as a single girl!"

"I guess you're right," I said. "So – anything I should know about the single life these days?"

"Hmm. Well, we're going to an adults-only resort, and you won't be walking around with a guy, so everyone there is going to assume you're single, and every guy there is going to want to sleep with you."

Her frankness caught me off guard, and I laughed. "That easy, huh?"

"That easy," she said. "I know you and James go everywhere together, but now that he won't be around, you're in for an awakening. You'll be fighting off fellas left and right."

"Don't be absurd," I replied. "I'm sure it won't be like that. I don't know if an opportunity will arise, and even if it does, I have no idea how I'll respond if someone tries to flirt with me. I'll probably be scared to death!"

"Trust me," Jenny said, pulling a sleep mask over her face. "We'll find out pretty quick."

I took her sleep mask as a sign that she was out of tips for moment. I, for one, was too nervous and excited to sleep. I pulled out my in-flight magazine and started working on the crossword puzzle – which I completed, by the way! – and anxiously awaited the next step in our journey.

***

Everything in our travel itinerary went off without a hitch. The rental car agency had our vehicle, and Jenny's knowledge of Spanish ensured we got everything we asked for. From there, we got our car (the blue convertible Volkswagen Beetle you'd ordered us) and began the hour-long drive to our beachside resort. I must say, driving in Mexico is utterly *terrifying*. As I drove down the one-lane highway, setting the cruise control exactly at the speed limit as per usual, I realized the other drivers were horrible tailgaters. *What the frick?* There wasn't a passing lane, so I wasn't sure what I should do. I really wished you were here to do the driving, James, and with sadness in my heart, I realized it was the first of many times I'd be wishing you were here with me.

At one point, a truck crossed the center line and pulled up next to me, blaring its horn as it roared by. I watched as another car pulled over to the shoulder to allow the truck to pass. Lesson learned – shoulders in Mexico are for letting drivers pass.

Driving went more smoothly after I learned that little trick. We were soon at our resort, valet took our vehicle, and we received our room keys at the check-in desk. They also gave us pink wristbands to identify us as guests of the resort, as of course the amenities are all-inclusive. I noticed a few people at the end of the check-in desk receiving a green pair of wristbands instead.

"What are the green wristbands for?" I asked the desk clerk.

"Those wristbands are for VIP," she said. "They're for guests who purchase our deluxe suites; it ensures them premier service, additional dining options, and access to the VIP area in our nightclub."

"Fancy," I remarked, dreaming of the day when you and I can have the VIP experience.

***

Our room is standard but very comfortable. We're on the second floor, and our balcony provides a beautiful view of a swimming pool, one of many at this resort, and the sunny beach beyond. The room is furnished with two queen beds, and mine is the one by the window. The air conditioning is strong and feels utterly amazing, as it's a welcomed escape from the humidity outside. There's a mini-fridge in our room that the desk clerk told us they stock daily – free of additional charge – that includes water bottles, sodas, some cans of hard seltzer, and some bottles of beer. Jenny grabbed a seltzer almost instantly and handed another to me. "Time to start our vacation," she said.

It was time for a late dinner after our long day of travel, and we were pretty hungry. We decided to put on some pool clothes and grab food at the outdoor grill near the pools, sipping casually on our seltzers as we got ourselves ready. I expected Jenny and me to change separately, perhaps one of us in the bathroom, but good ol' Jenny just dropped her panties in plain sight.

"Geez!" I exclaimed, as her panties hit the floor. I covered my eyes with my hands, but not before I caught a glimpse of the rich, dark skin of her legs, her tan lines which are even more obvious than mine, and her neatly landscaped vagina.

"What's the big deal?" Jenny asked. "We're all friends here."

I uncovered my eyes and started to undress myself, realizing I might as well get used to having someone other than my husband see me naked. As I changed, I glanced toward Jenny to appreciate her beautiful body. I'll include a description because – who knows? – maybe that might turn you on, and that's kind of the point of all this, right? As you know, Jenny is shorter than me by a few inches. She's also curvier than me, with full, rounded hips and a narrow waist. Her ass is round, firm, and nicely lifted. Her breasts, I admit, make me envious. They're big, I presume D cups or double-Ds, but they definitely do not sag. Her nipples are a deep brown that's even darker than the rest of her tan skin. They're perkier than mine, and I couldn't help wondering if they were especially perky because of the air conditioning or because she liked getting undressed for me. Her tummy isn't as tight as mine, but she keeps herself in shape. Her large, doe-like, coffee eyes are a stark contrast to my "baby-blues" as you call them, and she has full, luscious, pouty lips that drive guys wild. The humidity has already done its work on her hair – while she usually sports big, looping curls that go down past her shoulders, her dark brown hair was frizzed and stood straight out against her will. "Fuckin' A," she said, looking in the mirror and running her fingers through her hair. "I should've known."

I awakened from my admiring daydream to select a bikini from my suitcase – the modest black-and-white striped bikini I know you enjoy – and pulled the bottoms up over my legs. I considered those fairly revealing bikinis we bought for our trip, but I wasn't quite ready to parade them out in public. *Baby steps*, I told myself. *Just baby steps for now.*

I pulled my jean shorts over my bikini bottoms and was ready to go. Jenny was wearing a thong bikini, and she chose a sheer pink wrap to wear around her hips. We each pulled our hair into buns – mine a bit less wild than hers – and made our way down to the grill for some dinner.

***

The grill is housed in a large hut, open to the sea breeze and with a grass roof. The food at the grill, served buffet-style, tasted amazing. I made myself a sensible salad at the extensive salad bar and went for grilled chicken and Spanish rice for my main course. They had soft-serve ice cream and various cakes and pastries for dessert, but feeling self-conscious with my tummy exposed, I decided to hold off for tonight; but I couldn't resist indulging myself with a glass of white wine.

Everyone at the resort was exceedingly polite. All of the staff spoke English, as I'm sure English-speakers are a majority of their guests. Despite Jenny's claim that everyone would be hitting on me, we were left alone for the duration of dinner. We ate our food, sipped our drinks, and enjoyed the dimming sky out over the beach. By the time we were finished, it was nearly dark.

"Hey," Jenny said. "It's been a long day. Want to find a hot tub and relax for a bit before bed?"

"Sounds good to me." Feeling the air start to cool around me, I imagined the hot, steamy water of a Jacuzzi on my skin.

We ordered some tropical drinks at the bar and took a walk around the pools. The crowds had started to dwindle by this time of evening, but nonetheless, the first Jacuzzi we encountered had several people in it, some couples and some single-looking men. The second Jacuzzi we came across had just two men in it, around our age or perhaps a little older. The tub was on the smaller side, but it had plenty of space for two more.

"Hey, guys," Jenny greeted them. "Mind if we join?"

The men looked up, and one of them uttered an audible "Woah" as we removed our coverings to get down to our suits. The other one, a tan-skinned man with light green eyes, replied, "Be our guests."

"Yeah," his friend replied, regaining his composure. "It's a free country. Wait – is Mexico a free country?"

Next, we introduced ourselves. The tan-skinned guy was Mark, and his friend, a barrel-chested White guy with short blond hair and a bushy beard, was John. We climbed in the circular hot tub and, I think intentionally, Jenny positioned herself between the two men so I had to pick a guy to sit next to. John seemed like a bit of a dweeb, so I sat nearer to Mark.

"Been at the resort long?" Mark asked.

"Just got in today," said Jenny. "Haven't even been in the ocean yet." Although I hadn't said a word, Mark's steely, green-eyed gaze was fixed on me. I couldn't help but notice he was handsome, but also a little intense. I wondered about his background and guessed he was a mix of White and Black. His body type was slender but toned. Although he was seated, I could tell from his long, wiry arms and torso that he was tall. His dark hair was closely cropped into a high fade, and it appeared that he must wax his chest, as he had no body hair in sight. He had a light amount of facial stubble that blended flawlessly up to his hairline and a tribal tattoo around his left bicep, the kind that walks the line between edgy and douchey.

We started with some small talk – where we were from, what we do for a living, on and on. The men, like us, were American, but I won't bore you with the rest of the details. Building up some liquid courage as I slowly drained my drink, I began to speak up more as the conversation progressed. When I did, Mark kept locking his eyes with mine. It was a subtle gesture, but the deepness of his gaze made my stomach flutter a little. It had been so long – were we just talking, or were we actually flirting?

Eventually, Mark asked, "So how come your boyfriends let you come to Mexico all on your own?"

"Oh," Jenny laughed, "We don't have any boyfriends." Technically that was true, but I felt a tinge of guilt when I didn't protest.

"Hard to believe," Mark replied. "You're both such lovely ladies." His voice dropped lower. "You came to Mexico to have some fun, right?"

Pushing myself to speak, I said, "Absolutely. It's all about fun and new experiences, right?"

"Absolutely," said Mark, mirroring my words and gazing again while moving slightly closer. How was he so close all of a sudden? Had he been slowly creeping toward me? Was I subconsciously moving toward him?

Jenny chimed in. "Samantha is especially looking for new experiences on this trip. She's a liberated woman!" Great, Jenny. Thanks.

"You mean, you're newly single?" Mark asked, smirking but never wavering in his gaze. A part of me wanted to shrink away, but a part of me wanted to engage!

"Something like that," I responded, trying to sound nonchalant.

"Then it's time to have some fun." Before I knew it, Mark was sitting directly next to me, and he leaned his mouth slowly toward mine. At the last possible moment, I tilted my face away from the prospect of a kiss on the lips, which I didn't feel quite ready for. Mark took it as an invitation to kiss my neck. His lips were warm and moist, at first pressed gently against my skin and gradually more firmly as it traced up toward my cheek.

It was happening, my first leap into exploring sexuality with a man other than my husband. Instantly, my mind jumped to you, James, wondering how you'd feel, whether you'd be happy, sad, angry, or all three. I remembered how you would kiss my neck when we first started dating, and how you turned me on so expertly with your light, strategic kisses. The mix of guilt and excitement was confusing, but not necessarily unpleasant. Mark knew what he was doing, and the neck kisses were definitely turning me on. Out of the corner of my eye, I noticed Jenny occupying the attention of John, who was sloppily trying to kiss her through his beard. Jenny could handle John, I knew, so that was one less thing to worry about. I closed my eyes, sighed softly, and tried to relax while experiencing this moment completely.

In no time at all, I felt Mark's hand fall lightly upon my upper thigh. I tensed for a second, but then it only increased my arousal, as his large hand squeezed softly on my skin. His hand moved slowly up to my inner thigh and toward the seam of my bikini. *Woah!* My arousal surged, but I didn't feel quite ready for this, so I placed my hand over his to halt his advance. I moved his hand back down toward my knee, but after a few more seconds of cheek and neck kissing, his hand began creeping upwards once more. I put my hand again over his again, but that's when he closed his hand around mine and guided it over to his crotch. I didn't resist; either he caught me off guard, or

I was simply ready to surrender. I gasped in surprise as I felt his hard cock bulging in his shorts. Eyes still closed, I explored the parameters of his length and width with my fingers, lightly tracing the outline of his dick. His penis muscles flexed with anticipation, and almost reflexively, I wrapped him in my grip through his shorts.

It was happening – I was holding a stranger's cock in my hand. The realization jolted me into self-consciousness, and I opened my eyes to take stock of the scene. The resort was empty, dark, and quiet, and all I could hear was the bubbling of the jacuzzi. Mark's eyes closed, enjoying the sensations as I casually fondled his cock. Jenny and John were really going at it, which involved kissing on both the neck and lips. And then I noticed the pair of men's swim trunks floating at the water's surface – apparently John had removed his shorts completely! Jenny obviously working his cock under the water with her hand. *When in Rome*, I thought, giving Mark's cock an extra squeeze.

Deciding to let go, I slipped back into my own little world. Mark's head was tilted back, fully immersed in the pleasures he was feeling. I closed my eyes, clumsily rubbing his cock through his shorts until he gradually untied the draw string and started to remove *his* shorts as well. I gave him a moment to remove them, then returned to feel what his shorts had concealed. I felt my fingers touch his skin. His cock was nice and hard, and it felt thick; it reminded me a lot of yours, James. I couldn't see what I was working with, but I felt it, smooth skin over a long, hard shaft. I stroked him slowly, feeling that strange power of having control. Every few strokes, I transitioned to massaging his balls, holding them lightly and then shuffling them like a sack of oversized marbles. I noticed the rate of his breath increase, and at times I heard him gasp or sigh, particularly when my fingers grazed the head of his cock. Noting his increased pleasure, I periodically paused my hand and tickled the tip of his head with my thumb, which he really seemed to enjoy, as it caused him to shudder and audibly moan. Eventually I realized his hand was back on my thigh, and I'm sure he would've found my womanhood wet and slick if he had worked his way up to it. I stopped his hand within millimeters of its goal, and the tickle of his fingertips near my labia made me yearn to give him more.

Suddenly, John started to moan loudly from across the Jacuzzi, presumably as Jenny had caused him to finish. Jenny leaned over and stuck her tongue down John's throat, probably to shut him up so he wouldn't disturb any passers-by. Amidst my momentary distraction, Mark moved his hand inward and make contact with my bikini bottoms. Before I could react, gently slid his middle finger back and forth over the thin fabric covering my slit. I gasped and then held my breath as the unexpected pleasure brought a hot, tingling sensation in my loins. My mind emptied of all but this sensation, my eyes closed in pleasure, and my mouth fell open with shock. I let him caress me for several seconds – maybe as much as a minute – before I snapped back to awareness and moved his hand quickly away. This either excited or frustrated him, as in reaction, he withdrew his hand completely, closed it around my hand that was still massaging his cock, and started pumping up and down furiously as he approached a climax of his own. He was more discreet than John was, but I could sense the intensity of his orgasm from the quickening of his breath, the throbbing of his member, and a low, deep moan that emitted from his throat. When the climax had finished, his breath began to slow, and he seemed to relax ever deeper into the foaming hot water around us. Sobering from the experience, I hoped that this hot tub was adequately chlorinated.

"That was fun," John said, while panting from across the tub. "And unexpected!"

"Samantha, that was amazing," said Mark, and he tried to pierce me again with his green-eyed gaze. But the spell was broken, and I looked away. "We have some more drinks in our room," he suggested. "Why don't you guys come on up?"

Jenny must have seen the panic in my eyes, as she cut in. "We're still settling in, and it was a long day of travel. I think we're pretty tired, right, Sam?"

"Right, definitely tired," I replied. "But yeah, this was lots of fun, guys. I mean – thanks!" I hadn't known what to say, but I felt totally lame about *thanking* this stranger for letting me give him a hand job. The comment must have stroked his ego, as he practically beamed.

"Really, you guys should come upstairs for a bit," Mark said. "We won't keep you late. Or you can sleep in our beds if you get too tired."

"Yeah," chimed in John. "We can even sleep on the floor, we don't mind!" Mark shot John a look of annoyance.

"We said *no*, guys, no thank you," Jenny said, growing sterner and standing up.

"*You* said no, but what about Samantha?" Mark asked, trying to catch my eyes again.

"I gotta agree with Jenny," I said. "Maybe we'll catch you around, okay?" I instantly regretted this, recalling my promise to not form any attachments. "I mean, well, bye!" I stood up.

"Let us walk you back to your room then," John offered. He stood up too, suddenly realized his junk was exposed to the world, and sank back into the water.

"Just a walk," added Mark. His face looked suddenly so serious.

"We know our way, thank you, let's go," Jenny said. As an afterthought, Jenny snatched up Mark's and John's swim shorts, which were still floating on the water's surface. She brought them outside the Jacuzzi as I stepped out as well. "Oh, and by the way," she said. "Don't get any funny ideas about following us, okay?" In one swift motion, she threw both Mark's and John's swim shorts over a row of beach chairs and into a nearby bush.

"Hey!" John exclaimed as he stood up again. We suddenly heard the growing voices of an oncoming stampede of tourists, as the nightly entertainment show must have just let out, and guests were returning to their rooms. John dipped quickly back into the water, stranded for now by the tourists, as Jenny and I blended into the crowd and made our getaway.

"You got us out of there fast," I remarked. "Quick thinking!"

"Thanks. I wasn't digging the vibe they were putting out, so I figured we should play it safe."

"Good idea. That was pretty exciting, but more than enough for our first night. I didn't expect anything like *that* to happen!"

"If I were you, I'd expect a lot more." Jenny and I broke off from the crowd as we approached our building. "Single guys come here hoping to get laid. And all the free booze can really boost their confidence."

"Makes sense," I said. "So, did you have fun as well?"

"Sure. My guy had kind of a small dick, though. And I'm trying to break my habit of hooking up with white guys."

I laughed. "You're a good wing woman, Jenny."

"Thanks," said Jenny. "I am, aren't I?"

***

We got back to the room, and before long, Jenny was fast asleep. It wasn't terribly late yet, and while my thoughts and emotions were still fresh, I wanted to type out my message to you. I miss you, James. Today was a mix of exciting, fun, and a little bit scary. Fooling around with someone was enjoyable, I admit, but I would never risk hurting you if you weren't 100% sure this was okay.

To be clear, tonight was not about Mark. He was nothing special, and I'd be happy to never see him again. After the stunt Jenny pulled, he probably wants to avoid us too! He was just some guy who happened to be there – but you're *my* guy, who is *always* there.

I know we agreed that this diary would be one-directional, as long as you still feel comfortable with what I'm doing. I only hope that this was as arousing to you as you thought it would be, and the thought of turning you on right now is making me love and miss you even more. But please – if any small part of you feels uncomfortable with this, tell me! I will abandon our plan in a heartbeat. The door will be locked, and I can throw away the key. But the other side of it is this – if you don't ask me to stop – I think I'm going to continue. Tonight was fun. It was empowering. It was – something I want to explore, that I think I want more of, but only if things are good between you and me. If you email me back and ask me to stop, I will understand, and I won't be upset. I will stop if you ask me to stop – but a part of me is hoping you won't.

Love,

Samantha

3: The Eager Young Suitor

Samantha

Monday, May 13, 2019; 12:43 a.m.

Dear James,

I woke up this morning, quickly rolled out of bed, and powered on my laptop at the desk. I knew that if I'd hear from you at all, the email already would've arrived. As I waited for my browser to load, cursing the crappy hotel Wi-Fi, my heart fluttered weakly, and my stomach felt ready to implode. *What if James wrote back? What would he say? What if I hurt him with what I had done?* My mind raced, and my hands were shaking as I typed my password into my email login screen. I waited – but no new emails from you.

I breathed a sigh of relief, and my innards returned to homeostasis. It was okay. No harm done. Just as you said, if you were okay with how things were going, you wouldn't respond. I pulled up the message I sent last night in my outbox and confirmed I sent it to your proper address. I saw the words, "Read receipt confirmed." It was official. You received my message of the events from last night – you read what I had to say – and you let it be.

Looking over at the clock, it was barely past 6 a.m.. Jenny was dead to the world – that girl can sleep! After the whole ordeal of looking for your email, my adrenaline was flowing, and I was too hyped up to return to bed. I decided to make use my energy to explore the resort.

I threw on some running shorts and a sports bra, tied my hair up in a ponytail, and strapped my smartwatch to my wrist. I connected my wireless ear buds to the watch – can't work out without a good playlist – wrote a quick note for Jenny, and quietly left the room.

I was out the door just in time for sunrise. The sky was a royal blue, faintly lit as the sun crept its way toward the horizon over the eastward sea. Between the resort and the ocean, the grounds are filled with tropical greenery. The bushes were trimmed low, but scattered palm trees stood tall and cast some shade. My first stop was the beach, and I jogged there in earnest to catch the first rays of sunrise across the water. Ignoring specks of dry sand, I laid back in one of the beach chairs lined up along the beach. Looking down the row, I saw a few other early risers scattered about, a couple, a group of friends, and some lonely souls like me. What I wouldn't give for you to be with me, James, holding my hand in the morning light.

In no time at all, the golden tip of the sun crept over the deep blue waves. Behind my sunglasses, I narrowed my eyes against the brightness of the light. The skyline above was painted yellow, orange, and red, reflecting shades of pink and purple against some low clouds. The waves moved in and out from the shore, and a morning breeze kept me cool and content. I closed my eyes, realizing I hadn't slept much last night, and may have even dozed off for a couple minutes; because as I opened my eyes again, the blinding sun had inched its way above the horizon.

Well, that was enough of that. Sunrise was a beautiful sight but fleeting, as the transition from night to day was complete. I stood up, stretched, and brushed sand off the backs of my legs. Time to resume my jog! With no set destination in mind, I set a leisurely pace along a winding sidewalk that ran parallel to the ocean. The resort buildings were lined against the shore, and I knew that various attractions were located in either direction. Running north, I came across a high row of steps that led up to another building. I detoured up the steps to check it out. The building was a large, white pavilion. Inside was a spacious auditorium with small round tables and chairs on levels leading down and facing a stage. On the top level where I stood, there was a bar area to my right where guests could order drinks to enjoy during the show. I read the marquis that was advertising for tonight: "Sunday night – Rock 'N' Roll music night!" *James would love that*, I thought, followed by, *Jenny would hate it!*

I continued my jog. Further north, I discovered an enclosure in which guests could swim with dolphins. An advertisement played on a screen overhead, showing ecstatic-looking guests suspended above the water, standing on the noses of two dolphins before crashing down into the pool. At the end of the resort, I found a small waterpark, which featured several waterslides and a section in which guests could ride against the current on a boogie board. It looked like fun – but it wasn't operational this early in the day.

I jogged back in the direction of our room, listening to my pump-it-up playlist and wondering what the rest of the day might hold. I passed our own building to see what was on the other side, and I came upon the gym and the spa areas. Checking my smartwatch, I'd scarcely covered a mile of ground so far, so I decided to finish my workout at the gym.

Like the grill, the gym was a large, round building topped by a grass roof. It was enclosed with clear plexiglass panels to keep the room temperature-controlled, and several ceiling fans hung from the rafters. The gym had a standard selection of workout equipment – treadmills, stair climbers, ellipticals, a pair of weightlifting rigs, and some free weights. I hopped on a treadmill to add some miles to my jog, and from my vantage point, I could survey the rest of the gym. Few people were here this early in the morning. There was a middle-aged woman using an elliptical and an elderly gentleman working with some free weights, but otherwise it was empty.

About 10 minutes into my jog, another guest arrived. He was a young man, Asian, dark-skinned, and in pretty good shape. Upon arriving, he removed his shirt and tossed it over a workout bench. *Oh my*, I thought. *This guy is pretty toned.* His body type reminded me of yours, James, but perhaps a bit leaner. His face was not as handsome as yours, attractive but youthful, almost pretty. He was clean-shaven with high cheek bones and large, pouty lips. He'd never have caught my eye if you hadn't encouraged me to engage people – but since you had, he appeared like he could be worth my while. I wondered what he'd be like to talk to.

I continued to observe him. Using free-weights, he performed some sets of curls, shoulder presses, and bent-over rows. I watched his muscles strain as he worked them, his well-defined ripples causing my face to flush with excitement. Before long, I decided to bring myself closer. Stepping off the treadmill, I approached the free-weight area, grabbed some light dumbbells, and started replicating some of his movements. Apparently, I caught his eye, because before long, he engaged me in conversation.

"You'll hurt your back that way, miss." He grinned shyly, examining me. I was bent over doing some dumbbell rows, and I suppose I hadn't kept my back straight.

"May I?" he asked, gesturing like he wanted to correct my form. He placed his hands lightly on my stomach and lower back, straightening me out. "There. Now you'll work the muscles in your core."

"Thanks," I said, feigning embarrassment. I really didn't care about my form, but I'm glad it caught his attention. "You look like you know what you're doing. Any other workout tips?" I felt so bold! Merely two days ago, the prospect of flirting with a stranger was a complete terror. Now, after one night of flirtation, I was acting like a natural.

"Sure," he said. "You'll want to pull all the way up to your chest on that row, don't cheat your own workout." I was a little self-conscious as he referenced my chest, and I realized that my nipples were starting to harden from the flirtation. I hoped they started to show through my sports bra, as I figured this might keep him interested. The young man returned to his workout at the next bench over, but every few moments, I caught him casting a furtive glance my way. My eyes were drawn to him as well, watching his skin stretch over his lean muscles. I imagined playing xylophone music on his ribcage as he flexed, shirtless, oily, and wearing tiny spandex shorts. I couldn't decide if my fantasy was sexy, comical, or deranged.

After a couple rounds of reps, I took a break from my workout, stretching my back and pushing my breasts forward, hoping to let him see. "Whew!" I exclaimed, and I saw him look over. "It's a lot more tiring that way," I said. "No wonder it's a better workout." Mission accomplished – his eyes darted straight to my tits.

"Yeah, well – glad I could help," he stammered. He turned away to resume his own workout. My mind whirred, wondering how I'd re-engage him.

"My name is Samantha, by the way!" The direct approach – smooth.

"Dillon," he replied, turning with a wave.

"Where are you from, Dillon?"

"I'm Canadian," Dillon said. "Oh, if you're talking about ethnicity, I'm half Vietnamese and half Filipino."

"Oh, cool," I answered lamely. "Have you been on holiday long?" Oh, God – apparently because he wasn't American, I decided to call it "holiday" instead of "vacation." Who was I?

"It's my last day, unfortunately," he said. I return to Ontario tomorrow."

"That's a shame," I replied, but in my head, I thought, *Perfect!* He was only here for one more day, so it would be easy to spend time with him but not form attachments. "Any big plans for your last day?"

"Probably just hang out by the pool. How about you? Been here long?"

"Just got in yesterday. A pool day sounds nice, I think I'll do that as well." I started to get butterflies in my stomach, not sure what to say next. Small talk was never my strong suit. It was time to escape before he realized I was awkward. "Well, anyway, maybe I'll see you around today, Dillon."

"Yeah," Dillon said. "I wouldn't mind seeing you again." He flashed me a wide, boyish smile.

I left the gym, finishing my workout with a quick jog back to the room.

It was 7:30 a.m. by now, and Jenny was still fast asleep. Setting my watch alarm, I figured I could go back to sleep at least until 9 before Jenny woke up. Thinking of Dillon, I drifted back to sleep.

***

After Jenny and I arose, we each took showers, made ourselves up for the day, and headed down to breakfast at the indoor buffet. The décor was fancier than at the grill, with full silverware sets arranged on open tables. I grabbed a sensible yogurt and some fruit. Jenny ate some cereal.

Afterwards, we changed into our swimsuits. Feeling emboldened and hoping to impress Dillon, I grabbed one of my sexier bikinis, the small, rainbow-striped string bikini. It would mark my first time wearing a thong out in public. I pulled my shorts over my bottoms for now, and Jenny and I headed out for a pool day.

The rest of the morning was fairly uneventful. Jenny convinced me to have a Bloody Mary with her – yuck, by the way – and I settled down in the sun to resume my book, *The Time Traveler's Wife*. Lying on a beach chair in my skimpy bikini, I figured I could at least work on these tan lines. I periodically dipped myself in the pool to cool off, then resumed reading, tanning my front side for a while and then my back. Meanwhile, Jenny – ever the extravert – was drinking more at the bar and making friends with an older couple.

Eventually, Jenny and I elected to grab some lunch at the grill – another salad and some authentic Mexican flan for good measure – before returning to the pool. A pool aerobics class was gathering, and an attractive male instructor was taking the lead.

"Do you want dibs on this one?" Jenny asked, referring to the hot instructor.

"No thanks, all yours." I went and seated myself at the swim-up bar, turning to watch Jenny as she placed herself at the head of the class in front of the instructor. I waited to get the bartender's attention when I heard a familiar voice in my right ear.

"Mind if I buy you a drink?" It was Dillon, and he was seated upon the barstool next to me.

I giggled at his little joke. "Sure!" We smiled at each other and I took in his image, shirtless once more, his hair now done in a short, messy style.

Dillon ordered a fruity cocktail for me and a Jack and Coke for himself. "Having fun?" he asked.

"Absolutely. This weather is picturesque. How about you?"

"Fun is an understatement. To be honest – I noticed you 30 minutes ago while you were sunbathing. You look amazing, I might add."

I'm pretty sure I blushed visibly. "Thanks!" I gave his body a suggestive glance. "Still without a shirt, I see?"

"You know it!" We continued some idle chit-chat for a while, sipping our drinks while sitting on our half-submerged barstools. Dillon's personality was warm and upbeat. He didn't seem like the smartest guy, but he definitely seemed genuine and kind.

"What do you think you'll miss the most about vacation?" I asked him at one point.

"Hmm. I think I'll miss the ocean."

"The ocean – I actually haven't been in it yet. Want to join me?"

"Absolutely. I couldn't turn down an offer from a beautiful girl like you." I glanced over to Jenny, who had initiated conversation with the instructor after her class. She was already working her girlish charms, laughing at his jokes and hitting him playfully. *She'll be fine*, I thought. I waved my arms to get her attention and pointed toward the beach, and she gave me a thumbs-up in return. And with that, Dillon and I made our way to the ocean.

We started simply by swimming around. The land around the beach formed a cove, with shallow water extending maybe a hundred yards out until it reached open ocean. The sand beneath our feet was smooth, and the water only came up as high as our elbows.

"This is nice," I remarked, bobbing softly in the waves.

"You're nice," Dillon responded, causing me to laugh.

"Is that so?"

"Yeah," he said, leaning in for a kiss. Feeling bolder since the events of last night and knowing Dillon would be gone in a day, I surrendered myself to his advance. His lips were warm and wet, and after a few seconds, his tongue darted deftly into my mouth. I returned the gesture, comforted by the fact that this was only for fun. I felt his hands upon my hips, and before long, he moved them to the bare skin of my ass. He pulled me close, and I felt a distinct bulge at the front of his swim shorts. *Kind of like Tommy-boy*, I realized, *only way sexier*. I pretended not to notice his erection but enjoyed the sensation, nonetheless. Before long, Dillon's hands slipped under my thighs, and he lifted me up in the water and wrapped my legs around his hips. My arms instinctively encircled his neck to hold on.

What a teasing sensation! In this position, my crotch was firmly placed against his, feeling his bulge along the crease of my vagina. There was a warm, diffuse tingle on the surface of my pussy. I continued to kiss him deeply as we grinded softly together. All of a sudden, I felt my top loosen as Dillon untied it.

"Hey!" I exclaimed, letting go of Dillon's neck to catch my top from falling off. Dillon's playful grin flashed broadly on his face.

"Oops! I guess my hands got caught in your strings."

I turned around, not wanting to expose my breasts to people on the beach. "You'll pay for that, Dillon," I warned. "Now tie me back up." I turned around, and he obeyed. Once I was put back together, he tried to kiss me on the lips again, but I turned away and took it on the cheek. Untying my top was a risky play, and it had backfired on him – I was no longer turned on.

"I'm here with a friend," I told him. "I bet she's wondering where I went."

"I'm here with my parents," he admitted shyly. "But I have my own room!"

"Good to know." *Here with his parents? How young is this guy anyway?* Examining his baby-face, I was relieved to know this was an adults-only resort. His voice snapped me out of my reverie.

"By the way, it's Rock 'N' Roll night at the theater. Want to catch the show with me?"

I considered for a second, realizing Jenny would not like that at all. Time to see what kind of wing woman she truly was. "Sure!" I replied. "What time?"

"The show starts at 8," Dillon said. "Join me at 7:45 for a drink?"

"It's a date." We waded back to the beach and rinsed off in the outdoor shower. The water caused Dillon's shorts to cling to his skin, I noticed the outline of his penis. I wondered if I'd see it in person later on. We parted ways, and I returned to the area where Jenny and I were sunbathing earlier. There she was, reading a book.

"Where'd you go?" Jenny asked, looking up from her book.

"I made a friend. We played in the ocean a bit."

"Sounds fun."

I told her about our plan to go to the show later. She groaned when I told her the theme, but she reluctantly agreed.

"How about you?" I asked. "Any luck with the sexy instructor?"

"Julian? He said he has a girlfriend. Freaking yuck."

"Aww, I'm sorry, girl. Plenty of fish in the sea."

"You got that right," she said, and we each resumed reading our books.

***

Evening came, and Jenny and I were in the room getting ready for our night out. I wore a tight pair of jeans that showed off my legs, as well as a low-cut turquoise tube top. Under my jeans I wore my tiniest little white thong, but nobody needed to know that – yet. Jenny wore a short jean skirt that was frayed on the end, an orange low-cut blouse, and heels. We were finishing hair and makeup at the bathroom mirror.

"So, tell me about this guy we're meeting," she said.

"He's good-looking. Not too smart but very friendly, great smile. Strong hands."

Jenny laughed. "You got to know his hands already?"

"Just a little. We kissed in the ocean and did some touching, but nothing crazy."

"I see. Well, it's good to know he has some potential."

"True!" I giggled. This all felt surprisingly natural – no butterflies just yet.

I finished straightening my hair in the mirror, and Jenny had tamed her own with some handfuls of conditioner. It now looked shiny and slick with large, looping curls; she was back to looking her best. She practically strutted on our way to the theater, taking long, powerful strides in her stiletto heels. The heels and the skirt complimented her ass, which looked toned and lifted under the tight denim cloth.

***

Dillon was waiting at the bar when we arrived. He apparently was watching the entrance, as he flashed me his smile and waved as we passed through the doorway. He wore tight khaki shorts and a tropical button-up shirt with rolled sleeves, left mostly open over a white undershirt. I was pleased that his undershirt was tight and exposed, as it gave Jenny a chance to see his muscles beneath. *That's right, Jenny, I snagged a looker.*

Dillon introduced himself to Jenny, asked for our drink orders, and turned to get the bartender's attention. Behind his back, Jenny winked and flashed me a thumbs up, signifying approval. After the drinks arrived – Dillon had ordered another beer, and Jenny and I each had a vodka RedBull – we turned to scan the auditorium for seats.

"Hmm," Dillon said. "Nothing much left, and the show's about to start."

"You came to the show alone?" asked Jenny. "Where's your group?"

"Oh." He grinned sheepishly. "I came with my parents. They're over there, but we don't have to sit by them. I mean, I'd rather not sit by them if that's okay." He laughed nervously.

I laughed a little too, and Jenny grimaced while looking back toward the audience floor. "There's a table over there, but only two chairs," she said.

"You and I can double up," I suggested, noticing that the seats were wide and cushioned.

"I don't think so," Jenny said. "Seeing as I have the widest ass here, I think *you two* should double up." Dillon blushed and started sputtering, so I cut in.

"Sure, that works! Your parents won't see us, they're way over there!" Taking Dillon by the hand, I followed Jenny to the small, candlelit table she had found. Dillon and I attempted to wiggle our behinds into the low, wicker seat, but it was kind of cramped.

"Just sit on her lap," Jenny suggested. She winked, and Dillon laughed.

Emboldened by the moment, I stood and repositioned myself across Dillon's legs, landing my butt cheeks on his upper thigh. I swung my arm behind his neck and onto his shoulders for balance. "How's this?" I asked.

"Perfect!" Dillon exclaimed, just as the lights went dim and the music show began.

The show was fun and campy yet seemed to be self-aware. They took us through a "history of rock," with impersonators of such artists as Elvis Presley, Buddy Holly, Kiss, Joan Jett and more. Of course, all the performers were of Mexican descent, and it was fun to see the cultural and linguistic blend of Spanish-speaking natives posing as English-speaking icons. The take on Bohemian Rhapsody was particularly unique, as five operatic singers dressed in evening gowns and tuxedos took turns belting out the memorable riffs and harmonies of Queen. Dillon occasionally bounced his leg to the rhythm, and before long, I noticed he had an erection in his shorts. *Does this young man have no self-control?*

We were only twenty minutes in when Jenny spotted the aerobics instructor, Julian, chatting with some tourists at the bar. "Excuse me," she said, and I'm sure she was glad for a reason to escape her role as the third wheel. Even though she vacated her seat, Dillon kept his arms around my waist, and I was content to stay upon his lap.

Eventually, the lights came up, and a booming voice announced the intermission. Dillon whispered in my ear, "Hey, wanna get out of here for a bit?"

"Sure, um – let's grab a drink?" Now the butterflies had arrived, and they moved around in my stomach both excited and terrified.

"Of course," he replied. The bar at the theater was packed, as guests were swarming for refills during the break. "The lobby bar is on the way to my room," he suggested. "Let's go there."

Leading Dillon by the hand, I brought him to a group of Jenny, Julian, and a few of Julian's friends who surrounded a high-top table by the bar. I whispered Dillon's room number in Jenny's ear, and she whispered back, "Have fun!"

When Dillon and I arrived at the hotel bar, I knew exactly what I needed. "Two shots of tequila and a glass of water, please."

"Make that four shots of tequila and two waters," added Dillon.

"Two shots each?" I wondered if he was as nervous as me. We pounded our first shots and paused before the second.

"Hey, Samantha," Dillon began. "You know I'm leaving tomorrow, right?"

"Yes, I remember. It's okay. I'm glad we have tonight."

"You want to come back to my room, right?"

I paused. "I do want to, yes. If you would like me to."

Dillon's face lit up like a kid discovering Christmas. "Of course I would, I'd love you to!" He grabbed his second shot, handed me mine, and we tossed them back together. "Viva la Mexico!" he said.

"Viva la Mexico!" I repeated.

***

Dillon's room was a little smaller than mine and Jenny's, and there was only one queen-sized bed. I scarcely had time to take it in, as he immediately grabbed me, started passionately kissing me, and pulled me toward the bed as soon as we got in the door. It was less than a minute before he pulled his shirt off and helped remove mine, and he immediately commenced with trying to remove my bra. His fingers fumbled with the strap, and I decided to undo it for him, worried that in his exuberance he might rip it. I let the bra fall to the floor, noting another milestone – the first time I showed my breasts to a man who wasn't my husband.

Dillon quickly resumed kissing me, pulling my torso close to his so that my breasts were pressed against his chest. Again, wasting no time, he reached down, unbuttoned my jeans, and undid the zipper. The top of my tiny white panties were exposed, but that's where I wanted to leave things for now. I felt more comfortable removing *his* pants first, so pushed him backwards onto the bed. He stared at me wide-eyed with excitement as I leaned forward and undid the belt around his shorts. His erection was prominently displayed against the khaki fabric, and I grazed it lightly with my hands before slowly unbuttoning his shorts and pulling them off from his legs. Next came his underwear, a grey pair of boxer-briefs, and as I pulled them down, his cock sprung loose from its prison and slapped lightly against his stomach. His penis looked rather unique to me, probably average in length but with much different proportions than I'm used to. That's when I realized – Dillon was uncircumcised!

Taking his cock in my hand, I held it up to inspect it. It was thicker in the middle and then thin around the head which was mostly covered in foreskin. I could massage the skin downward to reveal the head of his penis, which seemed small in relation to the bulk of his shaft. To be honest, I was more amused than impressed. Dillon was lying back on the bed with his eyes closed, breathing heavily as I explored his erection in my hand. Noticing his enjoyment, I started stroking up and down his cock, almost in slow motion at first, but very gradually picking up speed. I admired his well-defined ab muscles as they tensed with his deepening breaths, and occasional grunts or gasps escaped from his lips. Encouraged by his sounds, I leaned forward and touched my tongue to the very tip of his penis. His grunts became a loud groan, and much to my surprise, a string of semen launched forth from the end of his penis!

The semen hit me in the forehead and got slightly in my hair, and I sat back in surprise. Dillon, meanwhile, was grabbing at his pulsating dick with one hand, grunting frantically and staring at it in wide-eyed horror.

"I'm sorry!" he shouted, "I'm sorry!" He caught the rest of his cum in the palm of his hand, then rolled off the bed and scurried off to the bathroom. As I recovered from the initial shock, I could barely contain my laughter! The poor guy, I could tell he was extremely embarrassed.

I heard the faucet run from the bathroom, and then Dillon came back with a damp hand towel. He handed it me, saying, "I'm so sorry, Samantha. I didn't mean for that to happen!"

I assured him that everything was alright. "You're actually giving me a real ego boost," I said, smiling to help him feel better. I wiped his semen from my hair with the towel.

"But you must be really disappointed." He turned away, and I wondered if he may be tearing up.

"No, no, I'm not." I came up behind him and put my hand on his shoulder. "I've had a lot of fun already." A part of me was relieved that the encounter ended here. My butterflies had vanished, and I still had the endorphin rush of making this young man cum. It was a step forward from last night, but a small step, and I sort of felt relieved. *I wonder if James would feel relieved, too,* I thought, *or maybe disappointed?* I didn't know yet that more action was in store.

"Let me make it up to you," Dillon said, turning around. To his credit, his eyes were dry. He fixed his gaze on me. "Trust me, I'll feel better if I can make it up to you."

"Okay," I replied tentatively. "What do you have in mind?"

Dillon leaned forward, put one hand around my waist, brushed my hair aside with the other, and said, "I'll show you." He began kissing me again, his hands pressed against my exposed breasts. He worked his hands downward, sliding into my unfastened jeans and pushing them down and away from my hips. I broke from his kiss to remove my jeans completely, revealing my tiny white thong which scarcely covered my pussy.

Seizing control, Dillon resumed the kiss, took me into his arms, and guided me down onto the bed. The sudden initiative was arousing, and I felt light as a feather as he effortlessly lowered me down. Leaning over me, he playfully pecked at my neck while adding a couple gentle bites. He kissed his way down to my chest, stopping at each nipple to lick, kiss, suck, and nibble. While he did this, he began gently caressing my pussy over my underwear, lightly stroking up and down my slit through the soft cotton fabric. The friction drew my attention to the dampness of my flower, as the fabric was slick and then soon was fully drenched. *These will definitely need to be laundered*, I thought.

By now, my body was tingling all over, as shock waves surged from my stimulated nipples down to my hungry pussy. Dillon, keeping a steady pace, moved down from my nipples and gave me a few kisses on my abdomen, moving ever downward. The kisses tickled, but I tried not to squirm so he could advance more quickly to his final destination. When his lips arrived at the waistband of my underwear, he bypassed them and advanced to my legs, kissing and licking my inner thighs suggestively. My vagina burned with a need for attention, but the tension was strangely exhilarating, as my body responded with involuntary muscle contractions in my abdomen and legs. He ran his tongue upward along my inner thigh, all the way up to the tendon between my leg to my crotch. Suddenly, he pressed the center of his tongue against the middle of my underwear, applying pressure to the lips of my vagina and causing me to gasp and contract the muscles in my vagina and my ass. After what felt like an eternity of anticipation, he had finally touched down on the runway of my womanhood.

Once again, my mind leapt back to you, James. Here was this hot young man, so eager to please me, passionately servicing my vagina while my husband was over a thousand miles away. I imagined you watching me and hoped you'd be pleased, mounting an erection of your own and observing your loving wife seducing another man to arouse you. I was in two worlds at once, thinking of your affection while experiencing Dillon's vivacity as he stroked my underwear with his tongue. He quickly pulled my panties off and repeated the motion along the warm, wet opening of my flower, his soft tongue generating surges of pleasure, his saliva enhancing the eager slickness of my folds.

As things progressed, I realized that Dillon's strength was in his effort, not his technique. His tongue lashed my vagina furiously, slipping all around without much direction or purpose. At one point he used his tongue to insert me, pressing it as far as he could inside me and then pushing it in and out like he was fucking me with it. Don't get me wrong, it felt good, just – sloppy. He hadn't found my clitoris yet, and I wondered if he had much experience doing this. I recalled *your* first time going down on me, and I don't think it was all that different.

"That feels good, Dillon," I said softly. "Mmm, lick me right here." I gestured to my clitoris, gently pulling up on my skin to reveal it to him. To his credit, he did a fine job following my instruction. My arousal continued to build as he worked my clit, and I started to feel a hunger in my loins as I craved for even more. I pinched my nipples to enhance the sensation, and this unlocked a shockwave of pleasure that ran up and down from my vagina to my breasts, then radiated outward to my extremities, causing me to feel slightly lightheaded. I hadn't reached my limit yet, so again I made a request.

"That's so hot, Dillon," I said. "Now put two fingers inside me," I said. Dillon obeyed me once more, wetting his fingers in my natural lubricant and then slowly sliding them inside, stretching the lips of my pussy as they entered. He slowly fucked me with his fingers as he resumed kissing and licking my clit. This had been the missing ingredient, as I realized I was building toward a climax. My body became more restless, and I slowly writhed my hips to encourage Dillon to fuck me harder and faster with his fingers. Again, he took the cue, and his speed increased; before long, he was thrusting forcefully into my pussy, his knuckles grazing the cheeks of my ass as he pushed completely inside of me.

"Don't stop," I begged, and in no time, I felt my entire body tremble with ecstasy as I began to orgasm, the feeling originating in my pussy and clit but quickly spreading throughout my whole being. It was my first time having an orgasm with a man who wasn't my husband, and I hoped that you would be proud of me, and I wished you could somehow feel this pleasure with me. As I write these words to you, James, I pray that you can vicariously experience this thrill along with me, as I only wish to do this if *you* can enjoy it as well.

Before long, it was over. I laid panting on the bed, gradually recovering from the sensation that had just rocked my body to its core. Dillon stood up, and to my surprise, so did his cock. *Didn't he just cum a few minutes ago?* A sweet and innocent smile spread across his face.

"Did I make you cum?" he asked.

"You couldn't tell?" His eyes lit up, and again I wondered, *How old is this guy?*

"Oh, yeah, totally." He was trying to sound cool as one hand casually stroked his rock hard dick. "So, should I get a condom?"

I barely had time to consider this before we were interrupted by the sound of a heavy door closing nearby. Dillon tensed up with wide eyes, as a woman's voice called out, "Dillon? Are you here?"

"*You need to hide!*" Dillon whispered urgently. "*In the bathroom, hurry!*" He called out, "Yeah, I'm here, Mom! But I'm naked, don't come in!" I realized Dillon's hotel room was adjoined with his parents', and we were only a door apart.

Fully nude and still exhausted from the orgasm, I rolled off the bed. Dillon thrust a pile of my clothes into my hands and ushered me into the bathroom.

"Why are you naked?" his mother shouted.

"I was going to take a shower!" Turning to me, he whispered, "*Leave the lights off and try not to make a sound.*" I stepped into the bathtub and drew the curtains closed to avoid being seen from the doorway.

"At this time of night?" his mother called. "What's wrong with you? Cover up, we're coming in."

Dillon wrapped a towel around his waist and closed the bathroom door most of the way. I heard the door open from his parents' room. I held my breath.

"Dillon!" It was his mother again. "You were supposed to meet us after the show! Where were you?"

"I, uh, I wasn't feeling good, Mom. So I came back to the room."

"But you didn't even tell us, we were looking all over for you!"

"Now honey—" came a male voice, presumably Dillon's father.

"And we finally come back," his mom continued, "and you – Do I smell alcohol?!"

"What? No!"

This was getting weird, and his mom sounded really strict. What would she do if she found a naked woman hiding in the bathroom?

"Mom, please. Just give me some space, alright? I'm feeling sick, I need to take a shower!"

"Fine," his mother said. "But when we get back home, you're grounded!" *What. The. Fuck.* I heard her footsteps shuffle away.

"Son?" called his father's voice meekly. "You've really upset your mother – good work!" He cackled, and he must have left the room because I heard the door close softly behind him.

Dillon popped his head back in the bathroom. "You better leave fast – my mom might come back for more punishment!" He disappeared back around the corner.

I quickly put my bra on and pulled my shirt over my head. Looking around, I wondered, *Where the hell is my underwear?* I put my jeans on commando to save time, and holding my shoes in my hands, I crept out the bathroom door. "Dillon! Have you seen my—?"

"Dillon!" called his mother's voice once more.

"*You have to go!*" Dillon urged. "Just a second, Mom!" He coughed loudly, then gestured me toward the door. "I said I'm feeling sick!" He resumed coughing, and with his noises as my cover, I slipped out of the hotel room, closed the heavy door behind me as quietly as I could, and found myself alone in the hallway, shoes in my hands and my hair and clothing completely disheveled. I started the slow walk of shame back to my hotel room. I guess I'm never seeing those underwear again!

***

"Jenny, you're awake!" She was lying in bed, covers over her legs, reading a book.

"I know, right? Fuckin' A."

"Were you waiting up?"

"Of course I was! I had to make sure you got back in one piece."

"Well, I did! Uh, mostly." I told her the entire story, including the bit with Dillon's parents and leaving my underwear behind.

"Good for him," Jenny said with a grin. "The kid got himself a souvenir."

I laughed. "I know, right? How old was that guy, anyway?"

"19," Jenny replied. She looked at me with a half-smile.

"What?! How do you know that?"

"I met his parents at the bar!" Jenny said. She had stayed with Julian at the bar the show, hoping he might walk her back to the room. When he finally made an excuse to leave, Jenny spotted a pair of middle-aged adults who seemed to be looking around for someone. Noticing their resemblance to Dillon, she asked if she could help with anything, and learned about their missing son. "His mom seemed pretty pissed about it, but I think she was really just scared."

"Yeah, we just had the pissed off version when she made it to the room. The dad seemed cool, though. And the son – I guess he's okay for a kid."

***

I typed up this email as quickly as I could. There was a lot to tell, and as we agreed, I didn't want to leave anything out. I really hope you enjoyed this story. Although I'm having a wonderful time, rest assured that my heart is still yours, and at the end of the day, my body is too.

I wonder if things would've gone differently if Dillon's parents didn't come home. He suggested getting a condom for sex, but am I really ready for that? I'm not sure. I felt more confident about things today, so I think my boundaries are expanding as our experiment goes on. The next time I have an opportunity, I think there's a fair chance things will progress fully to intercourse. I'm telling you this because I want you to know the stakes. As you well know, I'm giving over the power here: it's up to you whether I stop or continue.

With forever-ever love,

Samantha

4: The Big, New Challenge

Samantha

Tuesday, May 14, 2019; 9:16 a.m.

Dear James,

Sorry for messaging you the morning after, but it was a long and exhausting night! My email should be worth the wait, however, because I think you're going to enjoy this one. I'll try to keep my introduction brief so I can get us to the good part. ;)

Today, Jenny and I decided to play tourist. We woke up at a reasonable hour, and I immediately checked my email. I had a "read receipt" notice on my message from last night but no response from you – perfect. We then got ourselves ready for an outdoor adventure to the Mayan ruins of Chichen Itza.

I let Jenny take the wheel of the Volkswagen convertible as we made the hour-long drive to the ruins. With our sunglasses on, the top down, and our hair blowing in the wind, we were the quintessential basic bitches. By following a brochure we received from the resort, we had no difficulties on the journey. Life was good.

We arrived in Chichen Itza to find an array of stands and food trucks set up around the parking area. It was nearing midday already, so I ordered a chicken-stuffed tamale while Jenny bought some chilaquiles fresh off the grill. We followed it up with frozen fruit bars from a shaded stand.

After our quick meal, we signed up for a tour. I noticed a fit, attractive male tour guide in tight khaki shorts, but alas – we were assigned to tour with someone else. The ruins were quite a sight to see, large stone pyramids built among the lush jungle terrain. Tourists were invited to climb to the top along some steep, rocky stairs – one stair each for all 365 days of the year – but we didn't wear the right shoes for *that* adventure! The Mayans also had designed a sports field with walls on either side. The walls had raised stone circles like basketball hoops, except turned on their sides. The tour guide explained that Mayan athletes tried to kick a ball off the wall and through the stone hoop, like a hybrid of basketball and soccer.

Following the tour, without much else to do in the area, we decided to head back to the resort. Jenny wanted to catch one of Julian's aerobics classes, and I was craving a frozen cocktail in the pool after our morning in the sun. From my barstool at the swim-up bar, I watched Jenny elbow her way up to the front of Julian's class. From his platform above the water, he bent low to greet her with a clasp of their hands. They spoke briefly before Julian pumped up the music to begin the class. Through his headset, he gave instructions and encouraged the patrons with his comments and cheers.

From my vantage point, I could tell that Julian was a charismatic leader. He performed various dance and fitness movements from his platform, and the guests in the pool, mostly women, attempted awkwardly to follow him, but of course, they were hampered by the water. The result was comical, and even Julian would laugh at times, shouting, "Looking good, ladies!" or calling out specific patrons ("I see you shaking those maracas, Jenny! Ay ay ay!"). Jenny seemed to be getting the most attention, and I'm sure I caught Julian winking at her!

I was on my second strawberry daquiri when a man took a seat next to me at the bar. There were plenty of seats, so I assumed his proximity to me was intentional. From the corner of my eye, I observed that he was stocky and had a long, bushy beard. He might've been attractive, if you find lumberjacks attractive. His barrel-shaped chest was hairy as well, which wasn't a good look, as I couldn't quite tell where the beard ended and the chest hair began.

"I'm Darren," said the man behind the beard.

"Hi, Darren," I replied. I gave him a glance and a smile but quickly turned back to watch the aerobics.

"Your name is?"

I really hadn't meant to be rude. He wasn't my type, but that was no reason to treat him poorly. "I'm so sorry," I said. I shifted back toward him. "I'm Samantha." We shook hands. *Now, how do I tactfully show him I'm not interested?*

"What brings you to Mexico, Samantha?"

"I came here with my – uh – my partner, Jenny." I gestured to the aerobics class. "She's the one in front wearing the white and purple top.

Darren shielded his eyes and peered into the crowd. "Nice," he said. "So when you said partner, you mean—?"

"My life partner, yes," I answered. Hey, this was kind of fun. "We're actually on our honeymoon."

"Congratulations," Darren said, unenthusiastically.

"Thanks!" I replied.

"Hey, um. Do you guys ever party?" Darren asked. "Like, with guys?"

"Uh, party?" I was genuinely perplexed.

"You know, like, swing. Like, do you ever miss the company of a man?" Wow. This guy was really going out on a limb here.

I decided to hit back. "Oh, like, for pegging?"

"What? No, not like – like—"

"I mean, we pegged a guy once. But he was tied up and blindfolded the whole time."

"Oh, no, I wouldn't want—"

"Yeah, that was fun. But that's probably the only thing I'd want to do with a guy these days."

"No, uh – I think I hear my friend calling out to me. I probably better go. Nice meeting you, Sarina!" He swam away.

"Nice meeting you, too!" I called. "Maybe I'll see you around!"

Well, that was fun! I slurped down the rest of my icy drink while the aerobics class was just wrapping up. Jenny lingered behind with Julian, of course, as the other guests dispersed from the area. Before long, another staff member called to Julian, and he grabbed his equipment bag to depart. Jenny swam back over to the bar.

"Hey, how was the class?" I asked.

"Great!" Jenny said. "Julian said he liked my dance moves."

"I wonder why! I mean, he had a pretty good view of you shaking those maracas," I teased.

"All part of the strategy," she said as she winked.

Feeling exhausted after an early morning start, we decided to take an afternoon siesta, so we dried off and headed back to our room.

"What would you like to do later?" I asked Jenny while closing the curtain over our balcony window. She was already in her bed.

"We could check out the nightclub," she suggested. "Seems like it's open every night. Julian told me lots of people head over there after the nightly entertainment."

"Sounds good."

I removed my wet bikini, pulled on a pair of comfy underwear, and climbed into the bed. "I think I'll skip the show tonight, but if I nap like I plan to, I'm sure I'll be ready for a long night of dancing."

Jenny didn't reply – she was already asleep.

***

As expected, by evening time we had plenty of energy for a night of dancing. It felt a little strange getting ready, knowing that I wouldn't have my usual dance partner by my side. *My gosh*, I thought, *I haven't danced with any man but my husband since high school!* I was wearing a hotel bathrobe and doing my makeup in the mirror when Jenny asked what I was going to wear tonight.

"Probably my black cocktail dress with the flowy skirt," I replied. I hoped the flash of my skirt when I twirled might catch some eyes on the dancefloor.

"Solid choice," Jenny said. She withdrew a small purple dress from her suitcase. The end of the skirt was ruffly and longer on one end, like it was used for salsa dancing. "What do you think, too showy?"

I gasped. "No, I love it!" In this setting, Jenny and her tropical attire would fit right in. I worried that *my* outfit might seem a little too Vegas-style formal.

I considered my underwear situation. Well, my tiny white thong was no longer an option, so I wondered if I should wear an equally tiny black thong or just go with some dark grey boy shorts. Out of the corner of my eye, I saw Jenny pulling up her own black thong under her purple dress. The skirt of her dress was form-fitting, and she could tease a little skin without being too revealing. My dress, on the other hand, was looser in the skirt and likely to swish up from my hips while I danced, revealing my upper thighs and maybe even more if I wasn't careful. *I did come here to live dangerously*, I thought. I retrieved the black thong and pulled it up under my robe, feeling the g-string settle between my cheeks. The bit of silky cloth in the front barely covered the line of my snatch while ending well below my waistline. I was grateful for the bikini wax James bought me for this trip!

Before long, our hair was done, our makeup was in order, and we were dressed to the nines in our dresses and heels. I went with some shorter heels, whereas Jenny wore stilettos. How she can dance in those things is beyond me, but the extra height was doing wonders to lengthen her legs and lift her ample butt. I hoped for her sake that Julian would be there.

***

When we got the club, we were in for a surprise – the place was nearly empty! One small group sat at a table on the periphery of the room, and a few more guests were seated at the bar. The club was 80s themed, with a disco ball that reflected colorful beams of light around the otherwise dim room, shiny black tile, and a dancefloor in the middle that was thus far empty. It was after 10 p.m. already, and we figured the nightly entertainment show would've finished by now.

"What a bust," Jenny said. "Oh well! We can at least get a drink while we're here."

I followed Jenny toward the bar. As I looked around, I realized we were overdressed; other ladies were wearing jeans and blouses, and the men were mostly wearing short-sleeved collared shirts and jeans or slacks. When we arrived at the bar, Jenny seated us near three gentlemen who appeared our age or a little older. There was plenty of space at the bar to spread out, so I figured her placement was strategic.

We ordered beverages – I chose a vodka tonic to avoid a sugar headache – and started chatting. Jenny was on my left, and the group of three young men were on the other side of her. Jenny and I were discussing plans for the remainder of the week when I noticed one of the men darting glances at me from time to time.

He was tall with meticulously-styled blond hair, a clean-shaven face, and baby-blue eyes. He had a slender build and wore a short-sleeve button-up shirt, designer jeans, and shiny black dress shoes. We made eye contact a couple of times, but I decided to play it coy for now. He wasn't particularly handsome, but his pretty eyes helped him stand out – and so far, it was his eyes that he was chasing me with.

Before long, the blond gentleman moved to the other side of me and perched upon a barstool. "Can I buy you a drink?" he asked.

Do all the men at this resort have the same pickup line? I thought. "Nice try," I said, looking straight ahead as if ignoring him. "But I'm afraid the drinks here are free."

"They are? Damn! In that case, I'll buy you two drinks!"

I had to give him credit for thinking on his feet, and he earned himself a side-eye glance and a half-grin. "Okay, then. I'll allow it."

"I'm Ethan."

"Samantha. And this is Jenny." I gestured behind me, but when I turned, Jenny was already talking to Ethan's two friends. "Well, that's Jenny over there."

"Nice to meet you, Samantha. What are you drinking?"

"Vodka tonic. I'm about ready for another one if you'd like to help me out."

"Sure thing." Ethan let out a sharp whistle, and although the bartender was in the midst of mixing a drink, he came straight over.

"Señor Hannigan, what can I do for you?"

"Vodka tonic," said Ethan. "And two shots of tequila."

"Right away, señor," said the bartender. He made our drinks first before returning to his prior task.

"What service," I remarked. "Does the bartender know you?"

"The bartenders tend to make friends with you when you're wearing one of these." He flashed a green wristband, signifying that he was a VIP guest. "Ready for a shot?"

"I guess I have to be." We clinked our glasses together and threw back our shots. I quickly chased it with a nibble of lime, but Ethan seemed unphased by the liquor.

"So where's your husband?" he asked.

I nearly choked on my lime. "Uh – what?"

"There's a tan line on your ring finger," he explained. "So either you're married, or you're very recently divorced."

Uh oh. I hadn't thought about what I'd say in this situation, but I figured I owed him the truth; then it would be up to him to decide if he were still interested. I tried my best to seem nonchalant. "My husband had to stay home. Something came up at work."

"You paused," said Ethan. "You thought about not telling me."

Is this guy a detective or something? He peered at me intently, but I refused to meet his gaze. Staring at the ice in my vodka tonic, I said, "I'm just trying to live in the moment, you know?" This time *he* was quiet, so I stole a quick glance. He was smiling smugly.

"Yeah, I think I know something about that. You only live once. Hey look, this place is starting to pick up. Do you want to dance?"

Somehow in just the past few minutes, the club had started to fill. The amount of people had tripled or more, and a pair of couples had made their way to the dancefloor. I took a hearty sip of my drink before answering, "Sure."

He took me by the hand and led me to the dancefloor. The music was standard club beats, techno or house music or whatever it's called, and the volume had increased as the dancefloor started to fill. At first, Ethan and I danced facing each other but without touching. I closed my eyes, allowing myself to feel the music as I shook and swayed my hips, sensing my skirt toss against my thighs. When I'd open my eyes from time to time, I'd see Ethan dancing along with random, jerky movements. He seemed confident, nonetheless, and he kept watching me with a sly grin on his face. He gradually moved closer and placed his arm around my waist. I kept my body movements contained, but even still, our bodies began to brush against each other. I felt his hand began to slide down my back toward my skirt. I could tell where this was going – I put my hand on his shoulder and raised my voice up toward his ear. "I think I'll need another drink!" I said.

I turned and walked away, avoiding his advance – for now. I was enjoying myself, but I didn't want things to move too fast, and I thought it might be fun to play it hard-to-get. Besides, this man was far too confident! I wanted him to work a little.

Ethan followed me back to the bar where his friends were still entertaining Jenny. Spotting me, she stepped away from Ethan's friends and joined me on my left with Ethan on my right.

"Hey!" Jenny said. "Things have started to come alive here. Having fun?" I could tell she was checking in with me, making sure I was comfortable so far with Ethan.

"Yeah, it's great! I'm glad this place is filling up. Need another drink?"

"Actually, I was about to go dance myself. You cool with that?"

"Of course! I'm grabbing a drink of water, but then I'll probably be back out there."

"Sounds good!" Jenny said. "Come find me when you're done with your drink!"

"I will!" I wondered about Jenny's request, if maybe she was worried about me being alone with Ethan. Had his friends said something to her?

I turned back to Ethan, who greeted me with, "Another vodka tonic, and another shot of tequila!" He held the drinks out toward me.

That was a little presumptuous. "I was just getting a water," I told him. "Enjoy your *two* shots of tequila!"

Ethan shrugged and then threw back the shots one after the other, again without a chaser. At least he didn't get pushy. I accepted the vodka tonic, and Ethan ordered me a water as well. When it arrived, I took a few long sips of the water before returning to my cocktail. With our backs to the bar, Ethan and I observed the dancefloor. I saw Jenny, sandwiched between Ethan's two friends, who were dancing close on either side of her. Jenny had a sexy Latin flow to her movements which was juxtaposed with the clumsy, jerky movements of her suitors. I laughed.

Ethan was laughing too. "I think my friends are out of their league!"

"Yeah, probably!" I agreed.

"You're not so bad yourself! Are you a dancer?"

"All my life!"

"It shows! I hope I get a chance to impress you with my own moves tonight."

"Oh, you're a dancer too?"

"Nope!" Ethan said. I shot him a suspicious look, and there was that confident grin again.

Before long, Jenny cha-cha'd her way over from the crowd and grabbed me by the hand, leading me back to the dancefloor. I gave in, ditching my half-empty cocktail on the bar. Jenny and I have a natural chemistry on the dancefloor together; I know you've watched us many times, James, and you've even been a bit jealous of our energy. Well, let me tell you, tonight we were on! We started off holding hands and doing a twist move with our legs and hips, and things got gradually more sensual as our bodies drew closer together. I could smell the perfume of Jenny's shampoo as we danced together face-to-face. I smiled at her as I began to run my fingertips over her shoulders and on the fabric on her waist and hips. Jenny was giggling slightly, and I noticed that our antics had started to draw some stares! Flowing with the energy of the moment, Jenny took my hands and led me in a full spin-and-a-half, resulting in her being positioned behind me. The crowd formed a circle around us as spectators whooped and clapped in our direction, so to give them a show, I leaned over and ruffled my skirt. Jenny began chugging in her heels behind me in a humping motion toward my ass, which the audience seemed to love. The music was building to a crescendo, which Jenny punctuated with a sharp smack on my ass as the music was ending! The crowd responded with whistles and applause, and Jenny and I devolved into laughter.

"That was fun!" I exclaimed as we left the dancefloor.

Jenny stopped me before we made it to the bar. "It was, and unexpected! But, I actually pulled you aside to tell you something."

"What's up?" I asked.

"I just wanted to give you a heads up about Ethan. His friends were telling me—"

She was interrupted by a pair of arms that wrapped around our shoulders. It was one of Ethan's friends, who was quickly joined by the other.

"That was hot!" the first one said. "You guys can really dance!"

The other guy winked at Jenny and said, "You should teach me some of those moves, Jenny." He gyrated his hips in her direction.

The first guy turned to me and said, "You can teach me your part if you like! Your name is?"

Ethan stepped in. "Her name is Outta," he told him. "Outta yo league!"

The second guy laughed, while the first guy looked challengingly at Ethan for a second before shaking his head and walking away.

"What was that about?" I asked.

"Nothing," Ethan said. "Just watching out for you, Dave's a little drunk."

"I think we're all a little drunk," I admitted.

"Even more reason to be careful."

The comment caught me off-guard. Jenny was about to warn me about Ethan, but here he was playing the protector. What's going on with this guy? The mystery had piqued my interest, but I knew I had to be wary.

"I'd love to dance with you some more," Ethan said, "but I have to square up with the barkeep real quick. Can you hang on in a minute?"

"Sure."

Ethan led me back to the bar. He withdrew a $100 bill from his pocket and got the attention of the bartender. "Manuel," he called. He handed him the bill. "For your help tonight."

"Thank you, señor," Manuel said. He tucked the bill in his shirt pocket, as if a $100 tip were no big deal.

"Ready to dance?" Ethan asked me.

"Of course."

This time around, Ethan started out by dancing close and hovering his right hand on my waist, touching me lightly from time to time. I tried to dance as if I didn't notice, but within a couple minutes, Ethan was even closer with his hand on my lower back. I then felt his other hand slide along my dress from my hip to the outside of my upper thigh. I could detect the faint smell of aftershave mixed with tequila on his breath – which wasn't necessarily unpleasant. Throughout the dancing, I caught glimpses of his blue eyes in the flashes of light from the disco ball above. They were always looking back into mine.

Things progressed. Ethan's hands continued to search me while we danced, grazing me at times as if by accident: upon my thigh, along the side of my breast, and gently on my ass. I knew that this was flirtation, and I was starting to feel turned on by it. He moved his right leg in between my legs, and with his hand on my back, he guided our hips close together. Something pressed again my leg, and I realized there was a distinct bulge poking against my upper thigh. Intrigued, I allowed him to continue, and he bumped and grinded the bulge against me. I tried to get a sense of what he was working with, but our movements were too chaotic. The next thing I knew, he was kissing me, and I felt his fingers graze the skin of my buttocks as he ran his hand under my skirt.

The promptness of his action snapped me back to reality. A line was crossed, and I needed a moment to decide how I felt about it. Disengaging from the kiss, I told Ethan that I needed to use the restroom. He said he'd wait for me back at the bar, and I agreed to return.

Arriving in the dim, black-lit bathroom, I could feel that my face was flushed. Rushing past booze-infused women touching up makeup in the mirror, I slipped into a stall for a moment to think. Things hadn't gone nearly as far as they had with Mark or Dillon, but there was something different about Ethan. He knew what he wanted, and he seemed like the kind of guy who knew how to get it. Once again, my mind turned to you, James. In my last email, I told you I might go further the next time I had an encounter. I gave you the chance to stop me, knowing where things might go if you didn't. And – you didn't. Was that your seal of approval? Or was this a test, and you want me to make the "right choice" on my own? A mix of excitement and dread filled me as I mulled where things might go. Best case scenario, I have a lovely time with Ethan, and James feels invigorated by sharing his sexy wife with a stranger. Worst case scenario, James never forgives me. With that thought in mind, along with an uncomfortable pit in my stomach, I knew what I needed to do. *When I leave this bathroom,* I told myself, *I'll grab Jenny and just slip out the door. If Ethan catches me – I can just tell him I got sick and need to go back to my room. Jenny will cover for me, I know she will.* In that moment, I was resolved. I stepped out of the stall.

"Hey, Sam." It was Jenny. "You good?" She was at the sink, watching me through the bathroom mirror.

"Yeah, I think so. I needed a quick breather."

She turned from the mirror to look at me directly. "About Ethan—"

"Yes?"

"I was talking to his friends. He's kind of – well – a slut."

"A what?" I asked. I laughed, as Jenny's presence and humor had started to ease my nerves.

"Yeah, a total slut. Apparently, they've been here since Saturday like us, and he's already had two women back to his room!"

"Uh, Jenny. I've already fooled around with two guys too, you know."

"Oh yeah." She tilted her head in realization.

"Look, I don't mean to stick up for the guy," I said. "I was already on the fence." *On the fence? Wasn't I just about to ditch this loser?*

"Oh, good," Jenny said. "James will understand."

"What do you mean?" The whole point of ditching Ethan would be to protect James.

"I thought James was kind of pushing for this, right?"

"Right. I mean, I guess."

"Look." Jenny put her hand and my shoulder and looked into my eyes. "I'm not trying to stick up for Ethan either. I think he's the wrong guy. Maybe.

But from what I could tell, James kind of wanted you to do this stuff. Like a hotwife thing."

"A what?"

"A hotwife, like a kink. Like – just Google it. So, what's your call, do we stay or do we ditch?"

I took a deep breath. "I'm having fun, and that's what James wanted. So, let's stay."

"Fine," Jenny said. "But if you change your mind and want to escape, I can blow chunks on his shiny designer shoes if you like."

"You can do that on command?"

"Sure! Girl, I was bulimic my whole junior year of college. And I'm sad to say, some skills you never lose."

"You never cease to amaze me, Jenny."

"Don't you forget it."

***

We returned to the bar where Ethan and his friends were waiting. Jenny went off with Ethan's friends, leaving me alone with Ethan.

"I thought you gave me the slip," he said. It was like he was reading my mind again.

"I thought about it." I shrugged, attempting to play it cool. My retreat to the bathroom had been rather sobering. "But I decided to have another drink – no shots though, please."

"You got it." He summoned Manuel.

"Still thirsty, señor?" Manual asked.

"Just a vodka tonic for my friend," Ethan said. "And a glass of water."

"Yes, sir. Be right back, muchacho." The drinks were ready in 10 seconds flat, and he gave the vodka tonic to me and the water to Ethan. Ethan slid the water my way as well. He then produced a $20 bill, seemingly out of nowhere, and passed it to Manuel who took it without a word.

"Have a seat," Ethan said. He gestured to a bar stool next to his, and I took it. It was time to make small talk – eek. I sipped my drink to calm my nerves.

"You're a good tipper," I said. "Do you come to resorts like this often?"

"Here and there."

"Not much for self-disclosure, I see?"

"To be honest, I don't think you and I are here to get to know each other." He grinned, and I was taken aback.

"Whatever do you mean?" I tried to sound nonchalant, but my voice quavered.

"This isn't a date, Sam," he laughed. "What was it you said? You're here to have fun?"

"Is that what I said? I guess that sounds like me." I felt his hand on my knee, and it jolted me a little.

"Then let's have fun," he said. He leaned in and started to whisper in my ear, and as he did so, his hand began to inch up my leg toward the hem of my skirt. "I have a suite in the building next door, the room is all to myself. I could use some company tonight."

A tingling sensation began at his fingertips and ran up my leg, causing a keen sense of warmth in my loins. Trying to sound in control, I whispered, "What did you have in mind?"

His fingers were halfway up my thigh. "There's a jacuzzi bathtub. 24-hour room service. And the view of the beach is stunning."

"It's nighttime," I said. "The beach will be dark."

"Then you'll see it in the morning."

His fingers were now three-quarters of the way up my leg, mere inches from the tiny cloth of my thong. I felt myself blush again, but the intimacy of waking up in his room caused panic. I realized that other guests might see that he was feeling me up, so I turned my legs away to face the bar.

"Sorry." I cleared my throat, and then took a long sip of water. "I want to get there. Just give me a little time."

"Of course." He was quiet for a moment, so I put my hand on his knee to reassure him. He put his hand on mine and said, "I'm digging this song. One more round on the dancefloor?"

"Good idea."

We made our way back to the crowd, and Ethan wasted no time getting close and personal with me. His hands were running up and down my body, and he took two or three opportunities to kiss me, short but intimate kisses, before rediscovering the music. The music I hardly heard, but I felt it, as if the beat moved rhythmically through my body and commanded my motions. By now, Ethan was hardly dancing – he was bobbing, and groping, and grinding his pelvis against me. I could feel his bulge again through his jeans, and it felt large. Curious, I began to move my body to invite more contact, and soon, he was rubbing himself continuously against my thigh and my hip. His hands had made their way up my dress again, and he was unabashedly fondling my ass.

I focused on his bulge as he moved it against me, and I could feel it running down his pantleg along his inner thigh. I thought I could make out the shaft, which was surprisingly lengthy, as it seemed to end nearly halfway down to his knee! It was clearly very hard, and I knew I wanted to see it in person. I also knew if we stayed much longer, Ethan would be doing pretty lewd things to me in public.

"I think we should get out of here!" I shouted up to him.

"Back to my place?"

"Yeah!"

"Ok, let's go!"

I scanned the crowd for Jenny and found her nearby on the dancefloor. Ethan's friends were moving on her like hounds, doing their best "Night at the Roxbury" impression, except clumsier and more sexual. She seemed a bit jostled, but nonetheless appeared to be enjoying herself. She squeezed out from between them once she noticed me.

"Hey, everything okay?"

"Yeah, Ethan and I are heading out!"

"What room number?" she asked. Ethan leaned in and whispered a room number to Jenny. "What's your last name?"

"What?" Ethan asked.

"It's Hannigan," I told her.

"Okay, Ethan Hannigan!" Jenny shouted over the noise. "Samantha better come home safe tonight, you hear me?!"

"Loud and clear!" shouted Ethan.

And with that, he took me by the hand the whisked me off through the crowd.

***

The walk to Ethan's was a bit of a haze. *This is it. I'm doing this.* Although I went to Dillon's room the night before, there was much less certainty about what would go down. I felt in control with Dillon, but Ethan had a way of getting what *he* wanted; and I knew I was ready to give it to him.

He took me through the path in the gardens to one of the larger, newer-looking buildings. He guided me up some stairs and through a hallway until he reached a room. He withdrew his keycard from his pocket and opened the door.

Ethan must have had the fanciest room in the resort. It was easily twice as large as my room, with newer carpeting, fancy paintings on the wall, and a larger, more luxurious bed. The wall-mounted television was enormous, and as promised, there was an indoor jacuzzi that looked like it could fit up to 6 or 8 people. The room was impeccably clean, and Ethan must have moved his belongings to the closet or the drawers because none of his possessions were in sight.

"Nice room," I said.

"Thank you." He leaned in and kissed me deeply, not a quick kiss like in the club, but a long and passionate kiss that probed my tongue and lips. When he finally disengaged, I blinked, struggling to catch up to the moment.

Next, Ethan opened his shirt in one swift move, revealing that it was fastened with tearaway buttons. I noticed his physique, somewhat doughy and not quite as thin as he seemed. He had love handles, and not much muscle definition. His chest looked bare, not like it was waxed, but rather in a blond peach fuzz kind of way. *He's not nearly as hot as James*, I realized. I felt a tinge of pride in that moment, recalling just how sexy you are and knowing you are mine. Ethan, on the other hand – if not for his eyes, his confidence, and his seemingly massive dick, I probably wouldn't find him that attractive.

He pulled off his shirt and approached me again, reengaging me in a kiss and slipping off the shoulder straps of my dress, revealing my bra-covered breasts. His movements were swift and deliberate, and he wasted no time unhooking my bra and tossing it to the floor. My breasts succumbed to gravity and my nipples touched the air, already erect with excitement. His hands began to grope me, and he alternated between kneading the skin of my bosom and massaging my nipples between his fingertips. I eagerly pushed my dress down until it was around my ankles, leaving me in nothing but my tiny black thong. I was exposed, but I willed myself to lean into the moment. Ethan's hands shifted gears and made their way to my ass. His erection must have been raging in his jeans, and when he grabbed my ass, he pulled me closer until his bulge was pressed up against the tiny cloth of my thong.

"This doesn't seem fair," I said, tugging at the waistband of his jeans.

He dropped his hands from my ass to unbuttoned his pants. "I think you're going to like this," he said.

What confidence! I was briefly stunned and almost put-off, until he pulled his pants and underwear down in one motion. Springing forth was the largest penis I have ever seen outside of porno movies – and it even had many of those beat! It pointed up toward me at a slight angle, and there was a manscaped tuft of blond pubic hair around his groin area. My eyes grew wide as I drank it all in, and he must have noticed my reaction.

"What do you think?" he asked.

He was fishing for a compliment. Should I give it to him? Should I feed his ego? My facial expression had already betrayed me.

"It's big," I said. I wasn't sure what else to say.

"Touch it."

I reached forward and gripped it in my hand, noticing that my palm covered just a fraction of its length. It was also thicker than I was used to, and I noticed the weight of it in my hand – it was hefty. I started to stroke it, slowly and gingerly at first. Ethan closed his eyes and breathed a bit more deeply, but after a few strokes, he moved my hand away and laid backwards onto his bed.

"Suck it," he said.

I obeyed his terse command without thinking. I sat upon the bed next to him, took his cock again in my hand, and debated how to proceed. How was this thing going to fit in my mouth?

Noticing my hesitation, he gave another instruction. "Get it wet. Lick it."

I leaned forward, held the base of his cock and balls in my hand, extended my tongue, and pressed it against the underside of his shaft, tracing it from the midpoint to the tip of its head.

"Mmm, that's good," he said. He was propped up on his elbows, watching me. "Keep going. Get it really wet."

I worked quickly to cover his cock with my spit. When I got to the head, I slipped the first few inches of his cock in my mouth, messaging it gently with my tongue and lips. I then returned to licking his shaft and repeated this pattern until he stopped me with his words.

"Take it in your mouth. Show me how far you can take it down your throat."

There was never a question if I would obey. I was never one for deepthroating, and even your cock, James, has never fit fully down my throat. This cock was longer and thicker, but I would have to do my best. Opening my mouth and dropping my jaw, I moved my head up and down his shaft, getting a little deeper each time. With inches still to spare, I felt the head of his cock press the back of my throat, and I fought against my gag reflex. My mouth was watering in response to this intruder, continuing to coat his cock in thick saliva to lubricate it against the sensitive skin of my throat. He put his hand on the back of my head and gripped me by the hair, pushing my head slowly but firmly until I was even deeper on his dick! The back of my throat began to expand – another inch, perhaps – before giving in to the reflex and gagging on his cock. He released me, and I withdrew to take in air, coughing and sensing soreness at the back of my throat.

His giant dick was soaked. "Good girl," he said. "Now it's your turn. Lay on your back."

I did, and he kissed me again on the mouth before trailing his kisses down my body, on my chin, my neck, both breasts, my tummy, and down to my hips just above my thong. I could tell my pussy was warm and wet, and I imagined my fluid must be drenching my cotton panties. I instinctively opened my legs to him, and Ethan kissed me on the flesh of my inner thigh near my panty line, causing me to shudder with anticipation. He nuzzled his nose against the fabric covering my slit, and I could confirm that my panties were soaked! I hadn't felt this wet since I was a teenager and started fooling around with you, James. It was as if my body sensed Ethan's unusual size and was preparing for it.

"You're a dirty girl," Ethan said. "You're so wet for me, aren't you? Let's take a look." With his fingers, he pinched the fabric of my panties and pulled them to the side, revealing my pussy to him. My breathing accelerated as I felt the cool air touch the warm wetness of my flower, and I was nervous but thrilled to be fully exposed to him. Holding eye contact with me, he ran his tongue from the bottom of my slit all the way up to my clitoris. I gasped. This seemed to encourage him, as he set ravenously upon my pussy, taking long, swift swipes of his tongue across my opening and then flicking the tip of his tongue on my clit, sometimes gently and sometimes voraciously. The technique was a little sloppy and reminded me of Ethan's dancing skills; but nonetheless, occasionally he'd stimulate just the right spots, and I'd writhe or sigh against my will.

Then something unexpected happened. Placing he hands under my ass cheeks, he lifted and spread them a little, accessing my anus. As he spread my cheeks, I noticed that my ass was damp from the drippings of my pussy. He then stuck his tongue directly on my anus, and the sensation was a shock! It was slimy and almost tickled but was surprisingly intimate and arousing. He proceeded on my asshole with fervor, lashing his tongue upon its sensitive surface. Once or twice, he pushed the tip of his tongue against my opening, as if to penetrate. I massaged my clitoris with my fingertips, and in less than a minute, I'd had my first orgasm of the evening! The simultaneous stimulation of my anus and my clit was unlike anything I'd felt before. An electric sensation pulsed throughout my genital area, emanating from both my clitoral and anal focal points. My breathing accelerated, and I started to moan in a low voice. Ethan paused in response, but I begged him, "Don't stop!"

He continued, and a few moments later, the orgasm subsided, but an itch remained. "Oh \ God, I need your dick," I said. His rod was as hard as ever, and he climbed up over me on his hands and knees. He resumed kissing me, and he positioned his dick over my vaginal opening. I felt the head of his dick touch my lips, and I put my hands on his hips to stop him. "Do you have a condom?"

"Of course." He kissed me again, and the head of his dick was still touching my pussy. "Except I'm going to tease you first, make sure you're wet enough to take me."

He kissed me once more, and with my panties still pulled to the side, he traced the head of his dick along my slit. I kissed him back, feeling the burn of anticipation inside me and the warmth of his penis on the surface of my lips. Did the head just slip inside for a moment? For a split second, I felt myself open, stretching to take his unprecedented girth. I stopped him again.

"I'm plenty wet," I said. "Get a condom."

He rose from the bed and went to a chest of drawers as I removed my thong. He withdrew an open box of condoms – extra large – took one out of the box, and began to unwrap it. It was surreal. I was looking at a man who wasn't my husband, who was basically a stranger, and I was about to engage in an intensely intimate act with him. But then again, his tongue was just inside my asshole – is he really still a stranger at this point?

James is going to love this, I assured myself. *This is exactly what James wants. Ethan is nothing but a prop to me, a living, breathing sex toy. This will be fun, but beyond that, this means nothing.*

Ethan fit the condom around his cock and stood over me. "Have you ever had a cock this big, Sam?" he asked. Struck mute, I shook my head to indicate no. "Don't worry," he said, "I'll be gentle."

Holding his cock in his hand, he positioned himself above me. I marveled at the thing that would soon be inside me, and I realized I had butterflies. He rubbed the tip of his condom-coated penis along my crease twice more, ensuring I was damp enough to handle penetration. "Let me know if it hurts," he whispered, and he started to push his cock inside me.

The first few inches didn't hurt at all, and I actually felt a wave of relief come over me. My body was craving sex after all the foreplay, and I knew that I'd crossed another milestone – my first time having sex with someone new. The feeling was familiar, the warm, wet, pressure of penetration. My pussy expanded to accommodate its visitor, welcoming this big, new challenge. I closed my eyes and focused on relaxing my pelvis muscles to accept his thickness and length. It went in another inch, deeper than anything I've had inside me before. It then seemed to hit a wall of sorts, presumably my cervix, as his progress was halted, and I felt a dull, mild pain deep within me. Accompanying the pain was a sense of fullness, both pleasurable and slightly overwhelming. I couldn't tell if I wanted more of it or less, and the John Mellancamp song "Hurts So Good" played briefly in my head.

He continued in slow-motion, withdrawing his penis an inch or two before pressing it deeper, testing the limits of my depth. I held my breath, trying to cope with this feeling, and my mouth hung agape. Ethan gradually started to thrust with more force. By now he'd penetrated another inch farther, and both the pain and pleasure increased. He had ceased withdrawing much at all, keeping himself pushed deep inside me and pressing the tip of his cock against my cervical barrier. This felt a lot different than sex usually did, as I realized the cervix provides a different sense of pleasure than the vaginal canal or the clitoris. It was a deep, widespread pleasure accompanied by dull pain. Tension built inside me until I couldn't stand much more, realizing I might lose control and cry out. But before I could tell Ethan to ease up, my second orgasm of the night overcame me.

"Oh my God!" I exclaimed. I heard Ethan grunt in response, and he intensified his thrusting, keeping himself deep within me and pressing hard against me to penetrate, but he still could not push the final inch of his dick inside me. As I felt my vaginal muscles pulse and flex upon his shaft, I wet my fingers and started to stimulate my clitoris, attempting to enhance my pleasure and distract from the pain. The orgasm lasted for over a minute, before it finally began to subside.

Ethan relaxed as well, and though he stayed inside me, he stopped thrusting. He took a minute to catch his breath. Between gasps, he said, "You almost made me cum!"

"You *did* make me cum," I replied.

"I could tell." He shifted his weight, and I felt his dick move a little within me. "You're really tight."

"Thank you."

"How's my dick for you?"

"Really good."

"Intense?"

"Yes."

"I bet you aren't usually fucked like this."

"Maybe not exactly like this."

"How do I compare to your husband?"

"What?!" I nudged him off of me, and his still-hard cock slid out of my still-wet vagina. This topic was off-limits.

"Sorry, forget it," he said. He was watching me, grinning as if my defensiveness had given him his answer. Once again, his confidence both infuriated and aroused me. His right hand was stroking his dick through the condom, and his long, slow strokes seemed to emphasize his length. I think he was doing it on purpose to impress me – and it was working.

That thing was inside me, I thought. *Well, most of it.*

"Ready for more?" he asked.

"Yes."

"Come ride me, then."

"Okay." I sounded so meek, but the situation had left me speechless. He had been fucking me into submission, and I could do nothing but relent.

Ethan was on his back, stroking his dick with both hands to keep it hard. I crouched over him on all fours, and even on my hands and knees, his cock was poking me in the abdomen. He directed his cock toward my pussy and pushed his head against my soft opening. I sat backward slowly, easing my way down inch by inch. It was a quicker process than our first penetration, as my pussy was still a little elastic from being stretched. I couldn't sit all the way down at first, as his cock pressed once again against my cervix. But I realized if I shifted my weight a bit, I found an angle in which I could fit all of him inside me!

"Just a second," I whispered. I closed my eyes and sat still for a moment, acclimating to this full and intense feeling. If I shifted the wrong way, I felt a sharp pain. But if I was careful, I could move in a way that was exceedingly pleasurable. I didn't want Ethan to start stabbing my cervix again, but I noticed how enjoyable it was to simply move my hips back and forth, kind of grinding against him while his cock was fully submerged. My thrusting motion caused Ethan's dick to move and shift within me.

After a moment, I opened my eyes and saw Ethan watching my body move on top of him. He leaned forward and wrapped his arms on my hips, clasping my ass with his fingertips. He started to flow with my thrusting, squeezing my ass and pulling me even deeper onto his dick with each thrust. I released involuntary grunts when he did this, as not only did his dick press deeper, but I noticed my clitoris gained friction against his pelvis.

I was enjoying this multi-level stimulation and felt another orgasm start to build, when Ethan moved his hands up my back and bent me over him, pulling my face down toward his lips. I continued to ride his dick while I was kissing him, and the new angle allowed Ethan to resume a penetrative motion. Holding me forward with his arms and with his kiss, he used his legs to press against the bed and push his cock up into me, relaxing until his dick withdrew a few inches, and then pushing it back in to its fullest depth. His hips made a smacking noise as they pounded against my ass, and I felt a new, exciting sensation as his pelvis made contact with the lips of my pussy. His hands resumed their position on my ass cheeks, and he spread my cheeks apart as if pulling me open. My vagina already was stretched by his cock, but now it seemed like he wanted to stretch my anus. His fingertips were inching their way towards center, and before long, I sensed the tip of his middle finger massage the outside of my asshole. The area was still wet with my lubricant, and the additional stimulation was surprisingly enjoyable. His finger rubbed my juices on the surface of my anus, and he slowly started to penetrate my anus with a fingertip while still fucking me from underneath. He began finger fucking my anus, pushing his middle finger a couple centimeters in and out slowly. His cock had already left little room inside me, and my body strained to take both his cock and his finger in my holes simultaneously.

A third orgasm rushed over me in waves, and I disengaged from his kissing to let out a breath of ecstasy. "Oh my God, oh my God," I moaned. "Oh God, fuck me, fuck!"

He responded by pounding me harder, which was the first time he got truly aggressive tonight. Before he'd been moving gradually, mindful of my body's comfort and letting me get used to his enormous dick. But gentleness was out the window, as my excitement and my utterances seemed to push him to an orgasm of his own.

"Oh yeah, baby," he grunted. "Come for me. Come on that big dick!" His forceful thrusting prolonged my own orgasm, and gasping for breath, I thought I might pass out from lack of air.

"You fuck me so good," I cooed between breaths. He thrust again, hard, and pushed his finger deeper in my ass.

"You're making me come, baby," he said. "Oh God, I'm going to come."

His thrusting lost its rhythm as he started to come, convulsing wildly underneath me. I held myself still and squeezed my vaginal muscles, sensing the orgasmic pulses of his dick as he pumped semen into the condom. A few seconds later, Ethan relaxed his body, as his orgasm transitioned to a denouement. He removed his finger from my anus, and I lifted myself off his cock, feeling the length of it slowly withdraw from my pussy. There was a sense of emptiness for a moment, and I was sorry to feel it depart from me.

"How are you?" he asked.

"Really good. How are you?"

"Peachy. You're a hellcat."

I smiled, and maybe even blushed a little. "Thank you. You're not so bad yourself."

He sat up and removed the condom. It had a surprising amount of semen in it. He wrapped it in some tissues and threw it in the trash. Although his penis was growing flaccid, it was still long and snakelike as he moved around the room. I once again realized how unappealing his body was to me, so soft and pasty – not like the stud of man waiting for me back home. The oxytocin release from intercourse was making me want to cuddle, not with Ethan, but with you, James. The irony wasn't lost on me.

Ethan walked to the mini-bar. "Want a drink?"

"No thank you." I didn't regret the encounter, but thinking of my husband made me not want to be here. "I actually better go. Jenny will be waiting on me."

"She'll be fine. We'll call your room. What's the room number?"

"No, really, I need to head back. I had fun, though."

"Me too." I had just found my underwear on the floor and started to put it on when he approached me. "I usually don't say this," he began, "but I wouldn't mind seeing you again."

Caught off guard, I stammered, "But – but I have a husband."

"He doesn't need to know."

Actually, he does, I thought, *that's kind of the point*. Instead, I said, "Look, Ethan. I had fun. But I'm afraid this was a one-night thing for me."

He stared at me in silence, wearing the grim expression of a man not used to hearing "no." I pretended not to notice as I continued dressing, but I could see him out of the corner of my eye. He made me nervous, and I wondered what was running through his mind. Finally, he said, "Okay. Well, I'm glad I met you, Sam."

I stepped into my dress through the top and pulled it up over my shoulders. Relieved, I answered, "I'm glad I met you too, Ethan."

He walked me to the door and said, "Enjoy your vacation. Maybe I'll still see you around."

"Yeah, maybe," I replied. I walked into the hallway, not daring to turn around as I made for the stairs. I didn't hear the door close until I had turned the corner, so I presume he was watching as I made my escape.

***

I exited the building and stepped into the night air. Even at night the air was warm, and I welcomed it as I began the long walk to my building at the other end of the resort. *Back to the slums*, I thought, though the suites in our building were only slightly less fancy than Ethan's. The garden path was dimly lit with small foot lamps lining the path on both sides. I followed the path, with the buildings on my right and the beach on my left.

The resort felt eerie at this late hour. The guests must have mostly gone to bed, as I crossed no one on my journey. I looked out toward the beach and saw the moon, full and bright, with moonbeams reflecting over the waves. I decided to sit for a moment and gather my thoughts, so I removed my shoes, walked barefoot on the sand, and sat on the ground in my dress.

I was strangely numb at first. Seeking to ground myself, I focused my attention on my five senses – the sight of the moonlight reflecting off the clouds; the sound of the waves crashing on the beach; the friction of sand against my butt and my feet; the salty aroma of the ocean breeze; and a metallic taste in my mouth, a flavor I associated with being intensely nervous.

I couldn't avoid it any longer, I had to process what I'd just done. I'd had sex with another man, not my husband, for the first time in my life. The sex was good, thrilling, and pretty intense. If I thought about it, I could actually still feel a lingering soreness in my pussy, as I was just invaded by a larger penis than I'm used to. The man attached to that penis – was just some guy. Decent looking, a little arrogant, but otherwise just some guy. I felt nothing toward Ethan, not good or bad or anything. I thought of him standing there nude after sex, soft flabs of pinkish-white skin, a snaky, flaccid wiener, and a depressingly flat and bony ass. The image nearly repulsed me, and I had no desire to see Ethan again. But I still didn't regret what had happened.

I wondered what you'd be thinking, James. As Jenny said, maybe a part of you was hoping for this, and you'd really get your rocks off from what you'd read. But at the same time, I'm not exclusively yours in the same way I had been. I mean, of course I'm exclusively yours, but I'd let another person *borrow* me. Did that decrease my value? Would you love me less the next time you see me? Irrational thoughts ran through my head, but were they truly irrational? Emotions *aren't* rational often enough, and even if you know you *should* still love me, what if somehow you don't? I sighed. I guess there's no helping that now.

I stood and headed back to the room, straining to focus on the moment and let my irrational thoughts float past. *I had fun tonight*, I told myself, *and fun is all it was.* I took comfort in the fact that I felt nothing for Ethan. I realized I'd never actually had sex with someone and *not* fallen madly in love with them, so I was glad to know it was possible! Maybe it was possible for James to still love me after what I've done. Maybe he'd be proud of me; or maybe I'd get an email reply, telling me I'm only his and this was all a mistake, and we could go back to how things were. These thoughts and more raced through my mind as I shambled back to our suite.

***

I slipped quietly into our pitch-black room. I had just finished closing the latch on the door when Jenny's full-volume voice rang out of the darkness, causing me to jump.

"How was it?"

"Oh, hey. It was fun. You didn't need to wait up."

"Yes, I did. Did it happen?"

I paused for a moment. "It did."

"You okay?"

"I am."

"Do you need to talk about it?"

"Uh – not tonight."

"Oh, thank God." I heard Jenny's head collapse upon her pillow. What followed then was silence, and I was certain that she had fallen promptly asleep.

Love,

Samantha

~

James

Dear reader,

I could hardly believe it when I read Samantha's story about her tryst with Ethan. My body was tense from the first line, and I didn't relax until well after I'd read it through. I masturbated to the imagery, twice, rubbing my cock raw as I hung on her every word. Her encounters with Mark and Dillon were like warm-ups for this moment, and I'd already felt nervous reading about the foreplay she engaged in with these strange men. But reading about her having intercourse was a new level of feeling for me – I swear my heart ripped apart as she described the first moment of penetration, and I knew I could no longer claim Samantha's body exclusively as my own.

How to explain the duality of emotion, feeling gut-wrenchingly jealous while being carnally aroused? I imagined being a caveman with a club, watching another caveman fornicate with my woman, and then clubbing him on the head and reclaiming what was mine. I wanted to fuck Samantha – hard – harder than I'd ever fucked her before. Learning that she'd slept with a man with a larger penis – larger than mine – was maddening to think about. How could I, her husband, ever measure up to this stranger? What if as a result of this encounter, she started to view me as small, as inadequate, as forever less-than? The notion was ludicrous that my loving wife could ever feel differently toward me in this way, all because of a random hookup with some dumbass stranger. But just as Samantha had irrational thoughts to contend with, these ones were mine.

I considered Samantha's reflections on the night at the end of her letter. I was comforted to know Ethan meant nothing to her, but I was also saddened to know that she was scared about what this meant for us. I didn't want it to mean *anything* for us, apart from a little excitement. I knew I needed to comfort her, or I'd ruin the rest of her trip, she'd come home miserable, and our experiment would be an all-around "fail." Considering this, I wrote her the following email:

Tuesday, May 14, 2019; 6:39 p.m.

Dear Sam,

Thank you for your message. I love you. Your story was very arousing, and I'm glad to hear that Ethan meant nothing to you. A part of me hopes you'll sleep with someone else so he's not the only one. Is that weird of me? I know I wasn't supposed to message you, but reading your email, I wanted to give you some comfort. Follow the rules, and there's nothing you can do that would make me love you any less. Feel free to stay the course, but as always, the choice is yours.

Love and tenderness,
James

5: Playing with Fire

Samantha

Wednesday, May 15, 2019; 10:06 a.m.

Dear James,

First off, thank you so much for your email! It really put my mind at ease. Second, believe it or not – I already have another story for you!

Yesterday morning, after sending you the email about the events from last night, Jenny and I decided to use our meal vouchers to have a fancy brunch at one of the resort's premier restaurants. The hostess showed us to our seats on the shaded veranda overlooking a rocky stretch of beach. The waves crashing on the black rocks threw clouds of mist into the air, creating a pleasing ambience during our meal.

The menu featured tapas, including Spanish omelets, fried potatoes, bacon-wrapped dates, and a cheese and olive platter. I complemented my meal with a mimosa, while Jenny enjoyed a Bloody Mary. We talked about the previous night's events.

SAM

So, I had sex last night.

JENNY

Cool, girl! High five!

They high five.

                              SAM

              I think I want another drink.

                             JENNY

Me too. Waiter! Another round of drinks, please! And bring
                       more cheese!

At least, that's how it might've gone if we were men. Here's how it actually
went:

                              SAM

              So, about last night—

                             JENNY

           Oh my God, yes. Tell me everything.

*SAM tells her everything, leaving out no details. JENNY
asks a hundred questions. It takes about an hour.*

                             JENNY

            Oh, wow. So how do you feel?

                              SAM

         Conflicted. I think I need another drink.

                             JENNY

        Me too. Waiter! Another round of drinks, please!

The WAITER approaches.

                             WAITER

Right away, ladies. And would you like another plate of
                        cheese?

                        SAM and JENNY
                          (Ad lib)

No-no-no… I couldn't possibly… I feel so full!… Just the
                      drinks, thanks…

WAITER

Very well.

The WAITER departs.

JENNY

I can see why you'd be conflicted.

SAM

Right? It was fun. And it felt really naughty. But James—

JENNY

Uh huh.

SAM

What will he think?

JENNY

Well, it's not like he can be mad or anything.

SAM

He can't?

JENNY

No! If he has anyone to be mad at, it's himself. The way I
understood it, he practically begged you to do this.

SAM

I know, but - maybe he didn't think I'd go through with it.
Or maybe it'll hurt his feelings that I enjoyed myself.

JENNY

Sam, look, either he'll read the email and be cool with it,
or he'll have a reality check and call it off. Either way -
and I can't stress this enough - it isn't on you! Not only
did he ask you to do it, he told you to tell him the truth
about the experience, down to the last detail. If he can't
handle it, tough shit. You live, you learn.

SAM pauses to reflect.

                              SAM

Rationally, I get it. I "technically" didn't do anything
wrong. But what if this changes how he feels about me? What
if this hurts him, deeply, even though he *thought* it's what
he wanted? He could be wrong, you know. Not every fantasy
                  plays out how you think.

JENNY sighs.

                             JENNY

Then I guess that's the risk you guys are taking. But think
about how things have gone so far. You communicated really
clearly on the front end, put together some rules that were
very explicit, which you both agreed to. Then, once we got
here, you tested the waters with some foreplay – a little
handplay with Mark, a little oral with Dillon – James had
his chance to call it off, and he didn't! He *encouraged* you
to do this, and you full on *warned* him what you'd do. I'd
say as far as open relationships go, you guys have played
                       it pretty safe.

                              SAM

               I guess you're right…

*SAM takes a moment to think about things. She realizes that
JENNY made some really good points. She considers that
maybe this is what JAMES truly wants.*

JENNY belches.

                             JENNY

Woo! A little too much tomato juice. Anyhow, I know I'm
right, Sam. You and James are *crazy* about each other. Even
if you guys realize this was a huge mistake, there's no way
this situation will do actual harm to your relationship.
You'll make up, you'll move on, and you'll learn a bit
        about yourselves along the way. Everyone wins!

JENNY throws her hands up in a "victory" gesture, knocking items of silverware to the ground. She's a little tipsy, and she looks around to find the source of the clatter. SAM reflects.

SAM

You're right. You're right! Thanks for talking to me, Jen. This helped, a lot. I'm starting to feel a bit better.

JENNY

You're welcome. Oh, waiter! I think we'll take that cheese now...

Scene fades to black.

***

When we got back to the room, Jenny went to the bathroom to splash some cold water on her face. I checked my email and was surprised to see a response from you! Excited and nervous, I opened the message and started reading.

Thankfully, it was a short message. When Jenny stepped out of the bathroom, I rushed at her and gave her a giant hug.

"He isn't mad, he isn't mad!" I cheered.

"What the – huh?"

"He replied to my email, and he isn't mad!"

"Oh! Well, that's great!"

I brought Jenny over to my computer and let her read what you wrote.

"See?" she said. "What did I tell you?"

"You were right." I gave her a side-eye. "Why do you always get to be right?"

"Because I'm so wise," she said, tapping her temple. "Wisdom is born of experience, and I have *plenty* of experience."

"I won't argue with that!"

She stuck her tongue out at me. "Well, now that I've taken about six ibuprofens, what should we do next?"

I thought about James's message. Once again, he'd encouraged me to go out and find some fun. I wondered where that might be best accomplished. "Out to the pool?" I suggested. "Maybe Julian's working today."

"Something's telling me that he is," said Jenny.

And something was telling *me* that Julian would be the key to my next adventure.

We arrived just in time. Julian had just finished leading a water aerobics class and was standing on his instructor platform by the pool. Next to him was his boombox and a cute young Hispanic woman who must've been his co-instructor. He was waving goodbye to some patrons as we approached.

"Jenny! Good to see you!" Julian said. He was beaming. He put his hands on her shoulders, and they kissed each other on the cheeks. "And you must be Samantha, Jenny told me all about you!" I got the kissing treatment as well before he turned his attention back to Jenny. "You guys just missed my class, I'm so sad for you!"

Jenny laughed. "We'll get over it. Are you teaching again this afternoon?"

"No, no, my partner here has it covered." He gestured to the young woman nearby, who was speaking to some hotel guests. "She's my little protégé, she just started teaching classes on her own."

Jenny eyed the woman, who was tan like Julian with a pretty smile and a slender build. She wore a white one-piece bathing suit, and her hair was pulled back in a sporty ponytail.

Jenny asked, "Is she one of your girlfriends, Julian?"

His eyes widened. "Maritza? No, no! Like I said, she's my protégé. I only have one girlfriend."

Jenny rolled her eyes. "That's not what your friends told me." She changed the topic before he could reply. "So, what are you up to for the rest of the afternoon?"

Julian rolled with the change in topic. "I was just heading back to my villa before the show tonight. My housemate, Carlos, is performing. Hey, you guys should come along so you can meet him before the show!"

Jenny looked to me for approval.

I nodded.

"Yeah, sounds like fun. What does Carlos do in the show?"

"Oh, you won't believe it," Julian said. "He's a fire dancer. He and his crew put on an amazing show, you can even feel the heat from the front of the audience. If we get there early tonight, we can grab some front row seats."

"That sounds really fun," Jenny said. "Better than a rock 'n' roll show, anyway." She nudged me in the side with her elbow, and I chimed in.

"Yeah, sounds like fun. Just tell us where to go."

"Ok, sounds good!" Julian said. "I'll call up Carlos, let him know we should do a little barbecue for when you head over. Think you guys will be hungry soon?"

Jenny shrugged. "I'm sure I could eat." We'd skipped lunch and would probably be hungry for an early dinner.

"Ok!" Julian said. "So, Carlos and I live in the employee villas at the end of the resort. I have my car, so why don't you guys go get your things together and meet me in the lobby in, like, half an hour, say, 2 o'clock?"

"Two it is," Jenny said.

***

We met with Julian promptly at two. He drove a small pickup truck, and after he pulled into the hotel drop-off area, we all piled into the truck's single row, Jenny in the middle. She didn't have time to tame her hair before the journey, and her voluminous frizz kept brushing against both Julian and me.

"So who all do you live with?" I asked Julian.

"Just me, and Carlos, and *mi novia*," he said.

"Your *novia*?" I asked. I wondered if *novia* meant grandmother.

"His girlfriend," Jenny said. "So, is your girlfriend home right now?"

"Nah," he said. His voice sounded a bit distant. "She's visiting her family in Merida for a few days."

"I see," Jenny replied. The three of us were having the same thought, but it went unsaid.

"What are the villas like?" I asked.

"They're pretty nice," Julian said. "The houses are small, but they're well-built and new. A lot nicer than living in some of the towns nearby. And we have a pretty sweet backyard that's good for hanging out and cooking food, you know? And the community is all people from the resort, so we hang out, have little get-togethers, everyone knows each other."

"Sounds like a nice little community," I said. "Do you bring people around much? Like, guests?" I wondered if I was going to feel out of place.

Julian laughed. "We're not really supposed to bring guests from the resort. Jenny will fit right in, but we might have to smuggle *you* in the house, my friend!"

My eyes grew wide. He was joking, right? I laughed politely. "I'll, uh. I'll hide behind Jenny's hair."

"Yeah, thanks," she said. She elbowed me gently.

"What's Carlos like?" I asked. He had a cool-sounding talent, and I wondered if he was attractive.

"Carlos? He's a good guy. Kinda quiet. Oh yeah, and he doesn't speak any English."

Well, shit.

Following the short car ride, we arrived at a small residential area. None of the roads were paved, and a couple dozen houses were scattered randomly throughout. We were still in the middle of the jungle, and foliage grew all throughout the neighborhood. There were various outdoor amenities that were built by the locals, and I noticed a sand volleyball pit, a half-sized basketball court, a children's playground, and a soccer field. Some of the houses had small gardens attached. The residents had made this community their own without any of the master planning we see in the suburbs. It was charming and struck me as simple yet lovely.

Julian drove his truck up to one of the houses. I'd only seen a couple residents around the area, but I was still self-conscious about being a resort guest and infiltrating their private space. As quickly as I could, I got out of the truck and followed Julian to the side door, allowing his body to block my view from the road.

Once indoors, Julian whistled and called out to Carlos, adding a few sharp words in Spanish. A moment later, a tall, muscular man in a tank top and gym shorts emerged from a bedroom. He was bald, had a neatly sculpted goatee, and was covered in tattoos – oh, and did I mention that he had muscles? I'd say that his tank top was tight-fitting, but I'm pretty sure anything would be tight-fitting on this man. He was broad and barrel-chested, like a body builder in a strongman competition. His face was handsome as well, with a chiseled, masculine jawline, a heavy brow, and dark brown eyes.

Carlos smiled warmly and greeted us in Spanish. He then kissed Jenny and I each on the cheek, as Julian had done at the pool. As he leaned down to me, I could smell a mixture of aftershave and body odor, as if he had just been working out in his room. Although the scent wasn't exactly fragrant, it was nonetheless subtly arousing. Is this how pheromones work?

He disengaged and stepped back, smiling. Jenny said something in Spanish, and Julian cut in.

"Hey," he said. "Why don't we stick to English for Samantha since she's our guest? I can translate for Carlos, okay?" He repeated himself in Spanish for Carlos. Carlos nodded and looked to me.

Julian and Carlos had a brief exchange, and then Julian explained, "Carlos just said the barbecue and chairs are set up out back. Can I get you something to drink? Cervezas, margaritas?"

Jenny and I requested margaritas, and Julian went to the kitchen to whip up some drinks. Carlos went outside with some groceries to start cooking.

"Why don't you guys follow Carlos?" Julian said. "We have a place to sit out back."

The backyard was a patch of soft, damp soil with smatterings of wild grass growing here and there. It was partially encircled by tropical trees, creating a natural barrier between this yard and the neighboring ones. There was also a decent-sized barbecue and some clean but worn patio chairs.

Carlos went to the barbecue and said something in Spanish, gesturing toward the low-seated chairs. Jenny took a seat, and I followed suit. What ensued was a few moments of awkward silence. Carlos must've preheated the barbecue, as when he lifted up the top, a cloud of smoke issued forth. Jenny was reclining in her chair and enjoying the sunshine. I glanced around the yard, and before I knew it, my eyes drifted over toward Carlos. I observed his wideset shoulders, his barrel chest, his biceps flexing as he started to place and flip burgers on the grill. He was really attractive, but how would I ever manage to flirt with him? He speaks a different language, for goodness sake!

"Don't worry, you'll find your opportunity," Jenny said, making no attempt to quiet her voice. She must've noticed me staring at Carlos.

"What do you mean?" I asked, playing dumb for the moment.

"You know what I mean. I'm sure you'll find a way to communicate with him." She quoted *The Little Mermaid* in her best Ursula impression: "Don't underestimate the importance of – body language!" She shimmied her shoulders, causing her breasts to shake.

I laughed, which caused Carlos to look up from the grill. He caught my eye and smiled. I smiled back and waved. I guess that was a start!

Julian came out with some chips, salsa, and our drinks, margaritas for the ladies and Coronas for Carlos and himself. He took a seat next to Jenny.

"Ah," he said. "What a day to be alive! Perfect weather, refreshing drinks, beautiful ladies—"

He turned to Carlos and asked a question in Spanish. Carlos gave a terse reply, and Julian said, "Carlos agrees, he said you are both beautiful ladies." Carlos hadn't looked up from the grill, so I wasn't sure if I should trust the translation!

Soon enough, Carlos came over with some burgers, and we supplemented the meal with some of Julian's homemade salsa. We lounged in our lawn chairs, eating on plates held on our laps and resting our drinks on the ground when we weren't sipping them. The conversation was light and was slowed by occasional translation – although Carlos rarely chimed in and appeared content to relax and sip his beer, mostly ignorant to the chatter around him. He smiled affably, nonetheless.

At some point in the conversation, Jenny had migrated her chair closer to Julian's. As she leaned back, she playfully rested her legs on Julian's lap. Taking her cue, Julian started tickling the tops of her shins with his fingertips, gradually making his way up her legs until he was grazing her thigh.

Meanwhile, Carlos and I had locked eyes once or twice, and at one point I decided he was either really spaced out or was totally checking out my legs in my jean skirt. On my end, I couldn't help but admire his broad shoulders, his massive biceps, and his protruding chest muscles. I ceased tracking Jenny and Julian's conversation, and I was wondering how on Earth I might seduce this man who I could barely communicate with!

That's when I had a sly idea. Jenny and Julian were clearly distracted, and I was seated at a perfect angle to give Carlos a show. Mustering my courage, I opened my legs a little, giving Carlos a view of my panties up my skirt. He seemed to notice my flash of immodesty, as he quickly averted his eyes in a respectful manner. Was that a faint blush I could see? I left my legs open, and within seconds I noticed Carlos's eyes start to drift back in my direction. Was I really doing this? It was uncharacteristically naughty of me, and the idea of seducing Carlos like this started to arouse me.

Before long, we were engaged in a game of cat-and-mouse. Julian was telling some story or other – that guy sure liked to talk – and I pretended to listen while watching Carlos in the corner of my eye. I could tell he was staring between my legs, but when I turned toward him, he'd suddenly look away! I wanted to make it clear that I was tempting him on purpose, so I shifted in my chair and pulled my skirt up a little to give him a better view. As I did so, I felt my tiny grey panties ride up a little on my crotch. Were they fully covering me, I wondered? Or was part of my labia exposed? Could he tell that my panties were starting to get wet?

I realized that Julian had stopped talking. Somehow, Jenny had migrated to his lap and the two were kissing. When did *that* happen? I looked at Carlos and we both laughed a little. Holding his gaze, I opened my legs another inch and watched him glance downward with a surprised and guilty look on his face. I was both embarrassed and intensely aroused by my brazen act. Knowing it was now or never to make my move, I gently rubbed my inner thigh and seductively bit my lip. Body language, right? His eyes grew wider, and a dopey grin spread across his face. Jackpot. Now how could I get this guy alone?

Summoning up the tiniest bit of Spanish I knew, I pointed toward the house and asked him, "El baño?"

He nodded and gestured for me to follow him. He stood up carefully. Was he was trying to hide an erection in his shorts?

"We'll be right back," I called to Jenny, but if she heard me, she gave no sign. Her attention was fully directed toward Julian's lips.

I followed Carlos inside and he pointed out the bathroom, but I didn't go in. Instead, I put my hand on his bicep and looked up into his eyes. I tilted my head up toward him, and taking the cue, he kissed me. As I pressed up against him, I could feel the sizable bulge in his shorts.

"Tu dormitorio?" I asked.

"Aqui," he said. He led me by the hand into his bedroom.

I wanted to suck this beautiful man's dick – and since he was wearing gym shorts, the obstacle to me doing that was minimal. I kissed him once more briefly before dropping down to my knees. I pulled his shorts down in one swift motion and – oh my! Just like with Ethan, I was in for a big surprise with Carlos! His dick wasn't particularly long, but it was thick! I marveled at it for a second before taking it in my hand. It felt heavy, and when I wrapped my fingers around it, they couldn't even reach my thumb. How was this thing going to fit in me? For a brief moment, I wondered if it wouldn't.

I put it in my mouth, and it filled the empty space inside me. I opened my jaw as wide as I could to accommodate him, and I could only take a couple inches before it was too much. Being cautious, I decided to lather him with saliva before attempting to deep throat. I used a combination of strokes with my hand and lashes with my tongue to stimulate him. I noticed him taking off his shirt as I sucked on him, revealing a neatly waxed torso with beautifully defined abdomen lines. Looking up, we caught eyes, and he watched intently with a wide-eyed expression as I worked on his dick. *Wow*, I thought. *This is happening so fast!*

Once his cock was good and wet, I put it back in my mouth. This time, the saliva acted as a lubricant and allowed it to slip in deeper. Before I knew it, his cock was balls deep in my mouth, as my nose and upper lip made contact with his pubic hair. I'd done it! His cock was maybe 5 inches long, and it filled up my entire mouth. I strained to keep my jaw relaxed, as I was worried about skinning him with my teeth! He initiated a careful thrusting motion, fucking my mouth slowly, moving in and out by a fraction of an inch. I placed my hands on his ass to moderate his thrusting, and my fingers gripped two sturdy mounds of muscle on his backside. My fingernails dug into his skin and met his glutes, which were solid as a rock.

By now, my pussy was aching for attention. As if reading my mind, Carlos stood me up, began kissing me on the mouth again, put his hands under my buttocks, and lifted me off the ground! He carried me over to his bed and laid me down, kissing me for another moment before moving his kisses down my body. I took my shirt off, leaving only my bra, skirt, and panties. Carlos opened up my legs, fully revealing my wet panties that he had gotten only a glimpse of earlier. He touched the soft cotton fabric with his fingers, and he surely noticed the dampness that had been seeping through. The light pressure caused me to shudder, as I was desperate for this sexy man to please me. He took his time, teasing my pussy with a light massage over my panties that gradually increased in pressure.

"Please, don't make me wait," I whispered, unaware if Carlos had any idea what I was saying. Nonetheless, my words seemed to encourage him. He pressed his middle finger against my thong-covered pussy, and the soaked cotton slid effortlessly into me at his command. After another minute of stroking my crotch and teasing me, he pulled off my panties and tossed them aside, unveiling my bare, pink pussy. He inserted a finger and started rubbing my clitoris simultaneously. My copious amount of lubrication signaled that I was good and ready for penetration. He stopped the kiss and leaned in to whisper something into my ear.

"Tro-han?" he said.

"Um. Pardon?" I asked. Tro-han? What the heck did that mean? I gave him confused look.

"Tro-han," he repeated. He gestured toward his penis, and I caught on.

"Oh, Trojan!" I replied. "Yes, uh, sí. Por favor!"

He maneuvered to the edge of the bed and opened his nightstand. I watched him lean forward, baring his large, toned backside to me. I noted the contrast between his and Ethan's body from last night. There was a lot more here to appreciate!

When Carlos turned, I realized the condom he was holding was labeled "XL." It was an extra large Magnum condom, meaning his dick didn't fit in the regular Magnums! This guy must've been on the upper extreme of penis girth. I prayed he wouldn't tear me apart!

Carlos stood at the side of the bed and put on the condom. From this angle, I could admire the contours of his torso and the chiseled lines of his abdomen, down to the v-lines pointing to his sizable member. Once the condom was on, he leaned forward and scooped me up, his burly arms under my back. Effortlessly, he positioned me at the end of his bed, my legs splayed open towards him and my pussy now waist-high and aligned with Carlos's penis.

As I had the night before, I spread my legs as far as they went, opening my flower to him as best I could. I meanwhile prayed that the pleasure would surpass the discomfort of being stretched by such as large dick. Closing my eyes to focus on sensation, I felt him press the head of his condom-covered penis against my womanhood, and I noticed right away a thickness I was unused to. The head of his penis filled my entire opening, and when he slowly pushed inward, I noticed a sense of heaviness in my pelvis as my skin stretched to accommodate him. My wetness definitely helped, for although I felt very full, the friction was effortless and extremely pleasurable. When only two or three inches had been thrust inside me, I already identified a new sensation of being pushed to my limit. The pleasure was accompanied by a slight burn that jolted me at first but became tolerable after only a moment. It was like eating delicious but spicy food!

I sighed, enjoying the intensity of Carlos's large penis and feeling his hands on my thighs, pushing me open and assisting in taking him inside me. As with Ethan, he moved slowly, seeming to realize I needed to get used to him. But finally, after a steady, gradual progression, I felt our pelvises press together as he pushed his entire length inside me.

He paused his motion for a moment, which gave me a chance to take stock. This feeling was quite different than last night with Ethan – Ethan had seemed to stretch me lengthwise, whereas Carlos was testing my width. I noticed that my inner labia was gripping tight around Carlos's cock, as it seemed to fill every bit of space within me. Still fully submerged, Carlos began to adjust his position, and I felt his cock press against my walls at various angles. It was really different! With you, James, or with Ethan, your cocks would stimulate different nerves in my vagina based on the angle. But with Carlos, because of his girth, he stimulated nerves all the way through me!

After a few moments of adjusting himself, he started to thrust, withdrawing his cock only an inch or so before ramming it into me, his pelvis making a smacking noise against mine. He started to increase speed, and the repetitive friction throughout my vagina felt intense! The slight burn mixed seamlessly with the pleasure, and both sensations grew as he increased the force of his thrusts. I heard a low, deep-throated moan. *Was that my voice?* Somehow, his immense girth had caused me to moan in a way I'd never moaned before, as my body strained to accept him. It sounded guttural, primal even, and I repeated the noise involuntarily as he continued to pound me.

"Unh!" I tried to form the sounds into words to make them less unappealing. "Unh! Yuh! Yes! Unh! Uh God!" It was only half working.

My vocalizations must have excited him, as after just a moment of intense fucking, he paused as if holding back an orgasm. With his cock still inserted, he leaned forward over the bed and began again to kiss me. I seized the opportunity to touch his body, wrapped my arms around him, and clung to his muscly shoulders. He responded by slipping his hands underneath my lower back, and before I knew it, he was lifting me up into the air again! The motion seemed effortless, as he swooped me up and hugged me into his body. My legs wrapped instinctively around his hips, and his hard cock stayed inside me. I held on around his shoulders for dear life, while he shifted his hands under my ass to support me. I felt his fingertips dig into the flesh of my butt cheeks, his hands spreading my ass and pussy to ensure sufficient access to my vagina.

I kissed him in this position, and with his hands and legs in unison, he began to bounce me up and down on his cock. What a thrill! My pussy was already overwhelmed by his dick, but there was the added feeling of being tossed in the air precariously. My safety was literally in his hands, and the butterflies in my stomach were surprisingly a welcome complement to the pleasure in my vagina. Before long, I was overwhelmed to the point of climax, and I let out another carnal – if not slightly embarrassing – grunt as my body shuddered in its ultimate release. I gripped Carlos's back tightly as I weathered the intensity of my orgasm. I heard him start to moan as well in a deep, breathy tone. He stopped thrusting, and I could feel the throbbing of his cock inside me as he released his seed into the latex barrier between us.

The throbbing was incredibly sexy, and it was a satisfying crescendo brefore Carlos and I came down off our climaxes together. He lifted me off his cock to place me back on the bed, and his sexy body was slick with sweat. He'd really done his work with me! Lying on my side and catching my breath, I gave him a thumbs up as I breathed out a heavy, "Gracias! Uh, muy bueno!"

He laughed. "Muy bueno," he agreed.

He started to put his clothes back on, so I figured I'd better start too. Finding my underwear, I realized they were basically a cream-soaked mess. Oh my! I cringed as I pulled them on, feeling the dampness at the center of the panties but noticing stiffness where the moisture had dried. This would not be a comfortable car ride home!

Fully dressed, we now had to face our friends outside. What would Jenny and Julian think about my disappearance? I was glad they hadn't come looking for us! Carlos opened the door to his bedroom and stepped out. I listened carefully for someone in the home – no sound. Were Jenny and Julian still outside?

I followed Carlos out the back door, and there were Julian and Jenny – smoking a blunt!

"Sam!" Jenny called. Her voice sounded a little slow, and her eyes looked kind of sleepy. "Where were you guys?"

"Oh, uh. Just taking a break inside!" I replied.

"You wanna take a hit?" Julian asked. He held out the blunt to me.

"Oh, no thank you. What time is it? Doesn't Carlos have a show tonight?"

"Yeah, let me see. Yeah, it's almost 4:30." Julian seemed a little off as well. "Want me to drive you guys back now?"

"Um, can Carlos drive?" I asked.

"Huh?" Julian was definitely not himself. "Oh, no, I'm cool! I can take you."

Jenny chimed in. "Dude, we're high as fuck. You're not driving us anywhere."

"Ah, shit," Julian said. He laughed. He said something in Spanish to Carlos. Carlos shrugged and replied. "Okay, yeah," Julian continued, "Carlos said he can drop you guys off. But then he has to come back and get ready for tonight's show."

"Oh right, the show!" said Jenny. "Can we go, Sam?"

"Yeah, of course!" I *definitely* wanted to watch Carlos on-stage. "But you and Julian might want to sober up a bit first."

"Yeah, yeah, okay. Let's rest up at the hotel then. Julian, we'll meet you at the show around quarter to 8?"

"Sounds like a plan!" he replied.

✳✳✳

The car ride back to the hotel was interesting.

"Did you guys fuck, or something?" Jenny asked.

"Jenny!" I exclaimed. "What the hell, dude?" I started blushing. Would Carlos know what that meant? I was pressed up against him in the middle seat. Even if he had understood, the man hadn't flinched.

"Relax, I don't think he understood that. Here, I'll ask him in Spanish."

"No, don't!"

Jenny laughed. "Chill out! It's no big deal. I'm just a little jealous."

"Jealous?"

"Yeah! I've spent this whole trip trying to mack on Julian, and you sleep with his roommate in what, less than an hour?"

"I, uh – wow." Was I being a bad friend? I guess that was kind of insensitive. "I didn't think about that, Jenny. I'm sorry."

Jenny sighed. "No, it's not on you. Like I said, I'm just a little jealous. Well, not jealous. Envious?"

"Jenny, it's a different situation. Julian has a—"

"I know! I know. It doesn't mean I'm not still crushing on him. It just kinda makes me an asshole for doing it."

"You are *not* an asshole," I assured her. But I was quiet for a moment. How would Julian's girlfriend feel about the situation? Julian hadn't slept with

Jenny, but he certainly had kissed her. I imagined you cheating on me, James, and my stomach sank.

Jenny broke the silence. "Julian's an asshole. Men are assholes."

"Giant assholes," I agreed. "Big, smelly, gaping assholes!"

Jenny laughed. Carlos drove on in silence, oblivious to the chatter around him.

***

We went back to the room to clean up and sober up before tonight's show. While Jenny was in the shower, my mind drifted back to Carlos. He'd be performing his fire dance in the show tonight. We were going to meet up with Julian, so presumably, I could see Carlos again afterward. Was that allowed?

I consulted the Notes app on my phone for the official rules. Rule #4: Do not form attachments. Do not have an encounter with someone on multiple days.

I thought about that last part. Technically, I could have multiple encounters, just not on multiple days. With Dillon a couple days ago, we'd fooled around in the ocean during the daytime and then met back up at night. I guess that would be the same with Carlos, but I hadn't fucked Dillon. If I hook up with Carlos again tonight, would that be forming an attachment? How attached can you get to a person who doesn't speak your language?

Furthermore, was I even ready to sleep with Carlos again? My vagina felt a little sore, which was unsurprising, as in the past 24 hours, I'd fucked two different men who were *very* well-endowed. Would his penis break me if we tried again so soon? Would James be extra jealous if I fucked the same man twice, or would he actually like that more?

I decided to play it by ear. If it happens, it happens! I've already had my fill of Carlos – metaphorically and literally – but if a midnight snack turned out to be an option, maybe I'll just see if I'm hungry! Ugh, I think that analogy sounded better in my head.

Anyway, I spoke to Jenny some more about the Julian situation as we were getting ready for the show. She had sobered up by now, so I figured she could give me a clearer version of events. She told me that after they started kissing on the lawn, she noticed that Carlos and I were missing. That's when she made a move.

"I – may have accidentally unbuckled his belt," Jenny said.

"Sounds like quite an accident," I mused. "How'd he respond?"

Jenny was doing her makeup in the mirror. "Poorly," she said. "He stopped me, and he said that he can't."

"Because of his girlfriend?" I was deciding if I should wear jeans tonight, or maybe something a little more flirty.

"I guess. He didn't say."

"Well, that sucks. Didn't his friends say that he's cheated on her before?" I decided on the jeans. *If Carlos wants me tonight, he better come get me.*

"That's exactly my fucking point!" Jenny exclaimed. "It's not like he's ever been unfaithful before. Why is he suddenly Mr. Virtue?"

"Oh, Jenny." I stopped what I was doing and went to her. I put my hands on her shoulders from behind and looked at her face in the mirror. Her voice sounded angry, but her face was sad. I could see where her mind was going with this.

"I don't know," Jenny said. "I guess he just doesn't like me that much."

"Because he didn't sleep with you?"

"From the way his friends tell it, he sleeps with everyone *but* me!"

"You're selling him as a great catch, Jenny," I said sarcastically.

"Yeah," she conceded. "He *is* an asshole."

"He's an asshole," I said. "But I do think he's an asshole who likes you."

She turned from the mirror and looked at me in the face. "Oh yeah? How do you figure?"

"Well, he spends time with you. He invited you over to his place while his girlfriend was away. He never talks about his girlfriend around you. And I've seen those looks he gives you."

"What looks?"

"The way his eyes move when he looks at you. How he smiles when you talk, how his eyes are so focused when he's listening to you. He doesn't do that with me. When we were all together today, I felt like he was *with* you, and that Carlos and I were just part of the scenery."

"That's – that's real sappy, Sam. But, thanks." She turned back to the mirror. "It doesn't do me much good if he shoots me down, though. And it doesn't explain why he sleeps with other women."

Jenny was still a little salty, but I could tell the crisis was averted for now. I resumed getting dressed. "I'm sure there's part of the story you just don't know. Maybe he's trying to make it work with his girlfriend this time. Maybe she caught him and he's trying to be better. All I'm saying is that from what I observed, it isn't a lack of him admiring you. Trust me, the man admires you."

"Yeah, but it's not his 'admiration' I'm after. Were you seeking Carlos's 'admiration' today?" she teased.

I laughed. "It would've been better than nothing," I offered. "But no, I guess I wouldn't have been satisfied with admiration."

"Me neither, sister," said Jenny. "Me neither."

***

When we arrived at the theater, Julian already had a table reserved up front. We stocked up on cocktails at the bar and then took our seats.

"Is this show any good?" Jenny asked. "The only one we've seen so far is Rock 'N' Roll."

"Some people say this is the best one," Julian said. "In no small part due to Carlos. Man, that guy can *move*!"

"Really?" I asked. With a body like his, he seemed more solid than agile.

Jenny laughed. "For some reason, I thought you'd know that already."

I ignored her and sipped my drink.

When the time came, the lights dimmed, and the show was ready to start. The theme tonight was circus – and it included an array of acrobats, clowns, and animal acts. Some trained hawks flew around the theater, and I could smell the caged lion from our front row seats. Near the end of the show, it was time for Carlos's act to begin.

The lights went completely dark. Straining my eyes, I saw three shadowy figures take their places on the stage. On cue, they each lit a weight at the end of a chain – which I later learned is called a poi – causing balls of flame to ignite at the ends. A drumbeat began as they started to swing the balls of flame through the air. The fire show was on!

Carlos was the performer in the middle. He was shirtless, exposing his toned, waxed chest and the tattoos encircling his rippling biceps. Below he wore spandex shorts, which showed off his thick leg muscles and revealed the hint of his bulge at the front. He spun his poi with command and strength, which highlighted his straining muscles as the fire cast shadows on the contours of his skin. *Hmm*, I thought, *maybe I will try to sleep with him again!*

Carlos and the other performers had looks of deep concentration on their faces. They twisted and contorted their bodies in unison as they swung their pois, performing acrobatic leaps to the audience's shock and awe. Julian was right – despite his muscles, Carlos leapt effortlessly into the air, performing pirouettes and barrel rolls without ever losing control of the dangerous flame in his grip. We could feel waves of heat as the flames swung past!

I looked around to the other audience members, watching their faces as they marveled at the spectacle before them. Some must've been admiring Carlos's body as well, and I got a bit turned on thinking I might fuck that sexy body later. I could see sweat start to form on his skin, and it caused him to glisten in the light of the flame. *You're not the only one feeling a little wet, my friend!*

At one point, one of the fire dancers exited the stage. From the wings, someone tossed Carlos and the other remaining dancer a pair of staffs. They used the flames from the pois to ignite the ends of each staff, and then they swung the pois and launched them into opposite wings! Before I could wonder whose job it was to catch the flaming pois, the next exciting phase of the performance began. It was a battle!

Carlos and his partner squared off with their staffs, which each burst forth with fire at both ends. The battle must have been choreographed of course, but each man exerted himself with such vigor, it seemed like the fighting was real! Their grunts and cries added drama to the affair, as they dodged and parried each other's vicious strikes. One would swing low, and the other would jump over the flame. One would swing high, and the other would duck at the very last second.

At one point, his partner appeared to strike Carlos in the face with the center of his staff. Carlos staggered back, the crowd interjecting with a sympathetic "Oooh!" He touched his face and then shook his head, as if recovering from a bout of dizziness. He responded by going on the attack, locking with his opponent weapon-to-weapon, and then stomping on his opponent's foot. "Ahhh!" cried the crowd, who seemed to be in Carlos's corner! It was probably because he was the handsomer of the two.

They re-engaged, striking the staffs against each other once more with increasing ferocity. And finally, at the exact same moment, both staffs snapped in the middle! Carlos and his opponent paused, each now holding a stick in each hand with a flame at the end. The looked at the sticks, now makeshift torches, and then at each other. Their weapons now broken, they shrugged in unison then hugged, very carefully, in a show of peace.

That's when the third dancer ran in with his own flaming staff! With a warrior's cry, he executed leaps and aerials as he threatened to attack his two opponents. Carlos and the other watched impassively as the newcomer finished his flourish and then froze. Carlos handed his torches to his partner, walked over to the newbie, and snatched the staff out of his hand. The newbie looked astonished, as Carlos snapped the staff in half over his knee! He handed the pieces back to his opponent, and the crowd roared with laughter as the opponent looked dismayed at his broken implements.

The third dancer tossed Carlos's torches back toward him, and the three resumed a final dance in tandem. Now with both arms wielding a flame, they danced as wildly as ever, flailing their torches around to draw clever designs in the air. The dance ended with a dazzling crescendo, as the trio held their torches aloft and sprayed a flammable liquid toward them from their mouths, causing flames to shoot forth into the air. The very next instant, they somehow extinguished all six torches on cue as the drums sounded their final beat. The audience, once again in the dark, was all holding their breath in silence. The stage lights came back on, and Carlos and his crew stooped low in a gracious bow. The applause began, and excited audience members burst forth with whistles and cheers. I took to my feet and whooped in delight, catching Carlos's eye as he smiled broadly and waved down to me. I beamed. He was the star of the night, and he had singled me out as someone special.

***

Jenny, Julian, and I waited in the theater to see Carlos after the show. The crowds quickly dispersed, some to their rooms and some presumably to the club, as the night was still young. Jenny and I were chatting about our favorite acts from tonight's show, while Julian was suspiciously quiet for the moment.

Before long, performers began to trickle out from a side door that led backstage. No longer in costumes and makeup, they were casually dressed and even looked somewhat bedraggled from an intense night of performing. It reminded me of my days as a dancer, hastily hanging up my costumes at the end of the night, pulling my hair into a sloppy bun, and wiping a mixture of makeup and sweat off my face before racing home to rest. Performance can take a lot out of you!

Carlos was one of the last to emerge, now in plain clothes – a tank top, flip flops, and gym shorts. As he walked our way, we got out of our seats and went over to praise him, Jenny and Julian speaking in Spanish, of course. Feeling detached because of the language barrier, I stayed back a pace or two but smiled politely. Once Jenny and Julian quieted down, I chimed in.

"That was great!" I said. "You're amazing!"

Julian gave a quick translation and then punched Carlos playfully in the arm. Carlos answered, and Julian said, "He thanked you for coming and is honored that you had a wonderful time."

"I did have a wonderful time!" I gushed. "I knew you were strong, but I had no idea you could move so quick!"

After Julian translated, Carlos laughed. He spoke again and then winked. Before Julian even translated, I started to blush.

"He said if you like quick, he can show you some moves backstage!" Julian said.

We all laughed for a moment until settling into an awkward silence. Julian broke the silence, finally.

"Oh hey, uh. Sam, I was kind of wondering for a favor?"

I was taken aback. A favor? What could he need from me? "Uh, sure. What is it?"

"I was hoping I could talk to Jenny a bit, like in private. Would that be okay?"

Jenny and I exchanged glances. She seemed as bewildered as I was, but I saw no reason to protest. "Yeah, that's fine with me. Is that cool with you, Jenny?"

In a quieter voice than usual, she answered, "Yeah, that's – of course."

"Okay," Julian said. "Hey, Sam, maybe Carlos can show you around backstage?" He said something to Carlos, and Carlos nodded in agreement.

"Definitely, that sounds fun," I said. "Can I ask where you guys might go?"

"I was thinking of going to the beach maybe?" Julian said. He glanced quickly at Jenny, who nodded and shrugged. "Just a walk on the beach, 20, 30 minutes? Then we can meet you back at the room."

We all agreed. Julian definitely seemed nervous about something, but I trusted him with Jenny. A part of me wanted to ask what this was about – but a part of me was just happy for alone time with Carlos! Would this be a perfect opportunity?

Jenny and Julian departed. Carlos smiled at my shyly, and we were both painfully aware that our only two translators had just ditched us. Well, the body language angle worked earlier, right? Carlos gestured for me to follow him, and we proceeded through the side door leading backstage.

Carlos first showed me the backstage area, and we started in the stage left wing. The stage was a lot larger than it appeared from the audience point of view. Looking up, I could see set pieces suspended in the air, ready to be pulled up or dropped from the ceiling on command. Over in the stage right wing, I could see an elaborate fly system of ropes and pulleys used to maneuver these set pieces around. Here on stage left, there were tables and tables of props, and I recognized the fire implements from Carlos's act as well as several other pieces from tonight's show. There was still some bustle going on at the loading dock, as workers loaded some larger set units onto a semi-truck to make way for tomorrow's show. Walking to center stage made me miss the good old days of dancing in theaters in front of friends and family back home. What a rush it must be to perform in front of a hundred different people every night, all year long!

I smiled at Carlos. "Thank you, this is beautiful."

He must have recognized the word, as he repeated to me, "Beautiful," while looking into my eyes.

I smiled politely but then looked away. Something about that word seemed too intimate to me. I wanted this man to fuck me, not fawn on me! I needed a little distance. I pointed down toward the floor. "Downstairs?" I inquired. "Uh, el baño?"

"Ah, sí, yes," he answered quickly. He took me to a stairway that led down beneath the stage. We arrived in a corridor lined with racks of costumes on either side. Cork boards covered the walls with schedules and fliers, all in Spanish of course. The entire area was empty of people, so we avoided any awkward encounters with Carlos's cast or crew. He guided me into a dressing room and pointed out a women's restroom attached. I went inside.

I looked at myself in the mirror, and my face seemed oddly stressed. What was I doing here? Was I ready to make another move? Could another sexual encounter occur right here? The face in the mirror didn't inspire much confidence. Was I tired? Unsure of myself? Would having sex with Carlos again suggest to James that I felt attached? Does Carlos understand that this is just for fun, or was he starting to feel attached to me? I imagined him saying "beautiful" again as he gave me that boyish grin, and I felt my stomach drop out of me.

I turned on the sink and ran some cold water over my hands. I closed my eyes and dabbed water on my temples, hoping the cool sensation would help calm my thinking. What a crazy situation. Here I was, in the middle of Mexico, without my husband, alone with a stranger who doesn't even speak English, who I happen to have fucked earlier this afternoon, questioning if I'm going to do it again in a relatively public area. Who was I, and what had I done with the Sam I knew last week?

Not to say the situation wasn't thrilling. Everything I'd done so far was by choice, I found Carlos super attractive, and I really enjoyed the sex this afternoon. Plus, James gave me permission to do this, was turned on by the whole affair, and even encouraged me to keep doing it after last night. If only you were here, James, like a little conscience on my shoulder, helping me know right from wrong. But instead, you have to be a thousand miles away at home, probably in bed, fantasizing about these moments while I face the most awkward decisions of my life, with nothing to guide me but a few paltry rules! I ran through the rules again in my mind:

1. Only do what you want to do – so far, so good.

2. Only do what feels safe – yeah, I feel safe enough.

3. Always let Jenny know where you are and who you're with – check and check.

4. Don't form attachments, don't have encounters with someone on multiple days – this one made me uncertain, but *technically* I'd be following the rules here, depending on your definition of "attachment."

5. If things escalate to sex, always use a condom.

That's when I realized – did Carlos even bring a condom? Probably not – I mean, why would he? He had no reason to assume we'd be alone together again. This was perfect. If he doesn't have a condom, we can't have sex, even if we wanted to! It was a convenient little escape clause, my dilemma was solved, and I wouldn't have to make a choice tonight.

I opened my eyes. The woman looking back at me seemed *much* happier and more confident than the girl I'd seen before. I was shocked to realize the toll these decisions were making on me. I realized I needed to be *way* stricter with the rules moving forward. No more bending them a little – no more playing with fire.

I took a few final breaths and decided I was ready to face Carlos. He'd understand the situation – we really shouldn't fool around without a condom. He'd shrug, flash that dopey grin of his, and then walk me back to my hotel room. Crisis averted.

I stepped out of the bathroom and saw Carlos sitting in a chair in the dressing room. There was that dopey grin – right on cue – but he held something gold in his hand, a wrapper of some kind. "Tro-han?" he asked. Oh. Fuck.

∗∗∗

Well, it happened. I was so prepared with my excuse, that when Carlos flashed that condom, I didn't know what else to do. I stood there in shock for a moment before slowly nodding my head in consent. He arose from the chair and gestured for me to follow him into another room. Wordlessly, I obeyed.

He led me into an area I recognized as the green room. It's basically a lounge area where performers can relax before the show or in between scenes. This green room had several couches, a piano in the corner, two refrigerators, and a conference table at one end. It was brightly lit, but once we entered, Carlos flipped one of the light switches, dimming the room as half the fluorescent lights went out. He closed the door behind us and took me by the hand, leading me to a large, black leather couch at the center of the room.

The ambience did wonders to soothe my nerves. My excitement began to return, as gazing at Carlos in the dim light reminded me just how masculine he was. In the dark, his brown eyes seemed so deep, his brow so strong, his jawline so chiseled.

We sat side by side, and he started to kiss me passionately. He pulled my blouse up over my head, and I reciprocated with his tank top. We tossed our shirts aside. I put my hands up to feel his chest, while he reached behind me to unfasten my bra. And thus, mere seconds into our encounter, we were half-naked on the couch already.

Carlos was very interested in working my breasts this evening. He cupped them in his hands, his palms pressed against my nipples as he stimulated me with groping and squeezing motions. The sensations increased my arousal quite a bit, and in no time, I couldn't resist grabbing his dick through his gym shorts. We were on the fast track to fuck town.

He laid me down on my back and kissed my cheeks, then my neck, and traced my skin down toward my breasts. He put his lips to my left nipple, causing a shudder of electricity to pulse through my body. He continued to attend to me, flicking my nipple with his tongue and occasionally biting it, gently, through his lips. I tried to relax into the moment, but I kept being interrupted by joyous waves of heat throughout my torso. As soon as I felt I had reached my limit, he started working on my other nipple. *Could I actually have an orgasm this way?*, I wondered. It was pure bliss.

My pussy was craving to be touched. When Carlos finally let up on my breasts, I took the opportunity to remove my jeans and underwear. Fully naked in this somewhat public area, I felt a small thrill at the thought of being caught. There were crew members who were just upstairs. *Are we sure they wouldn't come in here?* I didn't want to be the only one naked, and as Carlos started kissing my stomach and fondling my ass, I started to pull off his shorts. We were both eager to fuck once again, and as soon as his shorts were off, Carlos began to put on the condom.

I figured it would be easiest to start riding him on the couch. I pushed him down to a seated position, turned my back to him, and began sitting backwards onto his erection. He rubbed the head of his penis against my opening, letting the lube of the condom combine with the lube of my pussy. Once it felt nice and slick, I resumed lowering myself down, recognizing instantly that I was still a bit sore from this afternoon!

"Oooh," I moaned, pausing and shifting my hips to adjust to his girth. His hands gripped my waist, and becoming impatient, he started to thrust slowly up toward me. I gritted my teeth in response to the pain. I moistened my fingers with my tongue and began to massage my clit, realizing that the distraction might help with the pain. After just another minute, his entire cock was inside me once more, as I felt my butt land firmly on his lap. I paused for a moment, letting myself experience this pleasing sense of fullness before I started to ride his dick.

I had to go slowly, or else the pain began to exceed the pleasure. Thankfully, Carlos reached up from behind and started pinching my nipples, giving me one more distraction from the intense stretching down below. With his hands on my nipples and my fingers on my clit, I could fully enjoy getting fucked by this monster dick!

The feeling started to build. "Don't stop," I cooed, forgetting that Carlos wouldn't understand me. He must have understood my tone, as he continued to stimulate my nipples while beginning to thrust from underneath. With the two of us moving together, the friction was enhanced, and I recognized the rush of an oncoming orgasm.

I cried out when it hit me, feeling the pulse of my vaginal muscles as they tightened against Carlos's shaft. Carlos's breathing accelerated as he fucked me with all his might, joining me in a climax and then sighing with his release. The sex had been just like his dick – short, but substantial and immensely satisfying.

"Beautiful," Carlos said.

"Beautiful," I agreed.

I still sat perched on his cock for a moment while we both caught our breath. The pain returned as I lifted myself off of his softening dick. *This might not feel great in the morning*, I realized. As before, my interest in Carlos ended with the sex. Now that I had what I wanted, it was time to depart.

I started to put my clothes back on. "Ready?" I asked. I pointed up toward the stage, signifying that I wanted to leave. Carlos looked surprised by my hastiness, but he took the cue and started to dress.

Not wanting to hurt his feelings, I said, "I had fun, merci beaucoup," then realized aloud, "Oh fuck, that's French."

"Je vous en prie," Carlos answered, which was French for, "You're welcome."

I froze. "Parlez-vous français?"[1]

"Ah, oui!"[2]

"Moi aussi! Un peu,"[3] I said.

We laughed together, clearly both surprised. To think, we actually could have communicated all along! We conversed in French as we walked back to

---

[1] Do you speak French?

[2] Yes!

[3] Me too! A little

the hotel. His French was better than mine, but he was able to dumb it down to my level. I confessed to Carlos that I had a husband back at home. I didn't know how to translate "open relationship" or "hotwife" exactly, so I left it at that. Carlos didn't seem fazed by that news, and he said he has slept with other men's wives before. A perk of living at a resort, I guess!

It was strange getting to know someone *after* I'd had sex with him. I learned that he was born in Cuba, and then as a teen, he moved with his family to French Polynesia. That's where he learned fire dancing, and he had been working at the resort for the past 6 years. He had no wife or kids, but he hoped to have them someday. For now, he was content to save his money and enjoy himself at the resort.

When we arrived at the hotel room, Jenny and Julian had not yet returned. I asked Carlos if he knew why Julian was talking to Jenny, but he said that he did not. I told Carlos he could wait in the room with me, but out of respect for my husband, I didn't want him waiting on my bed. He said he understood and sat on Jenny's bed instead. I changed into my pajamas in the bathroom for modesty, brushed my teeth, and then climbed into bed. Carlos seemed content to sit in silence, so I examined my thoughts as I waited for Jenny to return.

It felt like a really long day. What a journey it had been, from brunch, to the barbecue, to the show, and to all the extra-curricular activities. I not only met Carlos for the first time, but I had fucked him *twice* before realizing we had a language in common! My vagina was definitely sore from my adventures these past couple days, and I wondered if I should take ibuprofen before bed.

And then I thought about you, James. This whole trip was one big unknown, and once again, I really didn't know how you'd react to my story. I knew Jenny was right, that a part of me just needed to trust our relationship and trust in our agreement. We know how to communicate, and I'm laying my thoughts and feelings bare at your feet, as I always have and always will. I believe in you too, James, that if there's something you need to communicate, you will tell me. It's the only way we can make this work, and I hoped and prayed we we're making this work. I must've been more exhausted than I realized, as while thinking of you, I drifted off to sleep.

With love and joy,

Samantha

6: Working Out the Kinks

James

Dear reader,

I was tempted to respond to Samantha's last email – but after the previous day's exception, I didn't want to set a precedent that I'd reply after her every encounter or every time she felt uneasy. As long as she followed the rules, I wanted to stay silent so she could follow her desires without my influence. I already had urged her to continue – it was somehow important to me that Ethan wasn't "the one" who got to sleep with her. Plus, once I'd read her story with Ethan, I knew I wanted to read more.

Samantha's encounters with Carlos made me think about things. A lot. I masturbated all throughout her story, "edging" through the buildups – that is, keeping myself at the "edge" of orgasm but then stopping myself – and allowing myself to cum at the moments when Sam and Carlos did. I noticed that Sam's descriptions of the sex and foreplay made me jealous, but it was a hot kind of jealousy that stoked my arousal. I even enjoyed when she pursued him for another round, despite realizing it might be bending the rules. It was naughty, and it turned me on that her arousal overcame her. However, when Sam raved about how attractive he was, how talented he was, or seemed to enjoy spending time with him, it created a different kind of jealousy. I was less threatened by Carlos when he spoke a different language, but after they made a personal connection in French, I felt a pang of unease. It was her connection with him that bothered me, like enjoying him emotionally and not just physically.

Of course, I knew those things were inseparable. How could she enjoy an encounter with someone she didn't admire or connect with? I wanted her partners to be more than pieces of meat, but something less than romantic.

Where was the line? And how might I figure that out without Samantha crossing it?

Striving to understand my feelings, I searched the Internet for any information about the arousal I was experiencing. I researched the term Jenny had used for it – "hotwife." I discovered some online forums of other men who liked to have their wives admired or even enjoyed by other men. That sounded about right. I *loved* the idea of other men lusting after my wife – it was hot to know that other men wanted to pursue her. But there was a separate excitement from allowing Sam to explore her sexuality – acting like a "slut" – for pure carnal enjoyment. The fact she could be so driven by pleasure to give in to another man's advances was extremely arousing to me.

And then I stumbled across the term "cuckold." The word, I learned, was in reference to a type of bird who flies into another bird's nest, lays an egg, and then flies away. The bird who made the nest will think the hatched baby bird is one of its own and will care for it, leaving the actual parent the freedom to do whatever it wants. Applied to humans, "cuckolding" refers to the idea that a man can impregnate another man's wife, and the husband may never realize that he's raising another man's child. The term evolved to describe men who enjoy sharing their wives with other men and ultimately being belittled by the experience – being told that the other man is more desirable, more skilled in bed, or better endowed. For some reason, the shame of belittlement becomes intensely arousing to the victim or "cuckold." In more extreme versions, the husband is forced to watch a more dominant male have sex with his wife, often without a condom, and see the other man ejaculate in his wife's vagina. Further still, he would then have to lick the other man's cum out of his wife's pussy when they had finished. I read a few short stories about cuckold experiences on an erotica website, and I quickly realized that cuckoldry was *not* what I was interested in. No judgment towards those who enjoy it, but my pleasure was in no way driven by shame or a desire to be humiliated.

I circled back to the hotwife idea. Erotica stories about hotwives often emphasized a loving relationship between wife and husband that was rooted in devotion, trust, and mutual respect. The man was often shown as self-confident, which allowed him to share his wife with minimal jealousy and without feeling belittled. There was a clear juxtaposition between shame in cuckoldry and pride in having a hotwife. I related to the latter, feeling proud of how sexy my wife was and wanting her to experience casual sexual adventures without compromising her devotion to me. I'll admit, I was also influenced by voyeurism – visualizing Samantha being pleased by these strange, well-hung men was exhilarating. Receiving her stories was also a means to preserve our intimacy and ensure we both benefited from our arrangement. She wasn't fucking these men for *her*, she was fucking these men for *us*.

There was my justification. Samantha was able to "play" in Mexico only because I allowed her to, *invited* her to. She agreed to *my* rules. I wasn't a cuckold being humiliated. She wasn't fooling around behind my back. She wasn't out with other men because she was dissatisfied with me. I had the power to say "go" – and I had equal power to say "stop." Or so I believed.

~

Samantha

Wednesday, May 15, 2019; 9:31 p.m.

Dear James,

I didn't hear from you since my last message, but Jenny assures me that's a *good* thing. I know your last email was a happy surprise, so I shouldn't expect to hear back on a usual basis. I'll take your silence as agreement that our plan is going smoothly, and I'm totally good with that! Maintain your silence, baby, because when I finally hear your voice in person, it'll be all that much sweeter.

I meant what I said about doubling down on the rules. As much fun as I had with Carlos, I felt a tinge of guilt for sleeping with him twice. I hope-hope-hope-*hope* that you're okay with that decision. Nevertheless, from now on, if I'm not 100% sure of something, I'm not going to do it. I can have my fun but keep good boundaries as well. In fact, I learned a bit about boundaries today during my newest big adventure. Stay tuned. ;)

***

I'd fallen asleep the previous night before Jenny and Julian returned. It was morning when I awoke, Jenny was in her bed, and Carlos was nowhere to be seen. *Did I dream all that?* I shifted under the covers and realized my vagina was sore. *Nope, not a dream!*

I got up, stretched, and took some ibuprofen, deciding I better take it easy today. I checked the clock – only 7 a.m. – and knew I better get to work writing my story to you about Carlos. So much to tell, so little time!

Fortunately, Jenny slept in until nearly 10 a.m.. *How late did she stay out?* I was about to hit send on my email when she interrupted.

"What are you doing?" she asked.

"Sending an email to James," I said.

"Oh, okay." She yawned. "We got any ibuprofen?"

"On the bathroom sink. You good?"

"I think so," she said.

She thinks so? I gave her a sideways glance. "So – what happened last night with Julian?"

"It was, um, interesting."

"Go on."

"He said he just wanted to talk, but then he was being really weird and quiet on the beach. And he doesn't strike me as a guy who gets tongue-tied very often."

"What'd he say?" I pressed send on my email and turned back to Jenny. She was wearing a hotel bathrobe and holding a glass of water. Her eyes seemed a little glazed over.

"He didn't say much of anything until we got back to the bar and started taking shots."

"The suspense is killing me, Jen! What did he say?"

"Ugh, I have a headache, please don't raise your voice."

I lowered my voice and spoke through gritted teeth. "What. Did. He. Say."

"He – he said he's in love with me."

I nearly fell out of my chair. "What?!"

"I know, it's terrible, right?!"

"I mean, I guess. And then what?"

"And then we took some more shots. And – I don't know. It's hard to think, my head hurts." She held her glass of water to her forehead.

"Okay, I'm sorry. Come sit down." I took her by the arm and guided her to sit on her bed. Damn, she looked bad. "What do you need?"

"Ugh. Hair of the dog? Can we order room service?"

"We have booze in the mini-fridge," I said. I crossed the room and opened it. "What do you want, mango hard seltzer or beer?"

She sighed. "Gimme the seltzer, I guess."

"Okay. But once you kick this hangover, we should probably take it easy today." I handed over the seltzer.

"I'm good with that." She took a swig and then winced. "For a starter, how 'bout that room service? I think I'd prefer a mimosa."

"Works for me!"

***

100

Using the resort website, we ordered some breakfast platters with champagne and orange juice. We browsed the site while waiting for our meals and noticed we could book massages online.

"Oh, hey!" Jenny said. "We can book massages online!"

"Oooh, let me see." Jenny needed the pick-me-up, and I decided I could use a massage as well after all I'd been through the past few days. Not only was my body sore, but the stress was starting to get to me.

On the website, you could order a 30-minute partial massage or an hour-long full body massage. Of course, we wanted the full treatment. In addition, you could browse the site to select the message therapist you'd prefer. Each had a profile with a headshot and short bios, and selecting our therapist sounded like fun! Some of the more favorable therapists – the most attractive and those with the most experience – were already booked for the day. But they had plenty of options, and several had openings in the afternoon.

Jenny picked a masseur named Esteban, who reminded me a little of Carlos. With muscles like those, he undoubtedly had some strong hands. I took my time choosing my own – with the fooling around I'd been doing, I kind of had boys on the brain.

"Let's see. He's not that attractive. This one's a bit old. Maybe this guy?" This man, Dionisio, looked young, possibly the youngest massage therapist on the website. He had a thin, almost pubescent mustache in the photo, a wide grin, and pearly-white teeth. His shiny black hair was spiked, and his eyes were wide and youthful.

"Him?" Jenny asked. "You really don't have a type, do you?"

"Variety is the spice of life, Jenny! Besides, it's just for a little body rub."

"I know," she replied, "but you might as well have some eye candy."

"He's cute! And he looks, I dunno, eager to please?"

"Maybe you *do* have a type," she teased. "Does he remind you of Dillon?"

I laughed. "Nah. Read the bio. He's at least a little older than Dillon. He grew up in Mexico City and played college soccer for a year before enrolling in massage school. He seems a little more worldly, and Dillon's from *Canada* for Christ's sake."

"What's wrong with Canada?" Jenny asked.

"Nothing's wrong with Canada," I said. "But it's Canada!"

"Point taken."

***

Jenny started feeling better once she had some food and a little more booze in her. After the meal, we sat on our balcony finishing off the mimosas. The sun was behind some clouds, and the cool ocean breeze was the perfect remedy to the humidity and heat. For a while we sat quietly, listening to the breeze and the sounds of people at the pool below. At last, I broke the silence.

"You owe me an explanation," I said.

"A what?" asked Jenny.

"Your 'love' story," I said, adding air quotes on the "love" part. "With Julian?"

"Oh yeah, that." Her eyes reverted to that far-away look again.

"So? What did you do when he said that?"

"I told him he's crazy and that he already has a girlfriend."

I shrugged. "That didn't stop you from flirting with him. What did you expect?"

"I expected to him to *fuck* me, not to tell me he loves me!" I almost choked on my mimosa. Leave it to Jenny to be so direct. She went on. "It's just a dumb crush. I told him to go back to his girlfriend."

"And then you never saw him again," I said sarcastically. This was in jest, as they clearly stayed out all night and got trashed.

"And then we stayed out all night and got trashed," she confirmed.

"Did you even talk about it?"

"I tried my damnedest not to!" Jenny insisted. "The idiot kept bringing it up! He said he's never met anyone like me, he wants to find a way to be with me, he wants me to stay, he wants to visit me in the United States… It's all a big dumb fantasy."

"Yikes. Sounds like he's fallen pretty hard."

"I don't think so," Jenny said. "I think he just wants to leave his girlfriend and I'm a convenient excuse. I tried to talk to him about that – that's why we were out so late. But we were also drunk, so who knows how much of my wisdom got through."

"So where did you leave things?" I asked.

"I told him to get his head on straight. He asked if we could see each other today, but I told him we'd better not."

"Good call." I said. "So, did you kiss him?"

"Sam!"

"Just thought I'd ask!" I took a sip of my mimosa. "Well, did you?"

"Ugh, yes."

"Before or after you 'talked some sense' into him?"

She shook her head. "Eh, kind of intermittently throughout. There was a lot of kissing."

"Jenny!"

"What, we were drunk! And really emotional!"

"So it's like, 'I love you.' 'No you don't.' Mnumnumnum." I wrapped my arms around myself and simulated kissing.

"Yeah, fine, so there were some mixed messages."

"I'm sure you're both a little confused. Honestly, Jenny, no judgment. You'll figure out what to do."

"Thanks. Well, anyway, enough about me, right now," she said. "What about you? Did you get any action last night?"

"I may have," I said, trying to sound nonchalant.

"Do tell," Jenny urged, sitting forward in her seat. I took a deep breath and told her everything about what happened with Carlos.

***

We went to the spa in the early afternoon. It was in an enclosed area near the middle of the resort. We checked in, and the attendant, a prim-looking middle-aged woman, handed us robes.

"Here are your keys with your assigned locker numbers," she said. "Please find your lockers and undress to your comfort level. Then you must wear your robe in all common areas until you are in your private rooms. Once you are in your robes, please wait in the back lounge until your therapist comes to retrieve you."

Jenny and I followed her down a short hallway to the locker room. Once she departed, I turned to Jenny.

"Undress to your comfort level?" I asked. "Does that include being naked?" I'd never had a professional massage before and wasn't sure what to expect.

Jenny shrugged. "They usually cover your body with a sheet," she replied, "except for the parts they're actively massaging. So, if you're fully naked, they probably wouldn't even know."

I thought about the attractive young man waiting to caress me. Feeling a little devious, I slipped off my panties from under my robe and placed them in the locker along with my other things. Jenny was right – my masseur may never know, but I could still enjoy feeling a bit naughty.

Jenny and I proceeded to the lounge area, which was dimly lit and adorned with large, plush couches and sheer, flowing draperies. Cool air flowed about the room, and soft, soulful music was playing. The attendant returned and served us hot tea, which was delicious.

Before long, my masseur arrived. Right away, I confirmed he was rather cute. He had gelled black hair and a trimmed mustache on an otherwise youthful baby face. He was short and thin, but his arms looked toned, and I could see some pronounced veins in his forearms – probably a sign of ability at the massage table. What girl can resist a strong set of hands? He wore a cream-colored resort polo and form-fitting black gym shorts that went halfway down his thighs. As I inspected his physique, he gave me a broad, shy smile that emulated his website picture. He bowed his head, and with a slight accent and a gentle voice, he said, "You can call me Dio, miss. Please follow me to your private room."

I followed. He led me to a simple room, dimly lit with stone walls and a wicker basket filled with towels. The massage bed was in the middle of the room and was covered in a large sheet, which Dio promptly drew back.

"I will step out of the room in a moment," said Dio. His voice was kind of dreamy. "Please, remove your robe and lay face down on the table. When you are in position, you may pull the sheet up over your body, please." He bowed again and left.

I hung my robe on a hook and caught my nude reflection in a nearby mirror. Admiring my curves, I thought about how a stranger was about to caress my skin. I squeezed my breasts and ran my hands down my hips, preparing my body for the intimate contact I'd soon endure. I let my right hand slide casually down to my pussy, lightly brushing the crease of my lips. Was I starting to turn myself on? I blushed, realizing Dio might return to the room at any moment. With a quick sigh, I snapped into focus and moved into position on the table. I pulled the sheet up over my shoulders and put my face in the headrest opening. I closed my eyes as peaceful music drifted through the air. *Just relax,* I thought. *Don't get so riled up.* I focused on slowing my breathing, and I even started to doze for a moment before Dio came back in.

I heard him move quietly around me, and as he took his position, he trailed his fingertips over my body so I could sense his position. He first grazed my shoulder, tracing his way down my back and then stopped just as he reached the curve of my ass. "Just relax," he whispered, echoing my thoughts. "I'm going to rub some warm oil into your skin."

He slowly peeled the sheet off my shoulders, folding it over to reveal my back all the way down to the top of my glutes. I noticed the scent of eucalyptus and heard him rub oil into his hands before gently pressing them onto the tops of my shoulders. With expert grace, he lathered my back with the warm oil, applying a light pressure to certain muscles. I was hyperaware when he approached the more sensitive parts of my anatomy – as he sensually grazed the sides of my breasts, and as he firmly slid along the top of my butt.

I wondered what he thought of me. Here was a young man in his sexual prime who had a profession in which he touched numerous women, and men, most intimately every day. Did he admire his subjects? Was he admiring me? Or was this strictly professional and emotionless for him? I preferred to imagine him enjoying me, of course. As his movements and actions conveyed sensuality, I liked to think he appreciated my well-cared for skin, my toned muscles, and my feminine curves. Did he have dirty thoughts while giving a massage? Did he ever get an erection? Did he ever cross the line?

He started to massage my shoulder blades and worked toward my left upper arm. As he moved his way downward, he positioned himself at the end of my fingertips, using a pulling motion to stretch my shoulders and massage my forearms. With excitement, I realized he was pulling my arm in the direction of his crotch. If I happened to extend my fingers, would I graze his dick? Would I feel an engorged erection starting to form? He eventually moved around me and repeated the process on my right. How would he respond if I reached out and caressed the front of his shorts? Would he desire this? Would he take things further? I knew I could never be so bold, but the fantasy ran wild in my mind. And then what would he do? And then?

He traced his fingers up my right shoulder, and I heard his breath as he leaned toward my ear. "Señorita," he whispered, "How is the pressure?"

"Perfect," I moaned. Oh my, did I really just moan?

"That's good," he said, tickling me back down my spine. "Any particular area that is sore or needs attention today?"

My pussy, I thought. But I knew I shouldn't be so forward. "My glutes," I answered. At least I could be a *little* cheeky, pardon the pun.

I felt him rest his hand gently on my right buttock over the sheet, as if testing the boundary. "Do I have permission, miss?"

"Mm, yes," I replied, and he pulled the sheet back, revealing my naked ass and resting the sheet at the top of my legs beneath my cheeks. I heard the wet sound of massage oil and then felt his wet hands press gently and then firmly into my glutes. *Mmm, yes.*

The young man had an expert touch. I felt him work his palms and fingertips alternately into my muscles, stimulating them and melting the tension away. With certain lifting motions, he pressed my gluteal muscles upward in a way that shifted and opened my pussy a little. The motion piqued my arousal, and I could sense myself getting wet in response. I couldn't see his face or read his expression, as my view was blocked by the head rest. Did he know what effect he was having on me? Was he enjoying himself too? Or was this business as usual, and the electricity between us was all in my head?

He continued to work on my ass, and I felt a growing longing, an emptiness in my loins as my pussy hungered to be filled. I fought to contain a shudder of arousal through my body, but I squirmed nonetheless, writhing my hips and clenching my butt muscles involuntarily against his firm grip. He had to know what he was doing to me, right? I felt him place a hand on each of my butt cheeks and gently spread them apart. In swirling motions, he massaged my cheeks in opposition, rotating counterclockwise on my left and clockwise on my right. I felt my ass and my pussy lips open and close with each rotation. Could he glimpse my asshole from this position? Could he see my pussy? My face flushed hot with arousal and embarrassment. I was so vulnerable, so exposed. This man could have his way with me, and I'd be helpless to resist.

He finally gave me respite as he removed his hands from my bottom and placed the sheet back over my shoulders. Moving to the other end of the table, he lifted the sheet over my feet and folded it, so it covered my buttocks but revealed the length of my legs. He began massaging my feet. I had been breathing hard, and I'm sure he noticed that too. I focused on slowing my breathing and allowing my body to relax. *Slow, outward breaths*, I thought. *Slow, outward breaths.*

My heartrate and breathing finally slowed just as he arrived at top of my hamstrings. *Here we go again*, I thought. With incredible skill, he dug deep into my muscles with his fingertips and then ran up the sides of my legs with his palms. After thoroughly attending to the sides and the backs of my legs, his fingers worked their way inward. He opened my legs a little for access, and I opened them a little more, hoping to tease him with a view of my pussy from under the folded sheet. He moved upward along the inside of my left leg, working the tender flesh with his fingertips. He inched his way higher, and I knew my pussy was radiating warmth as he approached. Could he feel it? His index finger was centimeters away, now millimeters. I was breathing heavily again, knowing it was impossible for him not to notice. I wanted him to notice, wanted him to know the effect he was having on me. As if in response, I felt his finger brush against my labia.

"Mmm," I groaned. I knew I must encourage him, must communicate that his touch was welcome. He continued to softly brush against my labia under the pretext of massaging my inner thigh. I gasped faintly and arched my back a little, raising my hips to ensure he caught a view of my smooth, hairless pussy. No doubt, I was glistening with my own lubrication, and I prayed that he just notice. But just when I hoped he'd respond more directly, he removed his hands completely. What a tease! He moved to the other side of the table and began working on the muscles of my right calf muscle, crisply, professionally, as if nothing exciting had happened. But his hands approached again in an upward fashion, and I knew where this was leading. And I knew where I wanted him to take it.

As before, he brushed the bottom of my labia with his finger, now on my right. My breath came out in gasps and sighs, and I lifted my ass a little, urging him to continue. He responded boldly, and after a few modest strokes of my inner thigh, he relaxed his grip and then traced a fingertip directly along my vaginal opening! He glided gently, his finger slick with my juices as he pushed my lips a fraction of an inch apart. I could contain myself no longer, and without shame, I reached my right hand under my body and started fingering my clitoris. He turned up the intensity as well, letting his finger press millimeter by millimeter deeper inside my vagina. I gasped and then sighed, ensuring he would sense the intense pleasure he was bringing me. He moved so slowly, teasingly. I matched his pace on my clitoris, allowing the feeling to build gradually with the penetration. Soon, unable to contain myself, I pushed my hips back toward him, inviting him to press deeper inside with his finger. He obliged, finally pushing his finger its full length into my sex.

He fucked me slowly with his finger, in and out, tenderly, as if in slow motion. He was only using a finger, but the anticipation had intensified the feeling. My nerves felt every millimeter as he slid in and out. I held my breath to stifle my moans, and the lack of oxygen seemed to heighten my experience, causing the pleasure in my vagina to pulse throughout my body. When I finally inhaled, it was a desperate gasp, followed by an exhale of extasy and relief. Taking his cue, Dio introduced two fingers, turning up the intensity as he stretched me even more. Then he sped up, eventually plowing his two fingers deep into my flower so that his knuckles rapped firmly against my tight ass.

By now, it took all of my willpower to stay on the table, arching my back and flexing my core to contain myself. I abandoned my clitoris and squeezed the sides of the table with my hands, bracing myself against the onslaught from behind. Dio started to curl his fingers in a distinctive motion. *Is that my g-spot?!* The feeling caused me to lose myself to the hypnotic pleasure, my vision going hazy as my consciousness was consumed by simply feeling.

Until this point I'd stifled my voice, pressing my mouth against the cloth of the headrest and even biting down on it a little. But with Dio's new movements, I lost control, gasping, "Oh, oh baby, oh Jame – oh, Dio!" Yes – for a moment, I'd almost shouted my husband's name!

My exuberance seemed to inspire him, as Dio amplified his force, putting all his strength into pounding me with his hand. I felt an orgasm building, and I readied myself for impact, once again trying to hold my breath to make things more intense. And that's when it happened, I did something I had never done before – I started to squirt!

"Oooaaagh!" I exclaimed, half in excitement and half in shame. I felt a warm fluid spray out of me, hitting the massage table and splashing between my legs, soaking my inner thighs. Dio seemed unperturbed, as he maintained his pace and didn't stop finger fucking me. Eventually, totally out of breath, I lowered my body weight to the table, and Dio slowed to a halt. Too satisfied and exhausted to care about the wetness, I laid in my puddle and strived to catch my breath.

When I regained my senses, I realized the sheet was still draped messily over my lower back. I pulled it off, and noticed Dio was standing by with a towel for me.

"Miss, our massage is at an end," he said. "I can show you to the shower."

"It's over already?" I asked. I was blushing as I took the towel from his hand. Dio looked shyly at me too, and when I glanced down at his shorts, he appeared to be hiding an erection behind his folded hands. "Wouldn't you – like me to return the favor?" I suggested.

His eyes widened. "Oh, no, miss. I'm afraid that's not allowed."

And what happened is *allowed?* I wondered. Hell, why not say it. "And what happened *is* allowed?" I asked.

Innocently, Dio nodded. "Yes, miss. If a guest wishes to have this service, we are permitted," he answered. "Well – unofficially. But we cannot allow the guest to service us, you see."

"I see," I said. I gave him a sly look. "Would you want me to?"

He laughed uneasily. "Well, yes, miss, but – I have a girlfriend."

"That's good," I told him. "Good for you." He smiled. "And does this girlfriend know what you do at work?"

His smile widened. "Oh yes, she knows," he said. "How else would I practice my skill?"

Touché.

***

I met up with Jenny coming out of the shower. We both wore our robes as we walked to the changing area.

"How was it?" she asked.

"Pleasurable!" I said. "And yours?"

She furrowed her brow. "It was okay," she said. "My guy was a little rough with his hands."

"Mine too," I said. Had she received the same treatment as me? I couldn't tell. "I like it a little rough, though," I added.

Jenny didn't react. We changed back into our clothes in relative silence, and then left the spa to return to our room. I'm not exactly sure why, but we didn't discuss the messages any further. Jenny and I keep very few secrets from each other, but – maybe this one can be between you and me, James. ;)

***

The rest of the evening has been low-key. We stayed in the room watching movies and ordered room service again for dinner. I didn't pay much attention to the films, instead writing this email and reflecting on the events of the day. I had fun. After the whirlwind of the past few days, I was glad to dial things back but still enjoy a little adventure. Dio was skilled at bringing me pleasure – sexual and otherwise – and it was nice for my body to be admired. I'm glad he set a boundary, letting me know we couldn't take things further, in part because he has a girlfriend. Jenny's situation with Julian is somewhat messy, and I'd rather not cause people drama with my flings. If I can get a little attention, have a little fun, put on a show for my husband, and avoid hurting anyone – that's a perfect recipe for an ideal erotic getaway! Well, anyway, that's about it for tonight. I hope you enjoyed the story, babe. Until next time!

Love,

Samantha

7: Split

Samantha

Thursday, May 16, 2019; 10:25 p.m.

Dear James,

I fucked up. If you can't handle the suspense, you can scroll further down through this message. Otherwise, I'll start at the beginning.

It began with a morning yoga class. After our restive evening on Wednesday, Jenny and I were ready to start our day bright and early with a workout. We left our room at 6:40 a.m. wearing yoga pants, sports bras, and ponytails, and took a short walk down a quaint dirt path in the morning sun to the oceanside fitness studio, a round, white building with large bay windows facing out toward the beach.

When we arrived, the studio was already more than half full with around 20 people, mostly women of a variety of ages. How were there *this* many people willing to get up before 7 a.m. while on vacation? Shouldn't they have been out drinking and even fucking all night? Jenny and I grabbed some mats by the front door and claimed some space near the back.

While stretching my limbs, I surveyed the room in search of cute boys. *Who am I?* I wondered. I hadn't been this boy crazy since my early teens. A lot can change in just a few days! The guys around me were decent-looking, but none of them really caught my eye. Each were wearing loose-fitting gym shorts, and I wondered what they might be packing underneath. I chose a guy nearby who seemed nicely-built and snuck a peek at his crotch. Was that a slight protrusion at the front of his shorts, or just a naughty-shaped wrinkle? I looked up and caught his eye, realizing he might have just caught me staring. He smiled. Oh, God. I felt my face grow hot as I quickly turned away.

I brought my attention back to the room and noticed it had grown full with over 30 amateur yogis filling the space. The women around us seemed almost giddy – chatting, stretching, checking their reflections in the mirror, adjusting their bras – were some of them wearing makeup at this hour? What was going on here?

I soon had my answer, as the yoga instructor walked in, and the chatter died down quickly as everyone's attention turned to the front. This. Man. Was. GORGEOUS. He was late 30s and looked *very* European – Spanish, or Italian maybe? He was tall with a wiry build and tanned skin. His long, dark-brown hair flowed down to his shoulder blades. It looked damp and slightly sandy, as if he had walked straight out of the ocean. He wore tight, capri-style windbreaker pants and a tank top that showed off his sinewy arms and shoulder muscles. He had the face of a supermodel – high cheekbones, prominent brow and chin, and a day or two of masculine stubble. The women in the crowd were collectively drooling, and not necessarily from our mouths!

He put on a headset, and his voice issued forth from some speakers near the front. "Welcome to our morning yoga class on this beautiful morning in paradise!" He repeated himself in a few other languages, and his unplaceable accent was to *die* for. Put a strong breeze through his hair, and he could be the cover model for a romance novel. He resumed in English: "My name is Emilio," again, foreign but ambiguous, "and I will be your instructor today. Raise your hand this morning if you speak English." Many in the crowd, I'd say more than half, raised their hands. He inquired about a few other languages, and the remainder endorsed Spanish with a few who spoke German or French. He bowed to the minority language speakers and exchanged some pleasantries in their languages. He then said, "I will mostly conduct the class in English and Spanish. I will do my best with the other languages when I can. When in doubt, just copy everyone else, okay?" A few mother hens giggled near the front. He repeated his instructions a few times in other languages, and the class began.

It was a beginner's class, and we started with a light sun salutation. Although I hadn't been to too many yoga classes, I was familiar with some of the terms and poses, and my dance background and flexibility helped me breeze my way through. I caught glimpses of Emilio whenever I could. I watched his form as he demonstrated the poses and glared jealously as he walked through the studio, correcting women's forms with gentle touches on their backs, their arms, and their thighs. *When he gets back to me*, I wondered, *should I screw up the pose just to make him touch me?*

When he finally approached, the dancer inside me wouldn't allow myself to screw up. But *Jenny*, an accomplished yogi in her own right, suddenly couldn't master a downward dog! He placed his hands on her hips, shifting her body, and whispered, "Straighten those back legs, yes, that's right." He repeated the phrase in Spanish, and I decided he sounded like Antonio Banderas in the movie "Puss in Boots." *I'd like to be the puss in* his *boots*, I thought. Wait, did that metaphor make sense?

He moved past Jenny, and despite my perfect form, he attended to me anyway. "Yes, girl in pink pants. Very good, walk it out now on your toes, keep that backside lifted nice and high."

He noticed my backside! Wow, I hadn't felt so giddy about a guy since – well, *you*, James! And bent over in this position, I could turn my head and practically look straight up at his crotch in his tight pants. Striving to look out the corner of my eye, I noticed a bulge and imagined his cock pressing against the fabric from the other side. He seemed like the type to go commando, right? I watched him as he walked and could *swear* based on his movements, there was a dick bouncing around back there. And if so, it looked impressive!

A shock of shame jolted through me, filling my shoulders to my forehead with heat. *I'm happily married*, I told myself. *Should I be crushing this hard on some guy?* I hardly ever notice attractive men, let alone flirt with them, fantasize about them, or of course actually fuck them. The shame coincided with the feeling of being naughty – not the bad kind of naughty, but the fun kind, the sexy kind, the devious kind. Is this what you wanted all along, James, for your innocent wife to lust after other men? I thought to myself that it was. I thought, this is *exactly* what you wanted. For your wife – with permission – to act like a slut. Not the bad kind of slut, but the fun kind, the sexy kind, the devious kind. The kind who is overcome with animal lust, who doesn't repress her desires, but achieves them. You want me to discover the carnal side to my sex before returning to our loving, intimate sex. And maybe I'll bring a taste of that carnal sex back to our own lovemaking. Your words came back to my mind: *Your pleasure will be my pleasure.*

And with that, I was resolved to fuck this yoga teacher! And unlike my previous encounters, I wasn't going to fuck this guy for you, James. Oh, no, I was going to fuck this guy for *me*. Because I believe that's what you want, and from the moment Emilio entered the studio, a part of me wanted that too. And that part of me was growing.

And why wouldn't I be able to fuck this swarthy stud? I'd seduced every man I was interested in so far. My confidence, like my sex drive, had never been stronger. This time might be a challenge, I admit. There were currently two dozen pairs of hungry female eyes cast upon my specimen, but rule out the shy girls, the taken girls, the older girls, and the ones who weren't in shape, and I started to like my odds. But what would be my move? Helpless and coy worked with Dillon. Being forward worked with Carlos. Mark and Ethan had targeted me. I needed him to notice and engage with me, so I decided on playing it forward and direct.

I first adjusted my tank top to show a little more cleavage. It caught Jenny's attention, and she gave me a cynical look. "What? I feel hot," I whispered. She rolled her eyes and shrugged before resuming her "warrior two" pose. Meanwhile, I made an effort to lock eyes with Emilio. Could I seduce him with my body language? I couldn't exactly flash him like I did with Carlos a few days ago. I thought back to some flirting advice I received long ago, namely the last time I actually had a reason to flirt – in high school.

"Bat your eyes at him," my mom suggested. Standing in my parents' bathroom as a 14-year-old, I watched my mom flutter her eyelashes in demonstration.

"Mom, that looks ridiculous," I said.

"That was an exaggeration," she replied, "But you get the idea."

I remembered wanting to crawl out of my awkward teenage skin. Why was I asking my mom's advice about boys? Was I that desperate?

"Laugh at his jokes," she told me. "Find a way to touch him on his arm or his chest."

"Mom! I'm not walking up to Hunter and feeling up his chest!"

She sighed. "Not like *that*," she scolded, "find a reason. Hit him if he teases you, or put your hand on his arm while you laugh at his joke. Make it natural!"

As a freshman in high school, touching boys was *not* natural, not for me at least. And now, as a 26-year-old woman who had been married the past few years, touching a strange man was *still* not natural. But nothing ventured, nothing gained, right?

I needed to attract Emilio with my gaze. Of course, everyone was watching him teach the lesson, so I needed my gaze to be extra piercing. I needed to catch his eyes in mine, ideally while he was close enough to make the moment intense. He finally passed by our row of mats again, and I made my attempt. Glaring intently, I looked up into Emilio's eyes through my eyelashes. When he was just a few feet away, I felt his eyes meet mine, and they held. I batted my lashes, not grotesquely like my mother had done, but coquettishly and sly. Adding a little flair, I tossed my hair with my right hand and bit my lip.

He seemed – caught off balance, looking more shocked and concerned than intrigued. "Miss, are you okay?" he whispered, trying not to pull the focus of the room. I stopped and looked around, realizing I was standing upright like an idiot while everyone else was bent over in downward dog.

"Oh," I said, quickly dropping down into the position. I heard some laughter around me –my antics had caught the attention of nearby classmates who were jeering at my forwardness. Ugh, great. I tried to ignore it, feeling my face grow hot again and trying to hide my reaction in my hair while holding my downward dog. Mercifully, Emilio commanded the attention back to him.

"Okay!" he said, a little louder than usual. "One more breath in this position and then we walk our feet to our hands for our forward fold. Breathe in." He demonstrated, and the class fell back in line to follow. "And out."

He had rescued me. It was a small gesture, but I was grateful. And I knew exactly how I'd like to repay him, if I hadn't fucked things up already!

For the rest of the class, I was back on form. Having caught his attention in a negative light, I now was determined to impress. I conquered my headstand, engaging my abs and glutes and pointing my toes in perfect form towards the ceiling. Numerous students around me, Jenny included, lost balance and fell to the floor as I perfectly held my pose. When we did standing scorpions, my back leg was raised highest in the class, and I saw Emilio smile and nod in approval.

When the class ended, lots of the women approached Emilio at the door to smile at him and thank him for his class. He made light banter and grinned back at them, tossing about his wavy, sweat-strewn hair like a model in a shampoo commercial. I lingered toward the back with Jenny, who undoubtedly knew what I was up to, until finally the crowd had thinned and most had exited the building.

"Pink pants girl," he greeted as I approached. His warm blue eyes beheld mine, and he had handsome, masculine dimples at the corners of his grin. "Great job in class today!" And as quickly as he found my eyes, he moved his now to Jenny. "You also, *mi amiga*." He winked and spoke a quick line of Spanish to Jenny, who gave him a side-eyed grimace, said, "Hasta luego," and continued walking by. She caught my hand to bring me along with her, but I was on a mission, so I pulled free.

"You're a really good instructor, Emilio," I fawned, "I'm Samantha, and this is Jenny. How long have you been teaching?" A lame question, but I needed something to sustain the conversation. I fluttered my lashes and tried to catch his eyes once more. He didn't seem to notice.

"About 12 years now," he said. He avoided eye contact, instead looking over my shoulder in the direction of the resort. Was he distracted? Uninterested? "I also teach a spin class, which starts in 15 minutes at the gym." He looked back at me briefly. "You should come. I must head over there now to get ready, so I hope you don't mind if I quickly lock up." He ushered us out of the doorway and turned to lock the door.

Feeling dismissed, I nonetheless tried another desperate attempt, speaking to him over his broad, cold shoulder. "What are you doing after you teach? Would you like to grab a drink afterward with a few of your top students? I'm buying."

It was a bold play, and it would be clear what I was after. Would it flatter him to be chased by a woman? Would it excite him to know he could have me so easily, that at a whim I could be his? Or was I lowering my value by being so accessible, removing the thrill of the chase?

"No thanks," he said. "I'm – busy afterward." He dropped the keys back into his gym bag and looked ready to leave.

"Tonight, then," I said quickly. "We'll be here all night – of course." I laughed at my dumb statement and patted him on the arm, as if the joke was his.

He looked at where I touched him and cringed. "Sorry, miss, I have to run. Enjoy your time at the resort, okay?" He gave Jenny and me each a quick yoga bow and then hurried away, making it clear he didn't want to be followed. I watch his retreat in disbelief, lusting for his well-toned buns and feeling very much like the fool I'd just made of myself.

"What the hell was that?" asked Jenny.

"The worst moment of my life," I replied, and it hardly felt like exaggeration. Never in my life had I put myself out there and been so utterly rejected. Come to think of it, I'd never actually thrown myself at a guy before. I was way too shy in high school to approach someone. I'd never had a legitimate crush until I met you, James, and our flirtations had always been so natural, so effortless, like our stars were destined to align. I guess my stars and Emilio's weren't destined to align – nor were we destined to see each other naked.

"Fuck it," said Jenny. "Let's go get a drink."

***

Feeling in a slump, I wanted to look as sexy as possible to pull myself out of it. Back at the room, I put on my skimpiest bikini, straightened my hair, and applied a little more makeup than usual. I wanted to turn some heads.

Jenny was on a mission also. "Julian," she said. "That fucker's going down."

I laughed. "What does that even mean?" I asked. She was applying eyeliner in the mirror with intense concentration.

"Well, I told him I'm not fooling around with him as long as he has a girlfriend. And since he still has a girlfriend, I'm gonna make him wish he didn't!"

"By looking as sexy as possible?" I asked.

"Precisely," she said. Her eye makeup was now darker and more seductive than usual.

Soon, we were strolling into the pool area, wearing bikini tops, booty shorts, sunglasses, and sun hats. Clad in casual heels – yes, we were being *that* extra – we cat walked by the rows of deck chairs like models, flashing our long legs and tossing our hair in order to turn some heads. And it worked, as through my shaded lenses, I caught nearly every male specimen, as well as several females, ogling our physiques.

We found some empty chairs under an umbrella, just across the pool from where Julian held his fitness classes. It was about 15 minutes until his first class of the day. Ditching our towels and handbags, Jenny and I took a dip in the pool and then waded up to the swim up bar, where we swiftly got the attention of the bartender.

"Two strawberry daquiris," Jenny said.

"Make them strong," I said. The bartender nodded and started to mix the drinks.

"Sam," Jenny scolded. "It's not even 10 o'clock yet. Think you wanna pace yourself?"

I sighed. "Fine," I said. "After this one. But I'm drinking to forget my humiliation this morning."

"That's fair," she replied. "A strong one to take the edge off from this morning, but then we take it easy, okay?"

We watched the bartender pour two double-shots of rum into our daquiris, blended them up, and served them out. We clinked our glasses together.

"To being badass bitches," Jenny said.

"Hear, hear," I said. We sipped our drinks, which were strong indeed, and by the time I was halfway finished, I felt a little lightheaded. I realized we hadn't eaten breakfast.

We chatted for a few minutes, scanning the crowds around the pool and making some observations. This guy was cute, oh, but he was with a partner. Another guy had a pretty smile, but he looked like he might be gay. Soon, we saw Julian arrive in his resort polo and khaki shorts, and he began to set up his sound system for his aerobics class. He eventually noticed us and waved, and although I waved back, Jenny turned away and ignored him.

"Gonna take his class?" I asked.

"Not sure. Think I should?"

"You'd get more of his attention that way."

"Yes, but he might miss me more if I'm not there."

"Possible," I said. "But what if he accepts your absence and decides not to pursue?"

"His loss," Jenny muttered. Abandoning her straw, she poured the remnants of her daquiri down her throat. She turned and watched him for another minute. Her sunglasses were shading her eyes, but I could tell she was gritting her teeth. "Fuck it," she said. "I'm going. I'm putting myself out there, so then he'll *have* to address me." Without waiting for my reply, she swam over to where a group of women were gathering for the class.

I watched her for a moment, and when I turned back to the bar, I realized I wasn't alone. There sat Mark, the man from the hot tub that we met on our first night. He'd snuck up on me somehow, soundlessly approaching in the shallow water while I was distracted watching Jenny. He stared into my eyes.

"Hello, Samantha," he said. He smiled, but his eyes looked fiery and intense.

"Oh, uh – Mark," I said. "Hello."

"I was hoping I'd see you again," he said. His expression was strangely unsettling.

I broke his gaze. Seeking a distraction, I turned toward the bartender and called out, "Another daquiri, señor?" He nodded. "And – Mark, would you like something?"

He ordered a beer. "How's the vacation so far?" he asked.

"Good!" I said. *Oh my God, go away.* "How's yours?"

"It's good," he said. "Could be better but – maybe it's about to be."

Ugh, barf. "Yeah, you never know what might happen." What the fuck was I saying? I needed to get out of this.

"I forgive you, by the way," he said.

"Oh, yeah?"

"For throwing our swim trunks in the bushes. Well, for Jenny throwing them in the bushes."

"Oh, yeah." I forced a laugh. "Good old Jenny." My drink arrived. I took a sip. *Shit!* I realized. *He made it strong again. Of course.*

"But if you want to make it up to me," Mark said, "I'm sure we could work something out." Did he honestly think he sounded sexy? He was coming off as super creepy.

"Oh, no need," I said. "Well, anyway, I was just—"

Another voice cut in behind me. "Oh, hey!" said John. "You're that girl from the other night!" *Double fuck.*

"Yeah, John, this is Samantha," Mark said. "I was about to suggest we head to the beach together."

I was surrounded, John on my left and Mark on my right. I sipped my beverage nervously. "I have to wait here for Jenny, though," I said. "She's just over there."

"Oh, fuck *that* bitch," said John. "We almost got kicked out of the resort because of her."

"You – really?" I asked.

"Yeah," John said. "A staff member found us in the tub with no clothes on. They accused us of having sexual activity in there!"

"Wait – they accused you and Mark?" I asked. This time my laugh was genuine.

Mark's olive skin flushed red, and his smile turned to a scowl. "Very funny," he sneered.

"I mean, it *is* kind of ironic," I pointed out. "You *were* having sexual activity in there, just – not with each other."

"Of course, not with each other!" Mark said. "Look, like I said, I forgive you. But I think you kind of owe us for the other night." He pierced me with his steely stare, but what was sexy in the past was now frightening. "Let's just hang out, have some more drinks, and see what happens," he said.

"I'd love to," I lied, "but I actually have to—" *Fuck! What did I have to do?* I sensed them closing in, blocking my escape. *Do I – do I have to wait for here Jenny? No, then I can't get away.* "I have to run to the bathroom," I finally finished. I sipped my daquiri again, realizing it was empty. "Too many daquiris," I said. "Excuse me."

I squeezed past them and cut away through the water, feeling their eyes on me as I retreated from the pool. They were getting an eyeful as I climbed out of the water in my thong bikini, but I couldn't help that now. I scanned my surroundings for the nearest bathroom. Was I feeling dizzy? Those daquiris had gone straight to my head. I picked a direction but honestly wasn't sure where I was headed, until I heard a deep voice coming from one of the fancy, poolside cabanas.

"Hey," said the voice. "In here."

"What?" I asked. The curtain was merely cracked open, and I couldn't see inside.

"Come in here," the voice said. "They won't be able to find you." The curtain drew back and revealed the smiling, blue-eyed face of Ethan! This was getting out of control. But in contrast to Mark and John, Ethan felt like a godsend. I took his hand and slipped behind the curtain. Without thinking, I wrapped his bare torso in a grateful embrace.

"Oh my God, you saved me!" I gushed.

Ethan hugged me back tentatively and then stepped back. His short blond hair was lightly tousled, and he was dressed in swim trunks and sandals. "Don't mention it," he said. "You're lucky I found you. Who were those guys?"

"Some kind of creeps," I told him. "I met them a few days ago. Oh, hey, nice place!" As my eyes adjusted to the dim light, I started to scan my surroundings. Like Ethan himself, the cabana was rather impressive. It was spacious, and a gas lamp lit the room while the curtains were closed. We weren't alone. A male attendant stood by, and to the left was a table laden with a platter of cheese, crackers, and some fruit. To the right was a large, cushioned lounge bed.

"Can I get you a drink?" Ethan asked.

"Water, please," I replied.

"Ignacio, bring the young lady some water, please. And two shots of tequila." Ignacio nodded and left.

"I hope both shots are for you," I said.

"If you insist," Ethan answered. He told me to help myself to the snacks on the table, so I did. "So, in what context did you meet those guys?" he asked.

I blushed, but Ethan's calm tone and hospitality were disarming. I told him the truth. "We – kind of fooled around a few days ago. When we first got to the resort," I admitted.

Ethan's eyebrows raised. "Really?" he said. "I guess you're not as innocent as you look. What happened?"

He gestured to the lounge bed, and we sat next to each other at the end. Before I knew it, I told him about what happened in the hot tub, including when Jenny threw their swim trunks in the bushes.

"Some guys can't control their dicks," he mused. He smirked as he locked his eyes on mine. Shyly, I turned away.

"Some?" I asked.

"Only some," he replied. I turned back, and we shared a moment of silence as his eyes bore into mine. But then the curtain spread open, and Ignacio came back in with the drinks. He placed them on the table, and Ethan handed him a tip. "Can you wait outside, Ignacio?" Ethan asked. "And make sure we're not disturbed."

Warning alarms went off in my head – at least they should have. But somehow, I was at ease. Despite his playful looks, Ethan was exceptionally casual, a comforting contrast to Mark and John's attempts at intimidation. And the liquor had clearly dampened my defenses.

"So, what have you been up to since I saw you last?" asked Ethan.

I told him about the entertainment show and the massage, leaving out my encounters with Carlos and Dio. I sipped my water, not realizing that Ethan's tequila shots were so far untouched.

"What about 'living in the moment'?" he asked, echoing my words from a few nights earlier. "Have you done any more of that?"

His innuendo caught me off-guard. My mouth went dry, and I swallowed. "Maybe," came my weak reply.

His eyes narrowed, as if reading me. I tried to read him back. Was he curious? Jealous? He pursed his lips.

"Good answer," he said finally.

He stood up and retrieved the tequila shots, holding one in each hand. From my seated position, he towered over me. His crotch was right around eye-level, and I noticed the long imprint of his penis in his shorts. I strived to look away, to focus on anything else. Why did I feel tempted to look?

"To living in the moment," he said, and he offered me a shot of tequila. Distracted by trying to avoid his penis, I took it. I tossed it to the back of my throat, feeling the acute burn of liquor warm me from within. I was lightheaded again, and from that point forward, rational thought went out the window.

Ethan set upon me like a snake, leaning in and kissing me deeply even as the burn of liquor had not yet faded from my mouth. I kissed him back, and the burn was gradually replaced by a tingling arousal that started at my tongue and spread. In the back of my mind, I knew this was naughty and forbidden – but the front of my mind had *clearly* shut down by that point.

Ethan lifted me to a standing position before him. His hands went directly to my ass, pulling my hips closer until I could feel the protuberance of his hardening dick. Continuing to kiss me, he massaged his fingers through the flesh of my buttocks. I sensed my pussy getting wet, soaked even, as if it recalled his giant penis and anticipated its approach.

In no time, he'd removed his shorts, and his erection sprung free with a heavy slap against my thigh. He next untied my top and let it fall. It slipped between our torsos and landed on the shaft of his dick, dangling like it had been tossed on a coat peg. Ethan laughed at the bikini top hanging off his erection, but I could only stare, the unreality of the situation clouding any perception of humor. I watched in silence as he tossed my top to the floor, revealing that monstrosity of a penis that my pussy so hungrily remembered. He stepped in and kissed me again, muting any protest I might raise. His hard, upturned cock was now poking my abdomen just below my breasts. He took my hand and placed it on his dick, and obediently, I stroked its exceptional length.

"Mmm, just like that," he told me between deep-mouthed kisses. His hand slid between my legs and glided over my bikini bottoms, grazing my clit and down across my labia. I felt the fabric getting moistened by my juices. He hooked his fingertips under the seam, pulled the fabric aside, and repeated the motion of fingering my clit and then sliding along my slit.

"Fuck, Sam, you're soaked," he muttered in my ear. "You want this cock, don't you, Sam? Tell me you want this cock."

My breathing was shallow, and my eyes were closed in ecstasy. With hardly any air to spare, I whispered, "Yes."

"Say it louder," he commanded. He slipped his finger just past my lips, teasing the edges of my pussy.

"Yes," I said, with slightly stronger voice.

"Tell me what you want."

"I want your cock."

"Louder!"

"I want your big fucking cock!"

And with that, he grabbed me by the hips and pulled me across the room, bending me over the table. He held my bikini bottoms to the side with one hand and directed his penis with the other, pressing it right against my pussy. He ran the head of his cock up and down across my opening, marinading his penis with my juices. The soft flesh of his head slipped across the moistened surface, pleasing me, and yet teasing me for wanting more.

Another warning alarm failed to register in my mind. He had given me several moments to protest, to end the encounter, to insist he use a condom *at least*, but the thought never reached my conscious mind, let alone brought breath to my lips. He gave me one last opportunity.

"Tell me what you want, Samantha. I need you to tell me."

And my breath finally came. "Fuck me, Ethan."

The onslaught began. He pressed his cock slowly and firmly into my cunt, and once it was fully submerged, he started to pound me without mercy. Dull pain mixed with searing pleasure as he strained the walls of my delicate flower. Where was the gentle Ethan I'd met before? The one who'd eased me onto his cock, checked that I'd felt okay? He was gone, replaced by this aggressive, demanding version, the one angry that I'd left him a few nights ago, the one jealous I'd fooled around with other guys since.

It was like an out-of-body experience. I heard my whimpers and squeals as Ethan thrust himself fully into me; I felt the intense stimulation of nerve endings deep inside my pussy; I could see and smell the snacks on the table before me – was that brie? And yet I was detached, like an observer, the scene beyond my control, and I didn't feel the flood of emotions that should've been raging inside me.

I had a small jolt as Ethan slapped my ass, harder than it's ever been slapped. *That's gonna leave a mark*, I thought, and suddenly, everything came back into focus. I realized where I was, what was happening, and the numerous things wrong with this scenario. *How in the world did I get here?! How could I be doing this?!* But I was also more in tune with the pleasure I was feeling. *This is so naughty, so wrong, and yet it feels so good!*

Could I stop it? I'd recovered my wits, but I still hadn't found my voice. Ethan continued his barrage upon my sex, savagely thrusting into the deepest depths of my womb. I couldn't stop him. Tears welled up in my eyes and started to stream down my face, but I could do nothing but experience heartbreak mixed with the joy of a rising climax. *Oh, James. What have I done? What was I doing?* And then it came.

"Oh, fuck!" I exclaimed.

Ethan gripped my hips even harder, pulling me impossibly deeper onto his dick. "That's right, cum for me, you little slut," he sneered. "Cum on that dick you love. Cum on that dick you can't resist."

And I did. The orgasm was long and strong, and it consumed me for a few incredible minutes. I briefly lost myself again, absorbed only by the feeling of this climax as it emanated outward from my pussy, lightening the burden on my mind.

"Yes! Fuck! Yes!" a voice called, which I recognized as my own.

Ethan didn't stop or even slow down. He slapped me on the ass again, then leaned forward and slapped the side of my breast. He tweaked my nipple, causing another surge of pleasure to flow through me.

"And I'm just getting started," Ethan said.

As my orgasm started to ebb, I wondered if I'd have another. I'd resigned myself to the fact this wasn't stopping. My ability to speak my mind had abandoned me, and the pleasure sapped my will to end things prematurely. Besides, from the point that it began, the damage had been done. How much worse could it get?

Ethan lifted my right leg and put it up on the table. "That's right, babe, open up for me," he said. "Spread open wide so you can keep on taking this dick." I arched my back and lifted my ass, offering him complete access to my vagina. He penetrated now at a different angle, stimulating new areas within me and renewing my arousal.

How was I going to get through this? I tried not to think of Ethan. Despite his godlike penis sending waves of enjoyment, giving him my emotions would only amplify my transgressions. *Think of someone else*, I told myself. *Think of James.* And I tried. I thought of our love, of how you make me feel. But then I thought of how this will hurt you. Your disappointment. Your pain. *Is this what ends things?* I asked myself. *Is this what ends his love for me?*

The tears returned. I felt my pussy tense, the wetness starting to fade. Pleasure diminished as discomfort grew. This wasn't going to work. *How do I keep myself aroused? How do I keep my pussy from getting hurt?*

I turned my mind. *Don't think of James, think of – Emilio?* Yes, Emilio! The sexy yoga instructor from this morning! I focused on Emilio, imagining his rugged, handsome looks, his untamed hair, his toned muscles showing through his tight workout clothes – those shoulders, that ass, that bulge in his trousers. I imaged that beautiful Emilio was fucking me, that of all the women who threw themselves at him, he had chosen to sleep with me. Ethan was thrusting, but in my mind's eye, he was using Emilio's dick.

Arousal reemerged. *You're so fucking handsome, Emilio. Yes, give me your hot, foreign passion. Seduce me with that sexy voice, your exotic European sex moves.* I reached beneath me and started massaging my clit.

"Yeah, bitch," said Ethan, "Rub that dirty clit." But I translated the words to the sultry voice of Emilio. *Yes, beautiful*, Emilio whispered. *Love yourself for me.*

I started to pick up the pace of my fingering, noticing a second orgasm starting to build. I began to vocalize, "Mmm, yeah, oh God, yes –."

Ethan – or Emilio? – lifted my left leg off the ground, placing it on the table so my legs were spread wide. I clung to the table with my hands for dear life. My vagina felt stretched more than ever, and his cock was twitching inside of me, sending pulses of pleasure through me.

"Oh my God," I said. Here it came, orgasm number two. "Oh my God, oh fuck. E – Emilio. Fuck me, Emilio!"

"Emilio?!" roared Ethan. He kept fucking me, but he was clearly thrown off. "Who the fuck is Emilio?!"

I bit my lip. There was nothing to say. How could I explain this?

"Is Emilio your husband?" Ethan demanded. He smacked my ass again, then said, "Answer me, Sam. Is Emilio your husband?"

"Y – Yes," I said. What else could I say? I barely could think, I barely had breath, my orgasm was surging.

"Is he your small dick husband?" Ethan asked. I didn't answer, and my ass received another slap. "Does your husband have a dick like mine?"

"N – No. He doesn't. Yours is – yours is bigger."

"Does he fuck you as hard as I do?"

"No. No one fucks me like you do, E – Ethan."

"That's right, bitch, your pussy is mine." The pounding persisted. "I think I'm going to come soon," he moaned. "Do you want me to come inside you? Do you want me to come inside you with my nice, big dick?"

No! But my lips just wouldn't say it. Ethan wouldn't accept no, and I had no voice for no. My still-raging climax left no room for no. "Yes," I answered weakly. "Yes, please. Please, come in me. Please."

And he did. He grunted as it began, and I sensed his penis throbbing as it expelled its hot cum in me. I felt its heat as he filled me, and boy, was there a lot of cum. My climax roared like a cum-fueled flame, and then slowly it started to extinguish. The throbbing abated, and Ethan's cock laid still.

He slowly withdrew it from my ravaged vagina. The only sound was our gasping breaths as we sought to recover from the intense experience. I closed my legs and stood up on the floor. I adjusted my bikini, so it once again covered my sex. And then I turned around.

Ethan's jaw dropped at the sight of me. "Oh my God, Sam. Are you crying?"

His tone was suddenly different. As if the rage rushed out of him when he emptied his balls, he now seemed sensitive, even scared.

I picked up a nearby towel and wiped my face, forgetting that I was wearing more makeup than usual. I must've just smeared it all over, and I'm certain I looked like a mess. With the voice of a mouse, I squeaked, "Can you hand me my top, please?"

He rushed to acquiesce, his expression of shock and horror remained. "I had no idea," he said. "But – but why are you crying?!"

He wouldn't be able to comprehend, and he didn't need to. It really wasn't his business. "I have to go," I said. My swimsuit back in order, I turned to leave the tent. As I did, his voice trailed behind me.

"Sam – wait! I didn't mean to hurt you, Sam! Just listen!"

But I was gone.

***

The sun was blinding. I needed to escape, and I walked blearily toward my beach chair at a brisk but wobbly pace. My eyes were still adjusting to the light, and it was a mercy not to see the prying eyes of other guests as they saw me with my tears and makeup stains. I just needed to escape.

When I arrived at our beach chair, I found my bag, but Jenny's was gone. *Did she take it? Where was she? How long was I gone?* Though it felt like an eternity, it couldn't have been more than 20 minutes. Still, there was no sign of Jenny anywhere.

Fuck it. Priority number one was escape. I took my bag and headed to the resort – to my room – to safety. *Don't think. Just get there.* I noticed a slimy sensation between my legs, and I realized in disgust that Ethan's semen was pouring out of me. *Ignore it. Don't think. Just get there.* I felt the dull pain of being stretched by his giant penis, along with a satisfied, post-orgasmic heat that came with it.

I finally got to our room and opened the door. Jenny wasn't there. *Just as well,* I thought, *I should probably be alone with my shame for now.* I collapsed on the bed, and the cool air of the AC unit was kind on my skin. *Okay. Okay. I guess I'm allowed to think now.*

My thoughts started racing. I was so fucked! *This is it. I'm a cheater. James is going to be devastated. James is going to leave me.* I buried my face in my pillow, sobbing loudly into it, and the thoughts kept coming. I counted the ways I had broken the rules:

Do not form attachments. Do not have an encounter with someone on multiple days. The spirit of this rule was intimacy and trust. No one is special like James, and no one gets to enjoy me – and vice-versa – more than once. The rule set a clear boundary into cheating, and I'd crashed right through it.

Always let Jenny know where you are and who you're with. Always. A protection and a failsafe. Jenny could make sure I wasn't taken advantage of, or worse. She could help me stay mindful of the rules. And yet, where was she? Things had happened so fast. One minute, I'm escaping the harassment of thugs while Jenny was distracted. The next, I'm behind the veil, her protection vanquished by a curtain and a darkened room. This wasn't Jenny's fault. I'd stumbled out of her view, and there was no way she could've helped me.

If you decide to have intercourse with another man, he must wear a condom. Of course, the ultimate violation. Another man's skin had touched my skin, his seed was planted deep in my womb, even now. I was on birth control, but what about disease? What about the boundary of intimacy I had let Ethan cross? He took something that was meant for James alone, and unable to resist, I had given it to him.

I'm a slut. Why couldn't I stop it? Why did I go behind that curtain in the first place? How did this happen? What was I thinking?

I was suddenly taken by an urge to be clean, to wash it all off of me, to wash it all *out* of me. I started the shower, and in removing my bottoms, I noticed a pool of pearly white fluid on the fabric. I rinsed it away under the water, erasing a tiny remnant of my shame. I ran the shower hot – hotter than usual, and I stepped in the tub just as steam began to rise.

The water was hot enough to sting me, and I let it punish me and cleanse me. I scrubbed my skin with a bar of soap, harder than usual, as if scrubbing at my sins. I ran the hot water over my vagina, wincing, but wanting to purge every bit of semen that had entered me. The task and the heat were distracting, and I was grateful for it.

After the shower, I dried off, I wrapped a towel around my hair, and dressed in the warmest clothes I had, sensible underwear, pajama bottoms, and a baggy t-shirt – your Metallica t-shirt, James. I closed the curtains, darkening the room against the midday sun, collapsed back on the bed, and started to shiver. I climbed under the covers, a literal heap of despair, and the thoughts returned. *I ruined everything. What do I do now? I ruined everything. How did this happen?*

I was drunk. Not an excuse, but it didn't help. *I was scared, I wasn't thinking.* That was true. I'd just been intimidated by two creepy men, and Ethan had meant safety, or so I had thought. *I was sad, I was vulnerable, I was lonely.* That seemed closer to the heart of the matter. Emilio had rejected me, quite embarrassingly. I'd questioned my desirability, and Ethan's lust meant validation, a bandage on a bruised ego. He was filling a hole in me, no pun intended. *But I wanted it.* Ouch. Did I? Did I want to allow Ethan to take me? I reflected. A few days ago, I was pleased with how things went with Ethan, but I was also relieved to walk out of his life. He'd asked me to stay, but I left with no regrets. The next two days, Ethan never even crossed my mind. Carlos was more appealing to me than Ethan. And Dio – I'd wanted more than I'd gotten with Dio. But Ethan? He was done for me, used up, much like the condom he'd used with me that night. It was useful once, but then you throw it away and never think of it again. Then how did this happen?

He forced me. No. No, I rejected that idea. It was the easy way out, to externalize the blame. He was forceful, but he didn't force me. I was vulnerable, yes – I was losing control, and he was there to take the wheel at just the wrong time. I had every opportunity to put a stop to things, and I didn't. I kissed him back. I stroked his dick. I bit my tongue as he teased me with the tip, and in the end, I'd asked him for it, even begged him. His face at the end – his expression of shock and horror at my tears – was proof that he had no idea that anything was wrong with what we were doing. No, I couldn't blame him. I could only blame me.

Of course, this is the cleaned up, organized version of thoughts that were rolling around in my mind for hours. I fell in an out of sleep, worrying to the point of exhaustion, dozing for a bit, and then waking up from disjointed nightmares to continued regrets. I was awake and worrying when Jenny finally returned.

"Samantha," she said, "you're here." I sat up in bed beneath my heap of blankets and pillows. She caught sight of me and froze. "Oh, fuck!" she exclaimed, "What happened?!"

She rushed to my side and sat on the bed. I instantly started crying again, and she held me. It took a few minutes to get words out, but gradually, I told her what happened. Her eyes welled up with tears of her own.

"Oh fuck, Sam. It's all my fault!"

"No, it's my fault," I sobbed, and we cried into each other's shoulders. The scene must've looked melodramatic, but the misery was real.

"Sam, I shouldn't have left you," Jenny said. She explained what had happened. When Julian's class was over, I was gone. She took her bag and towel, leaving mine behind while she sat with Julian in the café. She was seated in view of the pool, so she could monitor my bag and watch for when I came back. She must have just missed me, because when she returned to our beach chairs, someone nearby said I'd grabbed my things and hurried off.

"I should have checked on you," she said. "I figured you went to grab food or went to rest in the room. That's when Julian – he invited me back to his place."

"Jenny!" I said. I wasn't mad at her about leaving me, but I was disappointed in her giving in to Julian. "You said you weren't going to mess with him!"

"I wasn't!" she said. "But – he broke up with his girlfriend, he even showed me text messages to prove he ended things last night. He swore it wasn't just for me, but by noticing his feelings for me, he just couldn't stay with his girlfriend."

"So, you went with him?"

"Uh huh."

"And you slept with him?"

"Uh huh."

"And was it good?"

"Oh yes."

I wasn't in the mood for details, but I nodded. "I'm glad."

"Thanks, but it was a mistake," she said. "I'd trade it all to have been there for you."

"You couldn't have known," I told her.

"I should have," she said. We shared a moment of silence. "Hey," she said finally. "You must be starving."

I should've been, but I didn't seem to have an appetite. "I'm not sure what I could keep down," I said. "I'm not really hungry."

"You have to eat, Sam."

"Okay. But I don't want to go anywhere. Can we order room service?"

"Of course!"

The rest of the evening was quiet. I had an important email to write, and Jenny was content to watch a movie on low volume and exchange phone messages with Julian.

So here are my final thoughts, James. I fucked up. I broke my own heart with what I've done, and I'm sure it's torturing yours. Please understand there was no emotion behind what I did – in fact, emotions were conspicuously missing. There was carnal pleasure, yes, but no intimacy, no joy. No *thinking* even, like a dreamy sleepwalk turned nightmare when I woke up. I can't imagine how I'll earn your forgiveness. I only hope you'll give me a chance.

Of course, our sexy experiment is over. It was fun while it lasted, but apparently, I can't be trusted to follow the rules. I don't want to do this anymore, I don't want to be with anyone but you. I won't even *look* at another man for the remainder of this trip. Just two more days, then we catch our flight home on Sunday morning. While I'm scared to think what will happen next – what you'll think of me, how you'll feel towards me – I can hardly stand to be here any longer. I want to face our future together, and I pray we still have a future to face.

With love, hope, and desperation,

Samantha

8: Aftermath

James

Dear reader,

I was stunned. When I sent Sam out on her erotic adventure, I never imagined she might violate the rules. My Samantha? My loving, devoted Samantha? The love of my life, the girl of my dreams, the Samantha whose eyes were only for me? Well, that was the woman I'd dropped off at the airport. Who was she now? What had this journey unleashed in her?

The day I read her email confession was a whirlwind of emotions. I had been waking up early each morning to read the latest update on her trip. I sat at the computer in my den in my boxer-briefs, coffee in hand, and lotion and Kleenex nearby in case of any – very probable – urges that might arise while I read. Sam hadn't failed yet to tell a supremely arousing tale, and I didn't expect her to disappoint. Lo and behold – she didn't.

I opened her message and was faced with her ominous opening line – *I fucked up.* Um. What? My heart sank. A chill ran through me. What could this mean?

The story invited me to skip ahead if I couldn't bear the suspense. I couldn't, but I forced myself to read on anyway, in the proper order, as the email intended. My heart pumped faster with each beat in the story. *Emilio. Did she grow too attached to Emilio? Was she telling me she'd caught feelings for him? Did she find she was in love with him?* Despite my panic, a part of me rooted for her to get with Emilio, casually of course. My erection agreed, and as her story built tension, it also built hardness in my cock. I liked hearing her lust for Emilio. It's exactly what I wanted – for her to feel lust, to explore her bodily cravings, and to bring the stories and the passion back to me. Anticipating a story, I stroked my cock to images of Samantha with Emilio –

of her melting into his embrace, of her writhing uncontrollably while riding his hard dick.

But no. She struck out with Emilio – and I sympathized with her, my poor wife, humiliated and rejected for wanting something so reasonable. I'm accustomed to supporting my partner, feeling her victories and defeats alongside her. But this time, it wasn't missing a promotion at work or second place in a dance competition – she'd failed to bag a dick – but I sympathized, nonetheless. *Go get him, honey*, a part of me had cheered. *Go get all of him.*

So, it wasn't Emilio. How had she fucked up? I read on. *Mark. Did she break the rules with Mark? Did she finish what she'd started a few days ago?* She'd only given him a hand job, but he'd wanted more. Did he get it?

Wrong, again. Samantha was wary of Mark, even frightened by his forwardness. I was afraid he and John would force her somehow, which of course would not be her fault. But she got away, she fled, right into the open arms of—

Ethan! Of course! Mr. "He-Meant-Nothing-To-Me" Ethan. The initial encounter had gone so smoothly. He was cool and assertive, but not particularly attractive, she'd said. Charming and disarming on the surface, but not the kind of person Sam might fall for. He was the ideal one-night stand, and the only thing exceptional about him was his penis. *His penis.* She had a thing about describing his penis and her body's excited reaction to it. I knew she couldn't love Ethan, but did she love his penis? I gripped my erection, thinking of Samantha fawning over Ethan's penis, drooling over it, lusting for it. What would it be like to be big like him? It would feel bigger in my palm. Would my fingers wrap all the way around it? Would I have to stroke it with both hands? Would my wife love me more if I had a bigger penis?

I read on. They kissed. She started stroking his dick. He pulled her swimsuit aside and started fingering her lips. *Why wasn't she stopping this?* And I thought I knew. *She needed his penis. She's addicted to his penis.* Inevitably, they fucked. This man's enormous penis was inside my wife's vagina. And he didn't wear a condom, it was skin-on-skin. He was stretching her, wider than my penis could stretch, deeper than my penis could reach. He stimulated her in ways I naturally couldn't. *Was it more pleasurable than mine? Was he more masculine to her, and me less so?* She orgasmed. *Was it more intense than what I could give?* The fucking continued. He commanded her, she obeyed. She called out Emilio's name – curious – now she was fantasizing about Stranger #1 while Stranger #2 was fucking her guts out. Ethan made her admit that his cock is bigger than mine, that he fucks her better than I do. *That slut, that dirty, cheating slut.* The thought was so strong, I'd actually said it aloud while reading. It was followed by a surge of shame. *The love of my life, how could I think of her like this? What has this all come to, how did we get here?* The fucking continued. She orgasmed again, just as Ethan came deep inside of her. I orgasmed too, the most depressing orgasm of my life.

And there it was. It was over. I checked the time. I was running late for work – I'd have to read her afterthoughts later. I cleaned up and got ready for work in a haze. *How could I focus on work today? Should I just call in sick?* Fortunately, I didn't have any client meetings, and my final meeting with my major client wasn't until tomorrow. There was no way I could be on my game in front of clients.

My thoughts swirled all the way to work. I needed to finish Samantha's email, and I needed to reply. But what would I say? Was I angry? Was I hurt? Was I shamefully aroused? Of course, I was all those things. But how to convey things cogently via email?

I arrived at work and sat down in my office. Pulling out my phone, I opened her email and hit "reply." I typed the following message:

Friday, May 17, 2019; 8:11 a.m.

Sam,

I can't believe what I've read. I don't even know what to feel or to think. I need some time for this to sink in – until then, I guess I don't know what else to say. Do whatever you want – nothing seems to matter right now.

Message you later,

James

It was a terrible message, I know. *Do whatever you want.* It was a slap in the face, a complete "fuck it, I don't care" type of response. I'm sure I wrote it to hurt her, to push her away. I suppose it seemed better than leaning into the anger (the "fuck you bitch" approach) or despair (the "woe is me" approach). Plus, that carnal part of me, the part that came so vigorously while reading her new with Ethan, hoped deep down that she'd act promiscuously again and produce another tale.

I thought that messaging Sam might lighten my burden while I was at work. It did, at first, and I thankfully got through my morning emails before she surged back into my mind. Little did I realize, all throughout my morning, I'd be playing out the various stages of grief.

Stage One: Denial. Fuck it. That's right, fuck it. I don't care. She can do what she wants. I sent her off on vacation to fuck other men, and she did that.

Sure, she broke the rules, but what did I expect? I'm sure I wanted this in some kind of way, and she sure did, so what the hell do I care?

It wasn't a very pragmatic approach, and of course, I couldn't keep that mindset forever. We'd have to face this together eventually, I couldn't just deny that it happened or ignore the consequences it would have for us both. But I guess for a while, it kept the anger at bay.

Stage Two: Anger. Yes, anger came next. I started to craft my next email to her in my mind. I imagine it would've gone something like this:

> Dear Cuntface,
>
> When I sent you out on your erotic adventure, we agreed upon rules for a reason – to prevent you from acting like a whore. But clearly, your craving for penis outweighed any love you ever felt for me. Fuck you, and enjoy slutting it up all over Mexico, or wherever the hell you go next, because you aren't coming back here to me.
>
> Regretfully and formerly yours,
>
> James

Thank God I never sent something like that, as anger seized the reigns of my rational mind and steered it into madness. Fortunately, these thoughts were short-lived, but they led me toward the equally destructive…

Stage Three: Bargaining. How can I make this right? How can I make us even? My thoughts centered on revenge. If she can cheat, maybe *I* should test the waters. Now that I'm the one at a low point, maybe *I* should seek some validation.

There was a woman I worked with in my office, a short, slender, young black woman named Olivia. She was cute, and while she was on the shyer side, we'd always gotten along quite well. It helped that we were close in age, two of the only twenty-somethings in the office.

Olivia was polite and soft-spoken with a faintly Southern accent. She wore her hair in long braids. She had a lovely smile and seemed to use it often when she was around me. Despite her thin physique and narrow hips, she had a perky little bubble butt and tended to wear tight pants. She was an executive assistant, and she was often assigned to assist the salesmen during a major pitch. She'd been helping me with my current high-profile clients, so we'd been chatting a little more than usual this week. I actually knew very little about her – her precise age, how she'd come to the company, and even whether she was single, though she didn't wear a ring. She wasn't available to assist with my meeting tomorrow, as she was going to a friend's wedding in

Jamaica. Today was her last day at work before her trip, so I'd been instant messaging her some final arrangements for our clients using our office's internal messaging service. I decided to ask something personal.

James: What time do you leave for your trip tomorrow?
Olivia: My flight is at noon, so at least I have the morning to get ready.
James: Need a ride to the airport?
Olivia: Nah, I'm good. But thanks :)
James: Jamaica, right? Ever been before?
Olivia: Nope. Should be an adventure!
James: I bet! I'm jealous. Mind if I stow away in your luggage?
Olivia: LMBO.
James: LMBO?
Olivia: Laughing my butt off.
James: "Butt"? LOL. So PG.
Olivia: There's certain things you don't say on your work computer, LOL.
James: So true. Text me?

I waited. A few tense minutes passed. Did I overstep? Was I getting too personal? My stomach dropped. I'd just asked a cute young woman – not my wife – to text me in a private conversation not appropriate for work. I hadn't transgressed yet, but I was starting to walk the line.

My phone buzzed. I checked the message.

Olivia: Better not bring you to Jamaica – you don't bring sand to the beach. :P
James: What? LOL.
Olivia: Almost typed that on the computer but deleted it… Probably not an appropriate response for work.
James: That joke went straight over my head… Am I the sand in this metaphor?
Olivia: Never mind! LOL.
James: Now I want to know!

Another pause in the conversation. What the heck did that mean? I started Googling the phrase when I got another message.

Olivia: LOL, yes… You're the sand.

Google came up with a hit. It was from Urban Dictionary, so of course, it was something crude. "You don't bring sand to the beach: You don't bring your girlfriend or women to a party or event where there will already be plenty of available pussy."

Wow. She meant it in the reverse gender sense, meaning Jamaica would be full of available dick, I suppose. Which meant she was referring to me as a "dick," as a sexual object in this scenario. Which meant *me* and *sex* were jointly on her mind. My cock started hardening in my pants. I shifted it toward my left pantleg, giving it some room to expand. Meanwhile, I crafted my response.

James: OMG, I just looked that up. LMBO.
Olivia: You just couldn't let it go, SMH, LOL.
James: Well, I was trying to figure out if you were flirting with me.

This lady sure knew how to use silence. While her previous responses took seconds, the minutes slowly ticked past on this one. Had I crossed a line? Did I scare her away? Did she get offended, or even creeped out? Here I was, a married man, asking an attractive woman at work if she was flirting with me. I was putting her in a vulnerable position, and I was putting myself in a dangerous one. The phone buzzed, and I was almost afraid to check her reply. I held my breath and unlocked my screen.

Olivia: There's no harm in a little flirtation, right?

She took the bait. She wasn't creeped out, she was *interested*. My dick was now engorged. I unzipped my slacks, pulled down the waistband of my boxer-briefs, and let my erection slip loose. My office door was unlocked, but I didn't get visitors often, certainly none that were unannounced. I imagined calling Olivia to my office. I'd be seated in my chair, and she'd open her blouse to reveal her petite, bra-covered breasts. She'd lean in for a kiss, and while our tongues made each others' acquaintances, I'd slip my hand under her shirt and unsnap her bra. Her breasts, in my imagination, were small but firm, and her nipples were exceptionally perky.

I realized I'd better reply. Now I was the one using the silent treatment, and she'd be particularly vulnerable after that last admission.

James: No harm at all!

Hmm. That wouldn't do much to advance the conversation, so I added:

James: Well, I can't stow away in your luggage, but you have 24 hours before you have to be on the plane. Maybe there are other ways to have fun?
Olivia: Depends. What are you good at?

Holy fuck. Was this an invitation to get sexual? She clearly wanted me. I stroked my cock some more in excitement, returning to my fantasy. Her shirt would be open while she stood over me, kissing me, pinning me down on my chair. She'd run her hands over my shoulders and chest. My hands would move to her lovely ass, groping its fleshy goodness through the thin fabric of her slacks. My cock would be out, just like it was now. She'd lower her pants, revealing tiny, brightly colored thong panties. Of course, she'd be wearing a thong, as panty lines were never visible on her pert and supple ass. I'd pull down her thong, eager to breathe in the sweet scent of her pussy. She'd step out of her clothing and turn around, giving me a stunning view of her round ass cheeks and her tiny, pink pussy lowering down toward my waiting cock.

The excitement was too much, my balls started to signal an oncoming climax. I edged, stopping myself from coming at the last minute to preserve the sensation. If I came now, I'd lose the mood. I released my grip on my penis, feeling the enticing tingle of an unrealized orgasm begin to fade. I needed to send my next reply. *What are you good at?* she'd asked. Was I supposed to reference something sexy? *I'm pretty good with my hands*, I considered. God, that sounded so forward, and getting blatantly sexual was the point of no return. I tried a more subtle tactic:

James: Maybe you can help me find that out.
Olivia: Maybe you should ask your wife.

Well, that was an erection killer. I pushed my softening penis back into my underpants. I was screwed. She was playing me, trying to get me to cross the line. What now? Would she report me to our bosses and say I was harassing her? Would she find a way to tell my wife? A sense of doom washed over me. I stared at the message on my phone, frozen, unsure what to do, unsure how to fix this. Maybe if I stopped right now, Olivia will let this all pass over? Maybe she'll never reference it again? Or did I need to do some damage control? But wait – what if this was her way of saying she knows I have a wife, and she's okay with that? Did kind, shy Olivia seem the type to play homewrecker? Clearly her message was a test, but of what? And whatever it meant, if I failed, the result could spell disaster. Thankfully, I was bailed out by another message from Olivia.

Olivia: Sorry, I had to get real for a moment. You are married, right? I mean, I noticed you wear a ring.

Well, her tone didn't seem too condemning at the moment. But how I'd respond could make all the difference. Was she okay with me having a wife? Did she want the flirtation to continue? Or was she offering me a way out? I knew I couldn't lie – if I said no, she could verify from just about anyone in the office that I *did* have a wife. I reviewed my options:

Immediate retreat. Admit I have a wife and say it was all a mistake. Apologize profusely, slink off with my tail between my legs, and hope Olivia is willing to let things lie. I'd avoid full-fledged cheating, and it was the safest option to prevent some type of retaliation from Olivia.

Double down with honesty. Admit I have a wife, but tell Olivia that she recently – *very* recently – had cheated on me. I'd let her know I don't know where things stand with my wife, but I'm hoping to settle the score to not feel so damned helpless and victimized. I was thinking Olivia would call things off if I admitted all this, but at least I'd maintain some integrity with my honesty, and perhaps she would understand.

Walk the middle path. Admit I have a wife and tell Olivia that we're trying out an "open relationship." It essentially would be a half-truth, as I wouldn't explain that things were open for Samantha but not actually for me. Perhaps Olivia would judge me less if she thought I had my wife's approval – besides, open relationships are increasingly common these days, and who's Olivia to judge me and my partner for our lifestyle choices? Either Olivia would back out politely, or she'd still be in. And a sizable part of me – my now resurging erection – was really hoping she'd still be in.

So, yes, I went with option 3.

> James: I am married, but we're doing an "open relationship" thing at the moment. Is that okay with you?
> Olivia: If it's fine with your wife, it's fine with me. :)

Holy shit, this was going to happen! My emotions were suddenly raging out of control. Excitement, fear, arousal, shame – what a reversal, how gratifying to be desired by Olivia when my self-esteem was at an all-time low!

But could I possibly go through with this? I thought of what Samantha had done. For all I knew, she already was doing it again. Did she go back to fucking Ethan already, enamored of his cock, unable to resist? Maybe she'd found someone new by now. I returned to anger, and a thirst for vindication.

> James: Are you free for a bit? Come to my office and discuss it? ;)
> Olivia: Sure. I can drop by in five minutes. ;)

And there it was. She was coming to my office *right now*. I slipped off my wedding ring and hid it in a drawer. Would Olivia make a plan with me for tonight, or did she mean for things to happen right here? How quickly would my fantasy of fucking her in my office be fulfilled? Was this instant karma? Was the universe paying me back for being cheated on?

I had five minutes to mentally prepare. It was going to happen, she was on her way. A week ago, even just yesterday, this scenario was inconceivable. I never would have cheated on my wife. I loved her, and she loved me, but suddenly the latter had been thrown into doubt. *How could she do this?* I thought. *How could she cheat on me?* I wondered, as I prepared to cheat on her. The irony didn't even occur to me. *I can't wait to tell her,* I thought. *I can't wait to shove this in her face.* Then maybe we'd be on a level playing field. Maybe then I'd have a chance to forgive her, but only if I first could hurt her back.

Someone knocked on my door. My angry thoughts were replaced again by the icy chill of excitement and fear. I had to clear my throat before calling out, "Come in!"

Olivia stepped in and closed the door behind her. She wore a grey cotton dress that was form-fitting, and her braids were wrapped in a bun atop her head. She looked good, though she had a curious expression on her face.

"Hi," I said.

"Hi," she replied. She smiled faintly. I couldn't quite read her, and I wondered how she might be reading me.

"Take a seat," I requested. I gestured to a chair in front of my desk. She sat. *Great,* I realized. *It feels like a business meeting.* I forced a smile, hoping to look casual. "So, um. Thanks for coming by."

"Yeah," she said. "It's probably better to have a conversation like this in person, right?"

"Right." How did people ever make this happen? It was so awkward! Didn't workplace trysts happen all the time, or is that just what the movies want you to think?

After a torturous pause, Olivia suddenly laughed. "Have you ever done this before?" she asked.

"Oh, uh, done what?" I asked lamely.

"Done the open relationship thing. Like, have you done this before, or are you just starting?"

I forced a laugh. "It's, uh – the first time, to be honest," I said. "Is it that obvious?" I froze, internally petrified.

"James – are you okay?" she asked. Her expression was genuinely curious. It wasn't judging or concerned, necessarily, just curious. What emotions could she read on my face? Could she tell how nervous I was?

"Yeah, I'm great, just -" I got out of my chair and hurried around my desk.

I leaned against it, now just a few feet in front of Olivia. "How are you?" I flashed her an eager-eyed grin.

She laughed again. "I'm good. Are you sure you want to do this, James?" She gave me a quizzical look.

"Of course!" I said. "I mean, Olivia, you're – a lovely woman. I've admired you for a long time, and – when we started flirting, I was like, yeah, that's great, let's do this!" *Who's speaking?* I wondered. *My voice isn't that high-pitched.*

"Okay, come here and kiss me, then." Her voice was so matter-of-fact. Was this really no big deal to her?

"I – what?"

"If you really want to do this, come here and kiss me." She stayed in her chair, one leg crossed over the other, waiting for me. Her face was oddly stoic.

I stared at her, immobile. *Do it!* I urged myself. *Now's your chance, just do it!* But I couldn't. I just stared, dumbly trying to smile.

"James, what are we doing here?" she asked at last.

"I – I don't know. I'm – I'm sorry." I couldn't do it. I hadn't even known I was conflicted, but when faced with the opportunity, I simply couldn't do it. Then – quite embarrassingly – I started to cry.

Stage Four: Depression. I cried silently into the sleeve of my dress shirt, trying to shield my shame from Olivia. It was humiliating. I felt her hand on my shoulder, and she guided me back to my chair. I sat and then buried my face in my folded arms atop my desk. After a minute or two, I heard a soft voice.

"James." I looked up, hardly recalling that Olivia was present. She was still in her chair across the desk, a solemn look on her face. "James, it's okay to cry while I'm here, okay?"

I blinked through tears and regarded her quizzically, surprised she hadn't fled my office and told everyone I was having a breakdown in here. *It's okay to cry?* Paradoxically, her words helped me stifle the tears, and I regained some composure. "I'm sorry I invited you here," I said.

"I don't know if you'd like to talk about it," she said, "but I'm here if you want to, okay?"

Why was she being so nice to me? She should probably think I'm a lunatic, if not just a total creep. I wiped my eyes. Her tone was so comforting. I wanted to trust her. "Thank you, Olivia," I said. "Would you – would you let me explain myself?"

"Of course. Go ahead."

So, I told her. I told her about how Sam and I had married young, how we'd never been with anyone else. I told her about my strange curiosity about her sleeping with other men, of the rules we'd set up for her on her trip, and how she just confessed that she had broken those rules. I talked about feeling betrayed and admitted that the relationship wasn't open on my end, that what I tried to do would've amounted to cheating. As I spoke, I felt a great weight lift off my shoulders, like the burden of secrecy was heavier than I'd known. I was mostly saying the words aloud for myself, but it helped that Olivia listened so patiently, so seemingly nonjudgmental. I rarely made eye contact while telling my tale, but when I did, she was nodding, and she regarded me with sympathetic eyes. She listened in silence, and once I finished, she finally replied.

"I figured it was something like that," she said.

"You – what?"

"Well, I couldn't have known all of the details, but I thought there might be some marital problems involved." I blinked. She continued, "To be honest, I didn't really come here to sleep with you, James. You're cute, and I wasn't closed off to the idea, but I knew I needed to talk to you first and figure out if something was going on."

"Really? What made you think something was going on?" She looked shy all of a sudden. Was she blushing?

"I've actually had a crush on you for a while," she said. "But you wear a ring and never seemed that interested in me, so I never thought much of it. Until today – the flirting seemed kind of out-of-the-blue."

I nodded. "Yeah, I'm usually a lot more boundaried," I said.

"But I like you, James," she continued. "You're a good person. So, if you were thinking of stepping out of your wife, I figured either you really did have permission, or something was up that you might need to talk about."

"You're very perceptive," I said. I smiled sheepishly. "I guess I should thank you. You helped me avoid a pretty big mistake."

"It's only because I've been there," she said.

"Were you married?" I asked.

"Engaged," she replied. "For almost a year." She told me her own tale of relationship peril. She described being cheated on by her fiancé and learning about it from a mutual friend. Before even confronting him, she sought revenge, and almost slept with her fiancé's brother. "And when I say almost," she said, "I mean it. We were actually naked together before I called it off."

My cock stirred at the image of her naked with her fiancé's brother, someone so taboo and yet apparently desirable.

"You'd gotten that far before ending it?" I asked. I was hoping to hear a little more detail. "Like, fully naked together? In bed?"

She pursed her lips. "Yeah, just about. We'd just taken our clothes off and were standing in his apartment, looking at each other naked for the first time, when I suddenly couldn't go through with it."

"Didn't like what you saw?" I teased.

She giggled. "Actually, he looked pretty good. My body wanted him, but my heart held me back. I realized how hurt I must've been to have stooped so low. The anger dissolved, and I was left with this horrible sadness and shame."

I nodded. "I can definitely relate to that," I said.

"I figured," she said. "It didn't work out with my fiancé, but I didn't need to be a villain too by acting out of anger. And who knows, have you talked to your wife yet? Are you sure you can't work through this?"

I shrugged. "We haven't spoken yet. Any advice?"

"Yes," she said. "Don't do anything drastic until you talk to her. Don't act out of anger, or desperation. Let your feelings settle a bit, and organize your thoughts before deciding what to do next. And be honest with your wife, even about you and me. She was honest with you about breaking the rules – you should give her a lot of credit for that, she probably could've gotten away with it if she didn't tell you."

She had made some great points. I thanked her for her wisdom and support – what a remarkable find, a faithful friend in the midst of my misery. She wished me luck. "I hope things work out between you and your wife," she said. "But if they don't, after the dust settles – feel free to give me a call. Even if just as a friend."

"I think I would," I said. We smiled at each other once more before she exited my office. As she slipped out the door, I peeked at her pretty, round backside in her tight, grey dress. *No panty lines*, I noticed. *I knew it.*

***

Stage Five: Acceptance. I clearly wasn't going to do any work today, meaning I'd be woefully underprepared for my client meeting tomorrow. *Oh, well,* I thought, *acceptance has to start somewhere.* After Olivia left my office, I pondered her advice. *Organize your thoughts,* she'd said. Earlier, my thoughts were crashing through my head like a raging storm. Voicing my thoughts to Olivia had been the first step toward having them make any sense. But how do you organize your thoughts?

I suddenly realized I hadn't finished reading Sam's last email. I opened it on my cellphone. I read about her leaving Ethan's cabana and feeling terrible. She returned to the room, and my heart sank as she cried into her pillow. She took a hot shower, hoping to wash off her horrible, guilt-ridden experience. She went back to bed and ruminated between fits of restless sleep and nightmares.

She reflected on how this all happened, practically against her will. It was like her rational mind had betrayed her, silenced by humiliation, booze, fear, validation, and lust. Did I not react the same way to my feelings of anger and hurt? Had I not sought a base, immoral, but easy solution to my woes? I, too, had ignored my rational mind in favor of carnal instinct. In Freudian terms, we had abandoned our superegos and succumbed to the id.

As I identified with Samantha, my anger dissolved. I came to understand her, to empathize with her, and to yearn to comfort her. How would I convey this to her? *Organize your thoughts.* Yes, Samantha had organized her thoughts and expressed herself to me via email. She'd said that writing it down helped organize the clutter in her mind. I had to get my thoughts down in writing, I had to email Sam. I imagined her sad and desperate, awaiting my response. I unlocked my computer screen to access my personal email.

My office phone rang. I answered, and it was Olivia.

"James, I have an update," she said.

"Um – what?" Did she have a change of heart? Did she now want to encourage me to cheat? Or did she decide to rat me out, or worse, blackmail me for coming on to her?

"The rep for the Sutterburg account just called," she said.

Oh, yeah, work. That thing I was supposed to be doing. "Yes?" I asked.

"They said they found a problem with the numbers. They're really upset."

"What? We didn't even come up with those numbers, we had an outside accounting firm handle that."

"I know, but apparently, they're pissed, and they're getting cold feet about this deal. They want to move the meeting up to tonight."

"Tonight? Shit! We don't even know what their issue is yet. How are we supposed to address it by tonight?!"

"I know, I know. Hey, don't shoot the messenger."

"Yeah, sorry. Did they say anything about their issue?"

"No, but they're sending over a data sheet right now. I'll forward it when it arrives."

"Thank you. Fuck. I guess we'll have to fix this one ourselves. What time do they want to meet?"

"Six o'clock."

"Okay." I checked my watch. It was 1:30. I guess my email to Sam would have to wait. Shit! "Hey, Olivia?"

"Yeah."

"Call up Bert in accounting and see if he can come look at this with me."

"Already messaged him, he's on his way."

"Thanks, Liv."

"Hey, you've never called me that before. I kind of like it. Bye, James." She hung up.

My brain did a 180-degree flip. While I once was panicking about my marriage, I now was panicking about my career. *How did they mess this one up?* I closed my personal email and switched to my work email, finding that Olivia had forwarded the file. I opened it, my eyes now glued to the screen. *Hang in there, Samantha,* I thought. *I'll get to you soon, baby. Hang in there.*

∽

Samantha

Friday, May 17, 2019, 10:56 p.m.

Dear James,

I wrote you a sonnet:

"Return to Spring"

A love that bloomed as eager as the Spring,
Our passion grew with every passing year,
As we matured, devotion time did bring,
'Til passion turned commitment to my dear.
Yet even perfect love, she has her trials,
And Spring begets a Winter time to time,
When mischief runs apace with all her wiles,
And traps me in the grip of lover's crime.
But what of lovers lost in Winter's storm?
Are they forever cast away at sea?
Can ever I repair our love's true form?
Or will you be forever lost to me?
I pray my penance brings me back to shore,
So we can live and love in Spring once more.

I know it sounds trite and melodramatic, but I don't know how else to express my yearning for you, James. I waited in the room all day, hoping to hear from you again. Your lone message tore into my heart: "Do whatever you want," you'd said, "nothing seems to matter right now." It came with a promise for another message, and I hoped it would come once you had time to clear your head. Alas, I've gotten silence.

I stayed in the room the entire day, fearful of going back out to the resort, which seemed to be crawling with men determined to tear our marriage apart. I ordered in for meals, but I could barely eat. Jenny's been worried, but I kept encouraging her to go have fun without me. Finally, around dinnertime, she left to spend some time with Julian. I spent the day napping, journaling, watching movies while paying minimal attention, and thinking of you.

Something interesting did eventually happen. Around 8 p.m., I got a WhatsApp message from Jenny: "Turn the lights off and get in bed," it said. "Pretend you're asleep, I have a surprise for you."

How curious! "Ok," I replied, and I did as she asked. I climbed in bed wearing nothing but may panties and laid on my side, facing the door. A few minutes later, the door opened and both Jenny and Julian walked in.

At first, they were only silhouettes. They held each other close and whispered to each other in Spanish. They kissed. They approached the bed, and Jenny turned on her bedside lamp. Their bodies were dimly lit, but I could see them well enough. They continued to kiss, and then Julian removed Jenny's shirt. He reattached his lips to hers, then reached behind her and smoothly snapped open her bra, causing her ample breasts to fall free with a satisfying bounce. His hands went immediately to cupping and massaging her breasts. I noticed my own nipples harden in response. This was turning me on!

Julian's shirt came off. He was nicely built, and his chest was smooth as if it had been waxed. He pulled Jenny close, and their torsos pressed together as they resumed kissing. They were so passionate, necking zealously and exploring each other's bodies with their groping hands. Julian was squeezing Jenny's flesh in his fingers, her breasts, her waist, and her bottom through her jean shorts. Jenny was feeling Julian's toned arms, his shoulders, his back, and his ass. She grabbed the bulge in the front of his slacks and sighed between their kisses. She grazed her fingertips over the bulge before kneeling on the floor and unbuckling his belt. He ran his hands through Jenny's hair while she unzipped his trousers and then pulled them down, revealing that he wasn't wearing underwear. Out sprung his very erect penis.

I shifted in bed – ever so slightly, ever so slowly – until my hand slid under my panties and between my legs. My vagina was wet, but not in a way that yearned to be filled. I was wet from pure enjoyment of the moment, from playing voyeur to Jenny and her unfolding sexual experience. I could relate to early sexual encounters with a new partner – that is, to my earliest memories of being with you, James – and I could feel Jenny's excitement right along with her. This wasn't just a man she found attractive, he was a man she admired and related to. Nothing is more exciting than the first rounds of sex with someone you're falling for.

She held his cock in one hand, stroked it up and down a few times, then held the base of his shaft while putting the rest in her mouth. My own mouth started to salivate as I imagined what she was experiencing: the taste of her lover's cock, the feel of soft skin over hard shaft, the force of his head pressing back against her throat – the power of knowing she's pleasing him. Watching it all unfold, I recalled doing these things with you in our youth, James, as well as recently, and hopefully in our future.

Her blowjob technique was different than mine. She was far more attentive to her lover's balls, massaging them in her hands, licking them, even taking one tenderly in her mouth and sucking it. *Maybe I should try these moves with James.* With you in mind, I massaged my clitoris with my middle finger. It was sensitive and immensely pleasurable, but I knew I had to modulate my movements to not arouse suspicion. Thankfully, Jenny and Julian were far too absorbed in each other to notice, as Julian's eyes were closed in ecstasy and Jenny was wincing at times to avoid gagging on his cock.

Eventually Jenny disengaged, and a string of saliva trailed from her mouth to his dick until she swiped it with her hand. His cock was drenched. He took her by the hands and stood her up, kissing her once more while removing her shorts. He revealed her beautiful round buttocks – bigger and fleshier than mine, but still perfectly lifted. She wore lacy, purple thong underwear, but not for long – he quickly pulled them down, revealing stark tan lines over a smoothly shaven pussy. While standing in an embrace, they fondled each other's genitals in anticipation of sex.

Soon, it was Jenny's turn to be slobbered on. He guided her onto her bed and leaned over her. "Wait," she said, and then repositioned herself lengthwise with her head on her pillow, improving my view. He climbed on the bed on all fours, putting his knees between her open legs. I watched them in profile, Jenny on her back while Julian loomed over her. He put his mouth and tongue all over her body, starting with her breasts – one at a time – and trailing down to her abdomen and her hips. He bathed her body in loving affection, making her glisten where his lips and tongue had touched. Eventually, inevitably, his face moved down to her crotch.

I was incredibly moist, but not as moist as Jenny must've been. He began his oral assault on her sex, running his tongue up and down on her slit and sucking on her clitoris. I mimicked their movements, alternating my own attention from my lips to my clit. In my mind, it was James stimulating me rather than myself. Soon, Julian started fingering Jenny's pussy while continuing to kiss and suck on her clit. His hand moved rhythmically, appearing to curl in an upward motion to help stimulate Jenny's g-spot. I attempted this as well, which was no easy feat with just my hands. I was moving around in bed considerably more by now, and I'm sure Jenny and Julian would've noticed if they weren't so absorbed in each other.

Soon, Jenny came, as evidenced by her sudden writhing and moaning. She flexed her butt muscles, pushing her hips off the bed in apparent loss of control. Julian stayed engaged with her pussy, pressing his fingers into her g-spot with increasing fervor. When the climax finally ebbed, he kissed her tenderly on the clitoris and then crawled back up on top of her, kissing her mouth with his firm erection resting on her abdomen. He murmured something in Spanish, and then crawled on his knees until his cock was right in Jenny's face. He pushed the head of his penis back into her mouth, then slowly started thrusting, using her open mouth as a pussy. His thrusts gradually became more aggressive, as he started pushing deeper and faster into her throat. Impressively, Jenny could take his whole cock in her mouth without an inch to spare! She gripped his ass while he thrust, and I admired the contracting muscles in his shapely buttocks. He finally got Jenny to gag once he pressed his cock fully inside and held the back of her head, holding it in her throat for several seconds. When she gagged, he withdrew his penis at last, covered with a thick new coat of saliva. Jenny took his wet cock in her hand, stroked it gently, and then kissed and licked the head playfully for a minute. Julian's eyes were squeezed shut, and the sensation seemed to cause small, involuntary jerks of his penis.

Julian whispered something to Jenny again and then climbed off the bed. He found his slacks on the floor and dug something from his pocket, a condom wrapper. He unwrapped the condom, which Jenny took from his hand. She put it in her mouth, her teeth pinched gently on the reservoir at the end. Using her mouth, she unrolled the condom over Julian's penis, as he watched with wide-eyed surprise. They locked eyes, his filled with admiration, hers filled with lust.

He laid her on her back and prepared to enter her, positioning his penis at her slit. Her legs were spread and her knees were up by her shoulders, giving him clear access to her waiting pussy. He pushed in tenderly, slowly acclimating her vagina to his girth. She cooed and whimpered softly, feeling the mix of pleasure and discomfort I was also so accustomed to. I continued to mirror them, now pressing my middle and ring fingers inside of me as best I could. My pussy was wet and slick so my fingertips slid in easily, but with my fingers and the angle, I couldn't match the length of Julian's penis. I briefly wished I had a dildo, or better yet, my husband's penis to fill me – but when I used my imagination, it would almost just as good. I pursed my lips to avoid a gasp of pleasure.

Meanwhile, Julian had picked up speed and started to thrust more vigorously into Jenny. I admired his biceps as he maintained his form in push-up position, and I watched as his abdomen and ass muscles worked his hips forward and back. Jenny was also an active participant, groping his body with her hands, massaging her own breasts, or shifting her legs and hips to create new angles. Soon, his rhythmic thrusts increased until he was pounding her, his pelvis clapping against hers as he slammed himself completely inside of her. I increased my intensity as well, pushing my fingers inside myself as deep as I could go, vibrating my hand to create stimulation. My palm brushed up against my clit, causing a rush of sensation all throughout my pelvis that started to surge through my torso, my limbs, and my head. I felt my face begin to flush with pleasure.

Jenny was uttering words of encouragement, forgetting to speak in hushed tones. Julian gasped and groaned with the strain of his thrusting, but he was determined to continue. Jenny let out a moan of pleasure, then grabbed Julian's ass and pulled him even deeper inside of her. I saw imprints of her fingernails digging into his flesh, holding him to her so he could not withdraw his penis more than an inch. He began convulsing his ass muscles, causing his cock to vibrate within her pussy. They now were face-to-face, and he slipped his tongue down her mouth in a passionate kiss.

"Oh, God," she exclaimed between kisses. "I'm coming."

And so did I. The rush surging through my body became electric, and I tingled all over with waves of pleasure. I'd abandoned inhibition, hardly realizing that my breath was coming in shallows gasps to enhance the intensity of my orgasm. I imagined you were giving it to me, the source of my pleasure, but also of safety and love. *James.* Your name was on the tip of my tongue, and I nearly whispered it aloud. I fucked myself with my fingers, eager to maintain this imaginary feeling of closeness as long as possible.

Eventually, I realized the action in the bed next to me had paused. Through heavy breaths, I heard Julian ask Jenny a question in Spanish. He turned toward me, and I froze, squeezing my eyes shut in mock slumber.

"No, she's asleep," I heard Jenny whisper in English. "I think she just stirred a little. Maybe we were a little too loud?"

"Maybe *you* were a little too loud," he teased. They resumed making out, Julian's cock still inside her but now idle.

"Let me go on top," Jenny said.

They rolled over, his cock never slipping from inside her. Now she had mounted him, and from this angle, I had a far better view of Jenny's body. She rocked her hips forward and back while Julian was fully inside. She reminded me of a belly dancer, moving and grinding in rhythm while her breasts swayed in mesmerizing fashion. In this position, she would be feeling his cock shifting inside her, stimulating various pressure points in her pussy. I craved that sensation of fullness, having a hard dick completely submerged within me. I continued my self-stimulation, matching their pace and their motions. Fresh off my orgasm, my body was still sensitive and prone to miniature aftershocks of enjoyment.

Julian pulled Jenny forward, locking lips with her once again. Her hard nipples were pressed against his chest, and with my off-hand, I pinched and flicked my own hard nipples with shuddering effect. He put his hands on her ass cheeks, holding her in place while he thrusted into her from underneath. His muscles flexed as he pounded into her, causing a wet slapping sound against her labia, the impact creating beautiful ripples in the flesh of her ass. He spread her cheeks with his hands, allowing him to plunge even deeper into her depths. It must have been intense, as Julian grunted in exertion and Jenny moaned with delight.

When Julian started to tire, Jenny assumed control. She sat up and started bouncing on his dick, lifting high on her knees before crashing down with a smack upon his lap. Her whole form was beauty, as her dark wavy hair tossed about, her nipples pointed up and down with the bounce of her breasts, and her ass and thighs quaked with the impact of their fucking. She rode impressively, lifting almost fully off his cock before falling completely upon it in a game of "hide the pickle." This was the best view of penetration I'd seen, as I could admire both his cream-covered cock and her tightly gripping pussy. Julian's hands stayed firmly on her ass, while her hands resumed fondling her breasts. Soon, Jenny leaned forward.

"I need you to come," she said to Julian, but I pretended she had said it to me. I redoubled my efforts at pounding my own pussy with my hand, and I noticed Jenny put her hands around Julian's neck. She choked him softly and repeated, "I said, I need you to come."

It was like she had said it to us both. Julian, straining from his limited breath, thrusted furiously upward from underneath. The flesh of Jenny's ass vibrated from his jackrabbit thrusts, and she started to gasp and squeal with pleasure.

"Come with me, baby," she said, full voice, gripping his throat now for stability.

We came, all three of us. Julian grunted and groaned, slowing his thrusts but slamming them deeply, powerfully into Jenny's pussy. I bit my lip, trying to suppress my whimpers of ecstatic delight. Thankfully, Jenny and Julian were too wrapped up in their own sounds and sensations to notice me.

Finally, Jenny collapsed forward upon Julian, her chest upon his, her chin resting over his shoulder as they both gasped for air. They stayed in these positions for a few minutes, muttering lusty phrases into each other's ears before Jenny finally climbed off and let Julian's softening cock slip out from within her. She removed the condom, then lovingly licked and sucked the cum off his penis. Surprisingly, his cock grew hard once again, and she gently stroked and sucked him while fondling his balls. It was hardly a minute before a second, smaller orgasm emerged. He held his breath as the veins on his shaft appeared to bulge, and his cock muscles contracted which each spurt of his cum into her mouth. She swallowed, and while his reaction was less intense than his initial orgasm, he still vocalized a satisfied, "Mmm."

For the next few minutes, I kept my eyes closed and focused on being as still as possible. I heard them shuffling around the room, putting clothes back on and speaking quietly in Spanish. Eventually, I heard the heavy main door open and close, as Julian had presumably left the premises.

"So what did you think?" Jenny asked aloud in full voice.

I stirred in my bed. "Hmm?" I asked. I moved around in the bed, stretching my limbs as if just waking up. "What did I think about what?"

She grinned. "Don't play dumb. You know I set that up for you."

"You what?"

"I made sure we fucked so you could see it!"

"Wha – But why?" I asked.

"For James," Jenny said. "To give him a story."

"Oh!" I said. I sat up fully in the bed, not caring that my breasts were now exposed. "You fucked Julian so I could tell James a story?"

She slapped herself in the forehead. "No. I fucked Julian because I wanted to fuck Julian. But I did it here so that you could watch and tell James."

I laughed. "But why?!"

"You are so dense," she said. She retrieved a water bottle from the mini-fridge. "It's an apology," she explained, "for ditching you the other day." She shrugged. "I wanted to pay you guys back."

"That's – that's really sweet of you, actually."

She blushed. "Well, yeah. Thanks."

We each giggled, feeling a little shy and awkward. I laid on my back to break the tension, looking instead at the ceiling.

"I think James will like it. The story," I said.

"Did you like it?" she asked.

"I did," I answered. "Very much." Now I was the one to feel a blush coming on.

She smiled and tossed her hair. "I could tell," she said.

"You could?!"

"Mm hmm. You could've been more discrete, you know."

I was mortified. "Could Julian tell?"

"Eh, I don't think so," she said. "He wondered if we woke you up at one point, but I think I convinced him you were still asleep. In any case, I don't think he suspected that you – enjoyed yourself so much."

I was relieved. "Thank goodness for that."

"So," she began. "Any word from James while I was gone?"

"No," I replied, "Not since his email this morning."

"I see," she said. "Well, it's not too late yet. Maybe you can send him your new story. As our joint apology."

"Good idea."

I got out of bed, put on pajamas, and sat down at the desk. Jenny ordered room service, and I was feeling brave enough to sip a cocktail while writing. My heart fluttered as I began to type, imagining your reaction and knowing that, like me, you'd always found Jenny very attractive. I was nervous, but also hopeful that I was taking the first small step toward contrition.

Love,

Samantha

9: The Last Hurrah

James

Saturday, May 18, 2019; 1:49 a.m.

Dear Samantha,

To begin with – I forgive you. I wanted to lead with that to avoid any unnecessary suspense. Like Darth Vader, I've searched my feelings, and I know it to be true. I still love you – and I hope, like Han Solo, you know.

Of course, I was badly hurt when I first learned of your transgression. It was like a stab in the back that penetrated my heart. But context is key, and I think I understand where you were coming from. It may take time for this wound to fully heal, but I'm committed to working it out with you. I love you today the same as I did last week, and nothing's happened that can or will change that.

I also have a confession. In my sadness, I made a mistake of my own, and it was nearly a fatal one. I now know how heightened emotions can impact sensibilities. While at the peak of my anger, I made a sexual advance on a coworker, and she actually seemed interested. Something nearly happened, but thank God, it didn't. I deeply regret even initiating it, and I can only imagine how terrible I'd feel now if I'd gone through with it. I'll save the details for later, but know this – I consider us on equal playing fields. Rather than quibble over whose offense was worse than the other, I'm hopeful we can call it a draw and move on, and you can forgive me, as I have forgiven you.

In that vein, I think the only way forward through these hardships is total trust and openness. When the time comes, if you have any questions about my mistake, I intend to answer them honestly and fully. By admitting what

I've done, I hope that earns me credibility, just as your honesty has earned it for you. I'm glad you were honest about your affair with Ethan, and I feel that I can still trust you moving forward.

In other news, there was an emergency situation at work last night, and that's why my reply is finally coming after midnight. In short, due to an accounting error, our client insisted we move up our meeting to clarify the mistake and amend our proposal. It was a grueling meeting, and long story short, we lost the account. It was a blow to the company, and I'm not looking forward to hearing from my bosses in the morning.

The disappointment really puts things into perspective. Of course, I'm sad about losing the account, but that isn't where my focus has been lately. Instead, my focus is on you, and any work matter pales in comparison to the health of our relationship. I regret missing our trip to appease these pompous assholes. I could've been on the beach, sipping Mai Tais and making love to my beautiful wife, but instead I'm covering for someone else's mistake at work and taking the blame. Such is life, but I intend to bring my renewed perspective to our marriage and focus on what matters most – us.

And finally, that story you just sent me was really fucking hot. It pleased me to hear you play voyeur to Jenny's love affair. It turned me on to see it through your eyes, your admiration of Jenny's body, the way it excited you and made you touch yourself. It was like I was viewing your lust through your eyes and touching myself along with you. And after the day I had, it was exactly the kind of stress relief I needed. Thank you, my love. And please, thank Jenny for me as well.

I'll keep this message short as it's late, and I expect a stern meeting with my bosses in the morning. As far as our little experiment – I have some mixed feelings, but I wonder if you're interested in continuing it on your last day in paradise. Once you're home, I want things back to normal, with your body and affection all to myself. But something doesn't sit right about Ethan being your last, and a part of me hopes you'll have a final encounter with someone new before your trip is over. Is that twisted? You may be in no condition to entertain that idea, and I can respect that. Once again, the choice is yours – one last hurrah on your erotic adventure, or save yourself exclusively for me. Either way, I can't wait for you to come home and again be fully mine.

Love,

James

~

Samantha

Sunday, May 19, 2019; 12:23 a.m.

Dear James,

Your message filled me with joy and relief. Of course, I'm nervous to hear the details of what happened with your coworker, but I trust that nothing serious occurred and that it's something we can work through. I long to come home to your embrace once more, so I can be fully yours in body as I always have been in spirit.

I considered what you said about "one last hurrah" and talked it over with Jenny in the morning. We decided that it was safe to pursue another adventure, and that as long as I followed the rules, it wouldn't bring any more harm to our relationship. However, with what had occurred, I couldn't envision even wanting a sexual experience with someone else, so I wrote it off as something that simply wouldn't happen.

I was terrified of going out in the resort. What if I saw Ethan, Mark, or John, or even Carlos or Dio? I didn't think I could face them at this point, not after everything that had happened.

"Let's leave the resort, then," said Jenny. "We've barely used the car, let's put it to use."

That plan seemed much more palatable, and after a lazy start to our day, we snuck out of the hotel, jumped in our blue Volkswagen convertible, and drove off toward the nearby city of Playa del Carmen.

Julian was at work today, but he recommended a local restaurant by the beach. It was very authentic, with no tourists in sight and no sounds of English to be heard. We ordered tamales and Mexican Cokes – no booze for me today, thanks!

We then went to a topless beach – or so I thought! We parked on a paved parking lot where the view of the beach was obscured by some dense, tropical trees. There was a sign in Spanish, and Jenny explained it was a topless beach. I had a bikini on under my tank top and white jean shorts, but I didn't anticipate taking my top off. I'd exposed my breasts to enough strangers on this trip, thank-you-very-much. Jenny dropped her top, though, and her beautiful, bouncing breasts dropped loose.

"Maybe I can even out these tan lines," she said.

When we made it down to the beach, we were in for a shock. Penis, penis everywhere.

"I thought you said this was a *topless* beach," I scolded.

"I did!" said Jenny. "But apparently no one cares around here."

The beach was crowded, and it took some searching before we found two beach chairs next to each other. The sand was gorgeous, and the water looked smooth and swimmable. People, maybe about three-quarters locals, were walking about, lying in the sun, or bathing in the ocean. Children weren't permitted, of course, but there were still some high energy young adults around, playing frisbee or beach volleyball with their breasts and dicks swaying in the breeze. *Aren't these people getting sand, like, everywhere? I wondered.*

"When in Rome," said Jenny, and she removed her bottoms. I felt a tinge of arousal upon seeing her snatch, which I quickly suppressed. She laid her towel on the beach chair and got on her stomach. "Can you rub some sunscreen on my back and shoulders?" she asked. "So I don't burn."

"Of course," I replied. I approached her naked form shyly with the sunscreen in my hands. I squirted some onto my palms and then rubbed it into her shoulders.

Her body shuddered beneath me. "Oooh, that's cold," she said.

I tried not to think dirty thoughts, but my face was so close to her naked body. I massaged the sunscreen around her shoulders and then wrapped around the sides, just grazing her breasts.

"Mmm," she said. "That feels good."

And it did feel good. I always knew I was attracted to Jenny, but I'd assumed it was more admiration than lust. And yet here I was, massaging sunscreen on the sides of her breasts, getting aroused. Was she getting aroused too? She certainly wasn't stopping me.

I continued down her back until I reached the curve of her ass. I had this burning itch to touch it, and I started testing limits but rubbing the sunscreen ever so slightly along the fleshy curve between her back and her butt cheeks. She interrupted me.

"Don't rub sunscreen there," she said. I drew back, embarrassed. "I want to tan there," she went on. "Can you use the oil instead?"

I blushed, but thankfully, Jenny couldn't see me. I rubbed some oil onto my palms and then started to massage her butt cheeks. The skin was smooth and soft, but the muscles beneath were firm. I massaged her ass in deep circular motions, occasionally pinching the skin or digging my knuckles into her glutes. The movements subtly opened her cheeks, and I admired her pretty asshole, similar in color to her tan flesh, which made it look cute and clean. I recalled hearing somewhere that porn models get their anuses bleached, and I wondered if it burned. Meanwhile, Jenny's asshole was small, tight, and beautiful. Spreading her cheeks a bit, I had a sneaky view of her pink pussy. Was it glistening with moisture just now? Was this turning her on like it was for me?

I couldn't go on, I couldn't keep ogling my best friend like this. I stopped rubbing her ass and gave her right booty cheek a playful slap. "All finished!" I said in a sing-song tone.

"Mmm," she replied. "That felt nice, thanks." After a brief pause, she asked, "Were you enjoying the view?"

"I, um – what?"

"The view," she said. "Of all the naked men and women around."

I was so absorbed by Jenny that I hadn't taken the time to look around. I did now, noticing a wide range of male and female body types. Fitness wasn't a prerequisite at this beach, but some people did have quite impressive bodies. I also observed variation in the dicks – some swung low against the men's thighs, whereas some were short, like cute little buttons at the tops of their scrotums. All were flaccid, swaying in the ocean breeze like leaves on a tree. The sights were amusing, but not exactly arousing.

Jenny's voice interrupted my thoughts. "Want me to get you now?" she asked.

"Do I what?"

"Do you want me to rub some sunscreen on you?"

"Oh, no!" I said hastily. Too hastily? I was not prepared for a sexual experience of any kind, let alone one with my best friend! "It's okay," I said, "I'm not gonna take my shirt off. I'll just put some on my arms and legs."

"Suit yourself!" she said. She laid back on the chair, burying her face in her arms, still baring her backside for the world to see. As I rubbed some sunscreen over my limbs, I noticed several men and women nearly breaking their necks to gawk at Jenny as they passed. A young man in a speedo, probably in his later teens, passed by at least three or four times, thinking he was slick. He passed along the side of Jenny's feet, trying to sneak a peek between her legs. The final time I caught his eye, then gave him a reproachful look. He stared back brazenly, his expression saying, "Whatcha gonna do about it, lady?" I shook my head in disdain, and once he passed, he didn't return.

I enjoyed watching people watching Jenny, wondering what went through their heads. Admiration, or lust, or simply a nice place to look? Were they judging her? Were they going home to masturbate to her image, or would they think of her tonight while fucking their husbands and wives? There's so much we can't know about someone's mind, so much we really shouldn't know. I thought of you, James, and how you confessed to making a move on your coworker. Was it purely impulsive, or was your eye on her for months? Did you fantasize about her while we were together? Did I really want to know? As your wife, was I entitled to know, or do you have the right to keep that private? I thought of the things I might not want you to know. Not secrets necessarily, but thoughts that might disturb you or thoughts you might misunderstand. *No, I decided. Our inner thoughts are ours, we're not required to share them.* You asked me to share my experiences on my adventure, and I did so willingly. My behaviors, yes, especially as they relate to fidelity. I agreed to share my behaviors, and I needed to tell you when I'd broken our agreement. But my *inner* experience? My thoughts, my feelings, my sensations, all the things that shape the inner me? I'm the gatekeeper to those. I share what feels comfortable and expect the same from you. Boundaries are healthy, and they keep us from chasing each other off with our crazy. Intimacy is born from what we're willing to share, not from what we're forced or obliged to. I was glad for the thoughts I'd shared with you, and I wouldn't insist on knowing any fantasies of yours that you weren't comfortable to share.

Lost in my reverie, I hardly noticed the time pass. Jenny eventually awakened from her nap. She groaned and stretched, her nipples perky in the salty air.

"How long was I out?" she asked.

I checked my phone. "About 30 minutes."

"Fuck," she said. "Now I need another 30 for my front." She repositioned on her back, her breasts and vagina exposed to the sun. Her eyes were closed behind her John Lennon shades. "You good?" she asked.

"I'm good," I said. "I think I'm going for a walk."

"Have fun," she said.

I took off my sandals and walked along the waterline, feeling the damp sand beneath my feet and letting the gentle waves crash upon my ankles. *I should have brought some music,* I lamented, but here I was, alone again with my nagging thoughts. What would happen when I arrive back home? You forgave me, but would things change? Would we feel distant? Would we be jealous, you knowing about my erotic affairs, and me knowing about your coworker? The questions brought no answers. *The answers will come,* I told myself. *You can't control it now. They'll come soon enough.*

What could I control? The present moment. Yes, I could control what I do now. But what should I do? Our vacation was almost at an end. Could I improve the situation? Could I do anything at all to improve my chance with James? I thought of your last email, how you'd asked me to sleep with someone else, to find one last fling to ensure that Ethan wasn't my last. I wouldn't pull that off, I realized. I wasn't in the mood. *Oh, well*, I thought. *I'll have to make another gesture. A crappy souvenir, maybe.* I knew you'd understand. You'd only want me to do it if I was really in the mood.

After my walk, I reconvened with Jenny. She was putting her clothes back on, and she said, "Hey, Julian got off work, he wants to meet up at a bar here in town. You game?"

I shrugged. "I'm game." I was glad to stay away from the resort as long as possible. It was like the place felt cursed.

We rinsed off the sand at a nearby spigot and shuffled back into the car. Jenny wanted some more photos for her social media, so we took a road along the ocean in search of scenic views. She took a beautiful shot in her thong bikini, ass out, leaning over a low stone wall overlooking the ocean. I wondered what this photo was for – simply a thirst trap on social media, or was she saving this for a dating profile? I asked her.

"Eh. Maybe both," she answered. "If I still like it when I post these later."

I grew up more conservative than her, so I'd never posted anything like this. "What's the point?" I asked. "Is there like an end goal?"

"Good question," she said. "I like when people 'like' them, I guess. And you can see who's snooping on your pics."

"So, like an ego-boost," I said. "But – doesn't that kind of cheapen it, like if just anybody can see your body?"

"Says the girl whose chasing dick all over Mexico," she retorted.

Ouch. My face grew hot with shame. "I'm sorry, I shouldn't have put it like that. Sharing myself is a whole new world to me. I guess it's something I'm getting used to."

"It's okay," she said. "I shouldn't have snapped like that. I guess my viewpoint is that it's my body, and if I want to show it off, that's my decision."

"Sure, it's good to be admired. I can relate to that, especially this week. But aren't you worried that creepers are leering at you? That people you don't like are lusting over your pics, or even fantasizing about you?"

"So, what?" she asked. "So, I'm renting space in their heads. Big deal! It's not too different than being ogled in the street. At least I'm in control of what's out there. And besides, sometimes it draws the attention of someone worthwhile."

"Oh yeah?" I asked.

"Oh yeah," she said.

We pulled into the parking lot of a restaurant near the beach with open patio seating and an outdoor bar. It overlooked a rocky stretch of ocean, and the sound of crashing waves competed with the steel drum music coming from the patio speakers. The late-afternoon crowd was composed mainly of locals. Julian sat alone among several occupied tables on the patio, and he waved us over.

"Hey, guys. Drinks?" he asked.

"Maybe an iced tea," I said. "I'm driving." I held up the car keys as proof of my excuse.

"Hmm. Could they make me a sex-on-the-beach?" asked Jenny.

"For you, there is always sex on the beach," Julian said. He winked, and Jenny rolled her eyes yet grinned.

We ordered the drinks, then began discussing our plans for tomorrow's journey home. Julian nodded along politely, but he kept staring wistfully off toward the darkening skyline over the beach.

"Julian." Jenny snapped her fingers. "Hey, Julian, are you listening?"

"Huh?" he asked. "Oh, yeah."

"Where did your mind go? We lost you."

"Oh. I was just thinking that you're leaving tomorrow, you know?"

"Exactly," Jenny said. "That's exactly what we're talking about."

"But, uh. Like, what does that mean for us?" he asked. I tried to shrink in my seat. Should I be here for this conversation?

Jenny actually blushed a little. "Well – I mean, it means we're leaving. And, of course, you're staying here."

His face fell. "I know that," he said. "But, like, will we stay in touch? Will you visit? Could I visit you in the States?"

Jenny, for once in her life, was at a loss for words. I knew they needed time to talk, so I abruptly stood up. "I'll be right back," I said. "Gonna get some air."

I left the table and walked to the end of the patio to take in the view. It was nearly dark now, and the ocean appeared almost black beneath the navy-blue sky. *My last moments of freedom*, I thought. No, that wasn't right. *Of loneliness. Of solitude. Of separation.* The ends of vacations were always bittersweet. I'd miss the scenery and the escape from responsibility, but there was comfort in the routines of work and home. Plus, this vacation was so atypical without my husband, not to mention the sexual freedoms I'd been granted this week. Normalcy would be welcome, though how normal would things be when I return? There was still so much to sort out. Will we feel awkward with each other? Will it be like walking on pins and needles? Will we need couples counseling to get through this? What if we've lost "the spark"? I knew I was ready to fight for our relationship, but was James?

I turned around and then gasped. My eyes caught a familiar profile at the bar, the strong brow, the wild locks of sandy hair, and the rugged facial stubble of our resort's resident fitness instructor, Emilio. He was alone at the bar and had just begun to sip a very full beer. My heart thumped in my chest, and I couldn't tell if it was from excitement or fear. He hadn't noticed me, and I covered my face as I hastened to my seat.

"Holy fuck," I said as I sat, grateful that my back was now to the bar.

"Yeah, we noticed him too," said Jenny.

"What's the big deal?" asked Julian, which meant Jenny mercifully hadn't told him about my failure to seduce him. "Did you fuck him or something?" I felt an impulse to start banging my head on the table.

"Quite the contrary," Jenny said, but she didn't explain any further. "Do you know that guy well?"

"Not really," said Julian. "I see him around. I think he has an apartment here in the city, since he doesn't live in the staff village."

"Does he have a reputation at all?" I asked.

"Like, is he gay?" Jenny chimed in. "My guess is that he's gay."

Julian laughed. "Nah, I don't think so," he said. "He mostly keeps to himself, not really plugged into the community, you know? Seems like an okay guy. Why, what's the big deal?"

"Don't worry about it," said Jenny.

"No, it's okay," I replied. "I – kinda tried to flirt with him, and he shut me down. Pretty hard."

Julian nodded. "Yeah, staff isn't allowed to mingle with the guests."

"You're one to talk," said Jenny. She backhanded him on the shoulder.

"I know, I know," said Julian. "But you gotta shoot your shot from time to time, right?"

"He didn't shoot his shot with me," I said, too late to realize the innuendo. Jenny must've noticed, as she started choking on her drink.

We ordered food. I distinctly kept my back to the bar, avoiding any chance to remind Emilio of my existence. But I had to go to the bathroom eventually. I slipped past him to the bathroom unnoticed. Before exiting, I checked my reflection in the mirror. *If he's gonna see me*, I thought, *I might as well look halfway decent.* My makeup was scarce, and my hair fell past my shoulders in a wavy, casual look. I tossed it a little to try to straighten it out, then braved the short journey back to our table. Which, of course, led me straight past the bar.

"Pink pants girl!" he called in his sexy foreign accent. Busted! I turned, hoping he wouldn't see my face turning scarlet in the dim patio lighting.

"Oh, hi! Um – you're the yoga instructor from the resort," I said, pretending to forget his name. We shook hands, and he held mine warmly for an extra moment as he smiled and met my eyes.

"Yes, Emilio," he said. "Remind me of your name, please?"

"Samantha," I said.

"Samantha, of course," he said. "And your friend, uh," he looked around, then spotted her with Julian at our table nearby. "Oh yes, Jenny. Samantha and Jenny."

I felt a tinge of jealousy that he'd remembered her name. "Yeah, that's right," I said. "It's so funny to run into you here."

Jenny suddenly popped up beside me. "Oh, hey, you're the yoga instructor!" she said, also pretending to forget his name. He reintroduced himself and shook her hand briefly. Was I imagining things, or was he less warm with her than he had been with me?

"I'm so glad you guys came out here," he said, "where you can see the *real* side of Mexico."

"Of course," said Jenny. "Julian over there is a personal friend." She gestured, and Julian waved.

"Oh yeah, Julian from the resort," said Emilio. He waved back and called something out to Julian in Spanish.

"So, Emilio, are you waiting here for a friend?" I asked. A swarm of butterflies awakened in my stomach. Was he waiting on a date? Was a beautiful woman about to walk in, elegantly dressed and with a perfect physique?

"Ah, no, not tonight," said Emilio. "I'm friends with the bartender, so sometimes I come here alone for a drink."

"I – hope we're not encroaching on alone time," I said quickly. I was giving him an out, a way to let me down easy.

"No, not at all," he said. "Sometimes when I'm here, I'm lucky enough to find people worth talking to." He winked at me. Oh, wow, what was going on? Just the other day he practically ran away from me, and now, with my rumpled hair and lack of makeup, he was ready to make a pass at me? I felt my sex drive reawakening. I so recently was closed for business, but now there was an opportunity, and chance for redemption. But also for a second letdown, I realized.

Jenny was studying my face, as if reading my reaction. "By the way, Emilio," she said. "We have another seat at our table, if you'd like to join." She glanced at me quickly. "That is, if Sam is okay with staying out a bit longer on our last night in town. Weren't you saying you felt a little sleepy, Sam?"

Brilliant! It was a perfect setup with Jenny making the invite but giving me plenty of space to accept or rescind it. The depth of her friendship cannot be understated. Now was my chance.

"Actually, I think I'm catching my second wind," I said. "And I'd appreciate not being the third wheel for a change." I put my hand on Emilio's bicep, repeating the move I'd made just two days earlier. This time, he didn't pull away.

"Fantastic," he said. "I'll let the bartender know I'm switching to your table."

Jenny and I returned to our table and shared a subtle high-five.

"What was that about?" asked Julian.

"Redemption," I told him.

He looked at me quizzically, then rolled his eyes.

Soon, Emilio took his seat on my right. "Good evening, everyone," he said. "How are we all doing on this beautiful night?"

We exchanged pleasantries, and the ensuing conversation found its natural flow. Food and drink were in abundance, but I continued to abstain from liquor. Nonetheless, Emilio's friendlier tone emboldened me, as well as my husband's entreaty to have one last night of fun. I laughed hard at Emilio's jokes, and I leaned in intently as he told his backstory of growing up in Spain and studying yoga in India and Northern Africa. I touched him when I could, including boldly on his thigh at one point. He didn't recoil, so I left my hand there.

"How about you, Samantha?" he asked. *Uh oh, here it comes.* How much of my backstory should I reveal? Should I lie about being married, or just artfully dodge the question?

"How about me what?" I asked, buying time.

"Where did you learn yoga?" he asked. "Clearly you are quite adept."

I smiled modestly at the compliment and fluttered my lashes. "Oh, I wouldn't call myself adept," I said. "But I took classes from time to time in college. I'm more of a dancer by training, I took ballet, tap, and hip hop lessons growing up."

"It shows," he said. "You're clearly very flexible."

"You should put that to the test!" Jenny interjected. She started laughing a little too hard, and I started to think she'd had one too many.

Emilio laughed too, then shot me a side-eyed glance. "I don't know," he said. "Should I?"

"Maybe you should." We locked eyes. He had those really pretty blue eyes.

"You two keep talking," Jenny cut in. "Julian's getting me another drink at the bar." She stood up.

"I am?" Julian asked.

"Maybe a water this time?" I warned. I gave her a stern glare.

"Yeah, fine, water," she said. She patted Julian on the shoulder, and he got up to follow her to the bar.

I turned to Emilio. "I like this version of you," I said, and I squeezed his thigh.

He grinned. "What do you mean?" he asked.

"You seem more open, more comfortable than you did at the resort. And more playful." I bit my lip and winked. Yes, I was being that forward.

He laughed. "Well, yes," he said. "Staff is not allowed to spend private time with guests at the resort. Didn't you know that?" Of course, I should've known that.

"But what about Julian?" I asked.

"Julian – he's kind of playing with fire, as you say." It made me think of Carlos, who also had been 'playing with fire.'

"I see. So – you weren't repulsed by me at the resort?"

"Not at all!" he said. "Look, I don't know if you'd guess this, but women flirt with me at the resort all the time. You know, they're on vacation, they're drinking, they want to have a good time – and usually it's easy for me to play it off, act smooth, maybe flirt back a little, and then disengage. But with *you*," he said, "I had my eye on you all morning."

"You did?" I asked.

"Oh, yes. Your bright blue eyes, your beautiful lips, your sexy body in those tight pink pants – and the way you looked at me, mm!" He swooned.

"Then why did you act so funny when I tried to talk to you?"

"Because I was scared!" he said. "You made me nervous. Like I said, most women, it's no big deal, I'm not interested, so a little flirting is like – no worries. But with you, I was nervous I wouldn't resist you."

I was flattered and relieved – and a little ashamed of how horribly I'd felt over a misunderstanding. "Well – that's a relief," I admitted. "I thought you didn't want me."

"Quite the contrary," he said. "But I never dreamed I'd run into you here. Out here," he gestured to our surroundings, "it's free game."

"Is that so?" I leaned in. "And does that mean you're hunting me?"

"It means I am on the prowl for you."

"Well, I think I'm already caught in your trap." I leaned in closer, and he took the bait. He kissed me assertively. His tongue moved swiftly past my lips,

161

then teased mine before departing. "You have some tongue skills," I said. "I may have to put *those* to the test."

Jenny and Julian returned.

"You guys seem to be getting along," Jenny said.

"We decided we should go somewhere more private," Emilio announced. I hadn't actually agreed to that, but I couldn't argue that that's where things were going.

"Great," said Jenny. "Julian has a house by the resort. Let's go there."

"We can't go there!" Julian and I exclaimed together.

"Why not?" she asked. Had she forgotten about Carlos, Julian's roommate who I had all-too-recently slept with? Her questioning look turned to wide-eyed surprise as she realized her mistake.

"What's the matter?" Emilio asked. "Something I should know?"

"No!" the three of us said together, followed by an uncomfortable pause.

"We could all go to my place," Emilio suggested. "I have an apartment in the city. Only one bedroom, I'm afraid. Perhaps we should split up?"

"No!" Jenny cut in, shooting me a look. I could tell she wasn't going to leave me. "Is there a living room? Julian and I can hang out in there if you guys need some space."

"What?!" exclaimed Julian. He gave her a look of disgust. "But wh – ouch!" She'd kicked him under the table. "I mean, yeah," he said. "That's fine."

***

In what seemed like no time at all, we arrived at Emilio's apartment. The building seemed new, or at least newly painted, and the units all faced the main street. It was located on a hill, and Emilio's second floor apartment had a lovely view of the city lights.

He opened the door, and we stepped into his quaintly furnished living room. We stood there for a moment in silence, before Jenny cut in.

"We'll wait for you guys out here," she said, collapsing on the cushiony brown sofa. Julian followed suit.

"Would you like a drink, or perhaps a blanket?" Emilio asked.

"Yes, and yes," Jenny said. He supplied Jenny and Julian with water, beers, and a large quilt, then turned to me.

"Shall we?" he asked, gesturing to a door that was presumably his bedroom.

"We shall," I replied, and to my surprise, he swept me off my feet, holding me under my back and behind my knees. My hair swooped through the air, and I cooed with delight. Being carried? Total turn-on.

He took me to his dark bedroom and closed the door. He set me down on my feet and then kissed me, his hands going directly to my ass. *They always go right for my ass*, I thought. The kiss lasted minutes as we probed each other's mouths. He was patient, and despite his hand placement, he didn't attempt to grope me or to take off my clothes, at least not yet, which was nice because it allowed me to melt into his kiss.

He disengaged. "May I turn on the light?" he asked.

"Mm hmm," I replied.

He reached behind me and flipped a switch. I didn't expect what I saw next.

"Are those – handcuffs?" I asked. Handcuffs dangled from both bedposts at the head of the bed, and silks were tied to the bedposts at the foot. "I hope those aren't for me," I said.

He smiled meekly. "Don't worry," he said. "They're for me. If that is okay with you."

"I – I've never handcuffed someone before," I said.

He took me by the hands. "I can guide you through it." He kissed me gently, and we resumed making out with building intensity, our hands now intent on exploring each other's bodies. He was muscular but lean, and I could feel the contours of his abdomen and chest through his shirt. His hands slipped under my t-shirt and caressed my lower back and my hips, gradually rising toward the bikini top I wore as a bra. My breasts heaved upon my deepening breath, and tension released as he untied my top and it fell through the front of my shirt. His hands found my breasts and began to massage them, teasing my sensitive nipples with intermittent pinches and flicks.

I grabbed his muscular ass, pulling his hips into mine, determined to feel his masculine bulge. Mission accomplished, as something hard poked through his jeans into my hip. I wanted to remove his pants but was wary of seeming too eager. My shirt and shorts were still on – shouldn't the guy start undressing me first? *Nah,* I thought. *I'm a liberated woman. I'm allowed to pursue what I want!*

I began by pulling at his shirt, and he assisted me with yanking it over his head. To my surprise, he had round piercings in both nipples. Edgy! We removed my shirt next and resumed our kiss, our bare chests now pressed together, my nipples grazing his chiseled pecs. I worked at his belt, and his buckle chimed the familiar tones of impending sex. I undid the button and zipper and then tugged down his jeans, immediately exposing his hardened cock. *No underwear,* I noticed. *How European!*

He reciprocated, unbuttoning and unzipping my shorts. He slid them off to reveal my thong bikini. He didn't remove it yet, instead enjoying the flesh of my ass cheeks with his squeezes while we continued kissing. Eventually, he paused.

"Chain me," he said. "I'll show you what to do."

He took his position on the bed, closed a cuff around his left wrist, then laid on his back. I now had a clear view of his cock, still erect and resting against his lower abdomen. It was modest in size, but aesthetically pleasing like the rest of him. His balls hung pendulous between his widespread legs. "Come," he said. "You can lock my other wrist."

I complied, my hands shaking with anticipation as I did. Or were those nerves? I was stunned by his appeal, but also his unusual requests. "Now tie my ankles," he requested, "Please." I followed his instructions on tying his ankles firmly with the silks. Soon, he was completely immobile and at my mercy. What now?

"Sit on my face," he commanded. I almost laughed. What a request! I started to remove my bikini, but he interrupted me. "No, leave it on for now, please." He certainly knew what he wanted. I imagined he'd done this with women before, but I shook the thought from my mind. *Stay focused*, I told myself, *Don't ruin this.*

I climbed on the bed, straddled his chest, and shimmied my pelvis toward his face. Looking down, I could see only his forehead and eyes, as his face was directly below my crotch. I lowered myself carefully down and then felt the tip of his nose graze the cloth of my thong. "Mmm," he whispered. "Yes." He ran his nose along my slit through the cloth, and I felt the material start to moisten with my juices. "So soft," he said. He traced his tongue along the seam of my bikini so it tickled my skin. I shuddered with growing anticipation. Such a unique situation, and yet such a tempting tease! He started working the cloth of my thong with his mouth, tugging at the material with his lips and then his teeth. It stimulated my own lips, increasing my arousal. I was melting, and I sensed my juices growing thick and gooey. He tugged my bikini aside with his mouth, exposing my pussy directly over his face.

"You're beautiful, Sam," he whispered. He lashed out with his tongue, tasting my well-soaked pussy. "And so delicious." He stroked and massaged my pussy with his tongue, giving equal attention to my vulva and my clit. His tongue penetrated as deep as it would reach, but it left me craving for more. After a couple minutes in this position, he requested a change.

"I want you to turn around," he said.

"Like, how?" I asked.

"Same position, but turned the other way."

I hesitated. Wouldn't that put my asshole on his nose? I realized he must know what he's doing, so I complied.

"Incredible," he said.

I lowered down and felt his mouth resume its affections toward my slit. I felt his nose poke my inner cheeks and briefly graze my anus, and I was instantly self-conscious. *Did I smell?* I wondered. *Oh God, I hope I'm clean!*

In any case, it didn't seem to bother Emilio one bit! He voiced his pleasure frequently, humming and moaning with delight as he continued to lavish attention on my lady parts. "Now, I'll lie still," he said. "I want you to fuck my face."

What?! What did that even mean? How would I – fuck his face? As if reading my mind, he answered.

"Just move how you like," he said. "Sit on me, grind on me. Use me for your pleasure."

Use me for your pleasure? That sounded good to me, but I wondered about Emilio. *Wasn't this degrading? Or – maybe that's the point?* I had a wild thought, wondering if he'd want me to fart in his face. I almost laughed aloud at the absurdity, but who knows if it might be true! Thankfully, he never asked.

I shifted around on Emilio's face, rubbing my genitals and my ass upon his nose, lips, and tongue. I had to proceed carefully, as his stubble tended to chafe. I was also mildly self-conscious. *It's been a long day. Was I even fresh down there?* I already knew I was dripping with lubrication. What did he think of my scent? Did it repulse him, or did it thrill him? The sounds and his words suggested the latter.

"Mmm, yes, baby. Fuck me, fuck my face. You taste so good."

It was exciting and stimulating, but it brought me nowhere near a climax. I may have been too much in my head, or perhaps it was my haphazard technique. Nonetheless, there was a certain satisfaction from having control, writhing upon his face while he was at my mercy.

I noticed his dick had softened from lack of attention. That wouldn't do! I got down on all fours, keeping my pussy pressed against his face and moving my mouth in the direction of his penis. It was limp against his skin, but when I licked it, it lurched to life as if shocked with a defibrillator. I felt Emilio's hot breath against my pussy as he spoke.

"Yes, suck me, baby. Get me hard so you can use me."

We held this sixty-nine position, and I felt his cock lengthen and expand against my tongue, my lips, and the roof of my mouth. He tasted salty but not unpleasant, and I wondered if baths in the ocean were part of his hygiene routine.

"Harder, suck me harder," he begged. This man was a freak! I added force to my movements, sucking harder than I'd ever dared before. I squeezed his cock with my lips and pressed it on the back of my throat. I pushed it between my inner cheek and my teeth, careful not to catch him on a sharp edge. Nothing seemed to satiate him, as he encouraged me further onward. "Oh, God. Punish that cock. Ravish me, Sam. Fuck me harder!" I'll admit, his accent was doing it for me, and I didn't mind his somewhat awkward word choice. But I was losing patience, and the oral stimulation would no longer cut it. I needed his dick in me!

"Fuck, I need this dick in me," I said, stroking his sopping cock with my hand. "Do you have a condom?"

"Yes, whatever you need. Over there in the top drawer." He gestured with his head, and I retrieved a box of flavored condoms from his dresser. Flavored? I pulled out a cherry. This could be fun! Recalling Jenny's technique from last night, I put the tip of the condom between my lips, taking note of the sweet cherry flavor. I climbed beside him on the bed and turned to him with the condom in my mouth. His eyes were wide with excitement. I lowered my mouth to his cock, attempting to unroll it without using my hands. This was tough! I held the base of his cock in one hand to stabilize it and used the other to massage his balls. I had to lock my lips quite firmly around his cock to unroll the condom, but eventually it yielded. I slid his cock deeper into my mouth, breathing softly through my nose and visualizing the expansion of my throat. And it worked! Before I knew it, his entire cherry-flavored dick was in my mouth, my lips just grazing the trimmed hair around his member. *I've never gotten James's cock this deep*, I thought. *Emilio must be a bit smaller.* I held it there as long as I could, perhaps several seconds, before I gagged and withdrew. Saliva ran from my mouth to his dick, and I knew we were lubed up and ready to go.

I took my place cowgirl style over his outstretched body, ready to mount him. *Here goes*, I thought. *My last hurrah.* I lowered down, feeling the tip of his penis brush against my lips before finding my opening and sliding in. He was a comfortable size, and he didn't stretch me like Ethan or Carlos. In no time, my ass and labia made contact with his lap, and he was fully inside of me. I rode his sexy cock slowly at first, but it didn't take much to acclimate to his penis. Soon I was bouncing up and down, creating as much friction as I could, intent on keeping him as deep inside me as possible.

"Use me, Sam," Emilio repeated. "Use me for your pleasure."

I looked into his eyes and admired his features. *Look how hot this man is, and here I am fucking him!* He wore a mischievous smile, and his eyes glistened as if admiring me as well. I felt the urge to kiss him, and I leaned forward to do so, causing his cock to find a new angle, pushing against the back of my vagina. I kissed him, and he kissed me back – but when I closed my eyes, I suddenly thought of James. I yearned for *your* kiss, not his. I wanted your *love*, not his lust. With my eyes closed, I imagined I was with you, being filled by you, being loved, cherished, and possessed by you. *Use me*, Emilio had said, and I *was* using him, using him as a surrogate cock for my husband.

It was a strange mixture of feelings. Eyes open, I could see and admire Emilio's superficial beauty – his rugged features, his chiseled torso, and his wild, flowing hair. Eyes closed, I could feel the marital intimacy I'd been longing for all week. I alternated, my physical attention on him, my emotional attention on you, James. Both combined in a flurry of arousal, and before I knew it, I started to cum.

"Mmm!" I bit my lip, and the name I was suppressing was "James," not "Emilio." What a turn of events! I had called out "Emilio" while getting fucked by Ethan. Now, I nearly called out "James" while fucking Emilio!

Emilio started bucking beneath me, his first contribution to the intercourse. *He really was like a sex toy*, I thought. *A beautiful yet emotionless sex toy, good for physical pleasure but not much else*. I appreciated his effort, as he assisted with maintaining and intensifying my climax. And lo, and behold, he actually started to come along with me!

"Fuck, you're making me come, Samantha!" he announced. He thrusted furiously, his rhythm more irregular as the sensations overcame him. After a minute he relaxed, his orgasm subsiding. I felt the last few pulses of his cock, and I squeezed him with my vaginal muscles for good measure before climbing off his already softening erection.

One climax, I thought. *Good, but not great. He's no James!* Or Carlos or Ethan, for that matter. But it would do. It was still quite nice as a last hurrah.

"That was amazing, Sam," he said through heavy breaths. "Your pussy is fantastic – I couldn't resist!" It was an excuse veiled in a compliment, but I accepted it.

"Yeah, that was really – good," I said. "So, should I unchain you?"

"The key is in the drawer," he said. Near the box of condoms, I found a small handcuff key, and I used it to release the handcuffs before untying his legs.

"Well, thanks," I said. He sat naked on the bed as I started to gather my clothing.

"Wait," he said. "Would you like to continue?"

I paused. He just came – was he already ready for round two? That would be impressive. But I didn't want that. I had used him like he'd asked, and it was fun, but now I was tired and ready to go home, ready to return to my husband.

"No thanks," I said. "Besides, do you really think you can continue?" I glanced at his limp dick, genuinely curious. He suddenly looked shy.

"Well," he said, "Maybe something else." I waited, and he seemed reluctant to go on. "Maybe you could – oh, what is the word?" He furrowed his brow, then started to gesture with his hands. He made one hand into a hole and inserted a finger, which I recognized as the international gesture for sex. I raised an eyebrow. "Ugh," he said, "no, wait." He waved his hands dismissively at his genitals and then pointed at me. He then took his thumb and pantomimed sticking it in his ass. He blushed. "God, what is the word?" he asked.

"Um – pegging?!" I asked. He clapped and pointed to me.

"Yes!" he said. "Pegging!"

Holy cow! I'd heard of pegging, of course, but only as a joke among my girlfriends. It was when a partner, usually a woman, used a strap-on penis to "peg" her man in his ass. Did people actually do that? *Dumb question*, I realized. *Of course some people do. I mean, clearly Emilio did!* I didn't judge him, but it was so far out of my limited experience that I didn't know what to think.

"The next drawer down," Emilio said. "Look in there."

Did I dare? Oh, I dared. I opened the drawer, and there was a bottle of lube and a large, flesh-toned, strap-on penis staring back at me.

"Pick it up," he said. "Don't worry. I clean it after every use."

That was a relief. I picked it up, and it was hefty, rubbery, and large, nearly as long as Ethan, and nearly as thick as Carlos.

"You – you want me to fuck you with this?" I asked.

"I'm *begging* you to fuck me with this," he said. "Please." He got on all fours, offering me his beefy, hairy ass.

It was surreal. A minute ago, I was admiring this man's masculine beauty, and now he was begging me to peg him in the ass! And would I? No, I would not.

"Sorry," I said. "Hard pass."

His face fell like a ton of bricks. I hadn't meant to be rude, but I needed to be clear. I didn't want him to think he could convince me.

"But – but why?" he asked.

"I'm tired," I said, pulling my bikini up to my hips. "And I just don't want to. But thanks for the fun time."

He took a deep breath and half-smiled, accepting his fate. "It was my pleasure," he said. "And I hope for you too."

168

"It was." I walked over and kissed him on the cheek, swiftly, so he wouldn't think to try anything else. He didn't.

We proceeded to get dressed, then cautiously peeked into the living room to not startle or interrupt Jenny and Julian. They were cuddled on the couch under a blanket, seemingly asleep. We woke them up, and Jenny bid goodnight to Julian, giving him a kiss and vowing to see him in the morning before we left the resort. I said goodnight to Emilio as well, but this time with a handshake. He held me warmly once more in his grip, and when he released my hand, we faded from each other's lives for good.

Of course, Jenny grilled me during the car ride back to the resort. "So, tell me all about it," she said.

"Jenny," I began, "THAT WAS REALLY FUCKING WEIRD!"

"What?!" she exclaimed. "Do tell!"

I explained that while Emilio was of course charming and had physical appeal, he was strangely submissive, even groveling in the bedroom. I described chaining him up per his request, as well as his pleas for me to use him like a sex toy.

"Not a bad analogy," Jenny said. "Since it was sex without feelings."

"True," I replied. "It actually felt pretty easy, having sex one more time before going home to James. But I didn't even tell you the craziest part. He wanted me to *peg* him."

Jenny nodded. "Sounds about right."

I expected more of a reaction than that! "You're – not surprised?"

"He just had you chain him to the bed. Pegging isn't *that* much more extreme."

"It isn't?" A thought occurred to me. "Wait – have *you* ever been asked to peg someone?!"

"Maybe," she said.

"And did you?"

"Well, sure! Why not?"

Of course, I should've known. "God, what haven't you tried?" I asked.

"The list is growing short," she admitted. "But you only live once. And, shit, I'll be 30 and married before I know it!"

"So – how was pegging?"

"Kinda fun, actually," she said. "Feels powerful. Must be how a man feels when *he* gets to do the thrusting. It's like – getting your aggression out, in a way."

"You think men fuck out of aggression?" I asked.

"Oh, sure, sometimes," she said. "Some of the best sex I've had was after a fight, or even in the midst of one. But I wouldn't do it with someone I didn't trust."

I reflected. "Do you think James will feel aggressive like that when I'm home?"

"Maybe," she said. "But you trust him, right?"

"Of course!"

"Then if it happens, I'd say go with it! Maybe a good, rough fuck is just what you guys need."

I pulled the car back into the resort. We parked, then enjoyed the cool night air as we walked the verdant path back up to our room. I wasn't quite ready to sleep yet. I had one last story to write before returning home to my love and putting this experiment to rest for good.

Longingly and lovingly,

Samantha

10: Homecomings

James

Sunday, May 19, 2019; 9:07 a.m.

Dear Samantha,
    A haiku:

> A lover on loan,
> Finds mischief then redemption
> Before she comes home.

Another:

> A beautiful girl,
> Explores the pow'r of her sex
> Then tells her husband.

One more:

> A hotwife has fun,
> Too much fun for her own good,
> I think I'll spank her ;)

I bet you thought you were the only poet in the family! You'll have to tell me which was your favorite when you get home today. Safe travels, and tell Jenny thanks from me for being such a great companion.

    Thank you for your final letter, by the way! Rest assured that I was delighted to read it. I especially appreciate you setting boundaries with Emilio, and I'm

171

glad you didn't do anything you were uncomfortable with. Besides – if you ended up pegging a guy, I'd never let you hear the end of it!

On a more serious note, I reflected on your conversation about "aggression" with Jenny. Will I feel sexually aggressive with you? I'm not sure. We have a lot to talk about, and many unknowns about where we go from here. But I do know that I love you immensely, no less than when you left, and I'm committed to keeping our marriage healthy and strong. Will we need counseling, you wondered? I'm not sure, but I'm open. I've been thinking of seeing a therapist myself, but more on that when we're together.

I'm really looking forward to seeing you. I want to be loving and excited only, but a part of me is scared that what happened this weekend will make things feel different. I really won't know until you're here, so please be patient with me, and know I'm striving to be optimistic. I love you, but the healing process is still in its beginnings. You likely have some resentments towards me too, and I encourage you to express them when the time feels right. I want to work through these with you, not just sweep them under the rug.

Wow – I'm sorry the tone of this letter turned so bleak! I'm really not pessimistic at all, I just want to make space for whatever we need to go through as this process moves forward. Maybe I'm overthinking, and everything will be fine. But whatever happens, I'm ready for it, and I'm hoping you are too. I'll be seeing you soon – but never soon enough.

Love,

James

~

Samantha

Our plane home arrived on time, and James picked us up at the airport. He wore sunglasses which concealed his expression. He greeted us each with a hug, and of course I got a peck on the lips.

"Welcome home, baby," he murmured in my ear. Did his hug feel a little bit stiff? Did his kiss feel a little bit cold?

The car ride home felt both cordial and strained, like the oxygen was thin and that breathing didn't quite feel normal. We talked about the trip – the weather, the scenery, the amenities at the resort – but there was a naughty elephant in the room we clearly weren't ready to discuss.

James parked the car in front of our house. We unloaded Jenny's suitcase, and James lugged it to her vehicle which she'd left parked on our driveway. He bid farewell to Jenny, then took my bags inside the house. Jenny gave me a final hug goodbye.

"You guys will be fine," she whispered in my ear. "Don't worry." She kissed me on the cheek, then got in her car. As I watched her drive away, I thought, *There she goes, the best wing woman a girl could ever know.* My swell of gratitude diminished as her car disappeared down the street. I felt strangely abandoned and alone. James was waiting inside, but what would I be walking into? It was time to face him, it was time to face *us*, whatever that might mean. I braced myself and walked through the door.

James was standing in the entryway awaiting me. His sunglasses were off, and I could finally read his expression, warm yet sad. He opened his arms, and I walked into his embrace. We kissed, not a hurried peck this time, but a lovers' kiss, deep, prolonged, and tender. I melted into him, and the emotional barrier faded until I was here with my husband once more, comfortable, familiar, and entwined. Something inside me had been missing all week, and finally things were coming back together.

~

James

I didn't know how we'd proceed when she came back. I'd rehearsed conversations in my head but never found the right words. I expected apprehension, for things to start slow, to talk things out with quivering voices and prolonged silences before deciding what was next. But when we kissed, all voices ceased inside my head, and the jolt to my brain reawakened my love, my passion, and my longing for her. *This is better than talking*, I thought as we kissed. *I'm glad we're doing this instead.*

The kiss went on, our tongues entangling, our lips getting nibbled. An image flashed of her doing this action with shadowy strangers, strangers named Ethan, Emilio, Carlos, Mark, and Dillon. Jealousy surged, and I kissed her harder than ever, now clutching at her body through her clothes. *She's mine*, my mind declared, *I'm reclaiming her.*

I tugged at her clothes, and she instantly gave in, assisting with removing her shirt and then mine. I maneuvered her up against the entryway wall, my bare chest pressed into hers as our kissing continued. My erection was strong and full, and she was determined to unleash it from my khaki shorts. Refusing to end the kiss, she fumbled blindly with my belt and zipper before removing my shorts and underwear in one downward shove. She followed them down onto her knees and held my cock in her hand, examining it like our first time once again, and then looked into my eyes with her own baby blues. I saw love in those eyes, and it comforted yet invigorated me.

~

Samantha

It was like we were possessed. I'd never been so outside of my head, even during sex with James, but the demon took over and my worries fell away. I held his erection in my hand, and it just felt right – the right size, the right shape, the right color – the right man. I kissed his penis. I didn't suck it at first, I kissed it as if making out, and his head was his lips, and his shaft was his tongue. It was an act of love, of *making* love, which had been missing from the sex I'd had throughout the whole past week. I was in love with this cock and the man attached to it.

James moaned. He was usually quiet while receiving blow jobs, but I actually got him to moan. Score! I took him into my mouth, engulfing his penis the best I could. At three-quarters deep, I felt his head press against the back of my throat, and I fought the urge to gag. *Definitely bigger than Emilio's,* I thought.

James was enjoying it. He started gyrating his hips, thrusting his cock gently past my lips and into my throat. I strained to accommodate him, but he started picking up speed until his thrusts were nearly full-force! *He's never been this forceful with me before,* I realized. *Something's come over him.* My ponytail was pressed against the wall, cushioning me against his thrusting blows. I put my hand down the front of my shorts to stimulate myself but also to distract from my impulse to gag. It worked, as when I focused on sensations in my clit, I could ignore the reflex in my throat. James's sounds grew louder, more frequent. Was he about to come? His long strokes shortened to deep vibrations against the back of my mouth. I pushed him back by his hips, forcing his spit-soaked cock out of my mouth.

"Please don't come," I begged. "I need you to fuck me."

~

James

I don't usually come from blowjobs, but I was remarkably close. I'd lost myself to sensations, intent only on scratching this primal itch, abandoning concern for her comfort as I face-fucked her harder than ever before. When I noticed her touching herself, that was the *coup de grâce*, as seeing her so aroused almost put me over the edge. But when she stopped me, when she begged me to fuck her, I knew I had to submit.

My cock tingled with sensitivity, as I was mere moments away from climax when she pushed me away. I held my breath for a second, intent on fading the sensation before it overwhelmed me. I knew I might come the moment I entered her, and I needed to get that under control.

Sam stood up, and I focused on getting her undressed. White shorts – gone. Cute lacy panties – gone. Now I kneeled, breathing in the familiar aroma of my wife's pussy. It was faintly floral – how did she achieve that tantalizing scent after spending the day on a plane? Was it pheromones, or did she spritz something down there like perfume? I'd have to ask her later, as my urge to lick overcame my urge to ask.

She leaned against the wall and spread her legs, granting access to her pink vulva and clit. It was a rush job, I'll admit – I only wanted to moisten her, to ensure that she was lubed enough to take me without too much pain. As I licked, I was interrupted by a thought. *Was that – cherry?* No, it couldn't be. It must be in my mind. It had been over 14 hours since Samantha was fucked with Emilio's cherry condom, and presumably she had showered since then. But still—

I couldn't take it. The mere hint of another man's presence lit a flame within me. She needed *my* scent, not his. I stood, turned her around, and positioned my penis to enter her.

~

Samantha

James was in a beastlike fervor, kissing me roughly, jostling my body, lapping feverishly at my pussy. Was this the aggression Jenny had warned me about? Perhaps this was his way of getting it out, of releasing his anger and frustrations from the previous week. It was gratifying to be wanted so intensely, and I flowed along with it, letting him control me and take what he needed. I adored it, giving myself over to someone I trusted, where I could get out of my head and just live in these sensations. James was outright sloppy, his oral techniques to both mouth and pussy were as unrefined as our very first time, driven by passion and lacking experience. But it was just as exciting as our first, like a *new* first, our first time together after an eternity apart and a world of experiences in between.

When he stood and turned me to face the wall, I winced, expecting a rough entry into my delicate little pussy. But when I heard him spit and then felt his moistened tip press against my labia, I thought, *He* does *care about me after all!* The lubrication helped but a little, as James entered me like a battering ram, lacking his usual tenderness. But could I blame him? I was grateful to be thick with lubrication, but still it felt raw, less seamless than when he would put it in slowly, spreading my juices comfortably through me. One quick thrust and he was buried to the hilt, and I cried out with pleasure and shock. I braced my forearms against the wall and pressed my forehead against them, arching my back and pushing my ass out as far as I could to open myself up to him. He pulled back and thrust once more, equally hard, and I cried out again.

"Yeah," he seethed. "Take it, baby. Give me that pussy, give it back to me."

He increased speed, pounding his bare cock furiously into my defenseless pussy. I couldn't believe it – he'd never been so dominant before! The unprecedented tempo excited us both, as we both began to come much sooner than usual. He grunted, and his cock started to pulse as he spilled his seed deep within my pussy. It was more than usual, and I sensed his warm semen spread throughout my vagina as he continued thrusting, just as vigorous as ever.

~

James

No! I thought. *Not this early!* But I couldn't help it. I had never been a one-minute man, but today was something different and new. My instincts took over, intent on filling my wife with my cum, intent on replacing the cocks of her lovers, especially Ethan, who came inside her despite our rules.

My orgasm was bigger and stronger than usual, and based on her reaction, Sam's was too. She bucked her hips back against me, as if craving more. *More?* came the angry voice in my head. *She wants more? More time, more size, more orgasms like the others had given her?* I continued thrusting, my cock staying hard. *Was this not enough? She desires more?* I envisioned her being fucked in this position by her suitors, by Carlos with the dick that stretched her wide, or by Ethan who fucked her deeper than I could reach. *Is this a trick of the mind, or does her pussy feel – looser?* It couldn't be. Fucking big dicks wouldn't loosen her pussy, would it? *It must be my imagination,* I reasoned. *Or my cum is acting like lube, creating less friction and the illusion of looseness.* But the devil on my shoulder whispered, *But what if it's true? What if she's thinking about them right now? What if she's lusting for them?*

It was this devil that spurred me onward, giving me second strength. I turned Sam around, causing my dick to slide out of her, and saw a bewildered look in her eyes. I kissed her again, willing her to think about me and only me. My dick was pressed against her hips, and while making out, I directed it between her legs and up to her gently parted lips which dripped with my cum already. I was going in for round two.

$$\sim$$

Samantha

His orgasm surprised me, but I didn't mind. I was flattered and excited that his lust for me hadn't gone away, and in fact it may have flourished. It sparked a climax of my own, which was enhanced by the intimacy of his warm cum and continued thrusting. When he turned me around – that surprised me too. His brows were furrowed with intensity, and his piercing eyes bore into my soul. *Was this – not over?* Usually, sex ended the moment he came, as his energy was depleted the moment he was drained of cum. But today a fire raged within him, and his erection wouldn't be tamed. He kissed me, not the tender post-sex gratitude kiss, but the pre-sex, mid-sex, passionate kiss.

His cock pressed against the bottom of my labia, rubbing against my still-moistened slit. He persisted with his kiss, pulling my breasts against his chest and groping the flesh of my ass, spreading my cheeks. He then placed his hands under my thighs and lifted me, pressing my back against the wall for support. His cock found the opening of my pussy once more and slipped pleasantly inside of me. Amidst these maneuvers, he never once broke our kiss. He held me under my thighs while thrusting up inside of me. I gripped him for support, hugging my arms around his neck and wrapping my legs around his hips. My back bumped against the wall, but I ignored it, attending instead to the overwhelming sensations inside my pussy. It was like my first orgasm never went away, and wave after wave of aftershocks surged through me. I whimpered at times but never cried out, intent on preserving our love-sealing kiss. It stretched on for many pleasurable minutes, and I never wanted it to end, until—

~

James

It wasn't enough – I wasn't going to come in this position. I broke the kiss, and I withdrew my cock from her pussy. This wasn't right – our relationship was so much more than impulsive, animal sex in our hallway. I withdrew, then shifted her body so she was cradled in my arms. Her head rested on my shoulder as I carried her to our bedroom – to our marriage bed. She was silent, and I felt her wide eyes watching my expression as I whisked her away – fueled by passion and a rush of adrenaline. I brought her in our room then laid her gently on the bed.

"I love you, Sam," I whispered.

"I know," she replied. "And I love you, too."

I climbed atop her in missionary, our most cherished position. It was tried and true – not wild, not fancy, but it was us. She spread her legs for me, and I pushed my cock inside her once more. I worked my thrusting to a steady pace, comfortable, familiar. It was like the thousand times we'd made love before, and I prayed the next thousand would be as intimate as this. I didn't even need to increase my speed, the perfection of her pussy was all the sensation I needed. I kissed her lips, then kissed her neck. After a few more moments of uncomplicated bliss, we came together once more. I was softening already when I finally withdrew, and I rolled over to my spot on our bed. We each were catching our breath when I found her hand and held it tightly in mine.

~

Samantha

It was a nice touch, a calming and comforting end to an unexpectedly wild adventure. Our lovemaking had paralleled the entire previous week and led to a proper and satisfying conclusion – exactly how it should be. I came home longing for things to feel familiar, and eventually, they had. If this was a sign of things to come, I was encouraged. I didn't know where things would go next, but I had hope, and that's what mattered.

Epilogue

James

Dear reader,

This is the part of the story where Samantha and I discuss what we have learned. As I write this, it's been almost a year since Samantha's grand adventure – and I'm pleased to say that we're still together and happy. Saving our relationship took some hard work, however, and personal therapy for each of us, but that's a story for another time perhaps. Suffice it to say, our love is going strong, and I might even call our experiment a success.

But what did I learn? Well, I learned more about my relationship, for one, including what it can endure. I knew I loved Sam of course, but you never know how a relationship will withstand a test of adversity until you've been through it. Can it withstand jealousy? Yes. Can it withstand some physical and emotional infidelity? It can, as long as we are honest, have empathy, amend our mistakes, and learn to forgive. We came out stronger, and our sex life has never been better. I can't get enough of my Sam – knowing she's desired by many yet mine, and mine alone. Every night in the bedroom is like reclaiming her anew, and I fuck with more vigor, more creativity than I used to. Lacking experience when we met, our sex life certainly benefited from this cheeky little jolt – and we're both left more satisfied than ever.

On that note, I also learned more about my kink – that is, my arousal by thinking of my wife with different men. Here I'll discuss the "what" of my kink, though I'll keep the "why" between myself and my therapist for now. As for the "what" – I think it starts at feeling arousal and pleasure by considering my wife's arousal and pleasure. I'm not so naïve to think she can only be turned on by me, and while social and psychological constructs keep her faithful, it was exciting to remove those barriers and consider where her sex drive would lead her. If she had sex with other men and it was not enjoyable for her, I'm certain it would not be enjoyable for me, so her pleasure is a necessary condition. There's also the jealousy, of course, of her being with another man – which amplifies my drive to be with her, to reclaim her, to possess her, and to dominate her. It recalls my "caveman" fantasy, imagining another man inseminating my wife, and feeling the carnal urge to cast out his seed in lieu of my own. I've discovered the term "sperm competition" – the idea that in promiscuous species, if two males copulate with a female, the male with stronger sperm will pass forth his genes. It's like the planned infidelity awakens that in me, an instinctual urge to sexually compete.

Regarding the rule violations with Ethan: of course, that hurt a great deal. And yet, it was one of the most exciting and arousing parts of Sam's stories! She was so overcome by lust and obedience that she couldn't help but give in, despite knowing at heart the possible consequences. There's a reason promiscuity can be arousing (note that the term "slutwife" sometimes replaces "hotwife") – it signals insatiable arousal, the prioritization of pleasure over risk. Don't get me wrong, I wouldn't want her to do that again, and the risks were not worth the rewards. For one, we risked sexual infections (though we both tested negative, thank God!). And for another, it damaged the trust between us, not only due to Sam's breaking of the rules, but due to my reaction of making a pass at a coworker. No, cheating is off the table in the future, regardless of how arousing it might be.

In addition to the excitement of her wanting, I also enjoy her being wanted. I'm proud that my wife is a head turner, and the thought of men pursuing her is gratifying. This is especially true when the pursuers are desirable themselves, men that Samantha would consider appealing. I wanted men to want her, and while I let them have her in a physical sense, they'd never get what I had with her emotionally – her devotion, her companionship, her love. They'd always remember the time they had with Samantha, but I'd have my time with her again and again.

Would I try the experiment again? I don't know. I haven't so far. It would take a long talk with Samantha and substantially more planning before we'd even consider it. I haven't felt the hunger for it yet – although, on some occasions, I'll ask her to recount a tale to me in bed, or I'll reread one of her stories while she is away. During sex, I'll admit, I sometimes channel that old aggression brought on by thinking of her past lovers, and it'll spark a powerful orgasm, for both of us if I'm lucky.

I tried to read more into the hotwife kink, nervous that the desire might grow into something more destructive. Sadly, there's little reading material out there, and most information resides in internet forums filled with testimonials rather than peer reviewed research. Some men have discussed how their kink lives escalated, how they started with an open relationship and evolved to requesting photos and videos of their hotwives with their "studs," who are usually more attractive men with larger penises. Next, they wish to watch the hotwife have sex live, either with the stud aware or while hiding in a closet or behind a hidden camera. Expansions of the fantasy involve the man being verbally humiliated by the hotwife, the stud, or both, as they ridicule his body, his genital size, or his impotence. It usually ends in makeup sex between the husband and wife, with or without additional humiliation.

Much of this seemed beyond what I could ever desire. Maybe a photo or video would be exciting, but I'd never want her to humiliate me. It infuriated me to hear Ethan belittle me while fucking Sam – but did it also stoke my arousal? The notion was unsettling. The arousal of humiliation could never outweigh the shame of it – at least, I'm pretty sure of it.

So, I think that's why I've repressed this interest for the past year. I'm afraid of where it might lead and the collateral damage it could do to my relationship with Sam. A sexual kink can become an obsession, and I wouldn't want to fan those flames. And yet, I still wonder. Does Sam fantasize about those men from last year? Does she now fantasize about men she sees on the street, meets at work, or passes at the gym? Dare I ask? Would she tell me the truth? Does she wonder what they're packing in their shorts, like she did in that yoga class last year? Does she take a peek? Would she want to be with them if I let her?

I may have opened Pandora's box, and I hope I have the will to keep it contained. Writing this down, like therapy, has been a pressure release valve, helping me suppress, to sublimate those feelings. I'm determined to move on, to let the fantasy live in memory alone. I think I'm satisfied. I think I have enough – for now.

~

Samantha

Dear reader,

You probably thought only James got to use that opener, right? Wrong! This is my chance to finally talk to *you* and tell you what I learned from my wild, erotic adventure.

First, a few non-sexual updates. My relationship with James is as powerful as ever. After the trip, our passion was renewed, and we were more determined than ever to show our love and commitment. It's altered our sex life, and in fact, it's enlivened it – but more or that later. We ultimately decided against couples counseling, but we both enrolled in personal therapy. It's wonderful, and I recommend it.

Next an update on Jenny. She's still in touch with Julian, but she's yet to actually see him again. It's basically a long-distance "situationship" – more than a fuck buddy, less than a relationship. They're still quite fond of each other, but given the distance and their circumstances, they haven't made any commitments. Jenny still goes on dates here in America, and Julian is free to sow his wild oats in Mexico. Perhaps they'll reunite someday, but I doubt it, and I think they're mostly content with where they are.

Now for what I learned. First, I learned the value of a true best friend and wing woman.

Jenny is the only reason my adventure was possible, as without a friend of her caliber, who knows what could have happened to me on my trip. Ladies, if you're out hunting for a hot new date, never go on the prowl without backup. Not only did Jenny keep eyes on my safety, but she made sure *I* didn't do anything foolish – for the most part. Pardon the PSA, but please find yourselves a Jenny in your life, and always let them know where you are and who you're with if you're entering a risky situation.

Second, I learned more about my relationship with James – what we're willing to do for each other, and what we're able to endure. Growing up in a conservative home, I'd never considered the idea of an open relationship. A woman was meant to love, marry, and have sex with just one man her entire life. I'd followed this tenet to a tee, marrying my first love while I was young and not exploring sex with anyone else. It was working, as I love James very much and never felt compelled to be with anyone else. But I was willing to open my mind for James's sake and to indulge his fantasy to make him happy. Of course, I reaped my own benefits as well, but at the end of the day, my adventure was more for him than for me. We make sacrifices for love – and I expanded my comfort zone to please my man.

We also learned lessons in trust and forgiveness. My actions with Ethan were major rule violations, and I had equally major regrets. I shouldn't have been so vulnerable, I shouldn't have given in. And yet I did. I'm glad I came clean, as honesty was the only way to clear my conscience and seek forgiveness from James. Had I been dishonest, the guilt would've eaten away at me, consumed me, until I was a shell of myself around my own husband.

You see, in relationships, secrets lead to more secrets, and honesty sets you free. If you can't trust your partner with hearing the truth, then you can't trust your partner. The truth hurt James and led to a transgression of his own, but it gave us a chance to learn from it, heal through it, and grow stronger in response.

Third, I learned more about my own sexuality. By trying out new partners, I expanded my sexual experiences by sampling men with different bodies, different personalities, and different sexual interests. Variety is the spice of life, and sampling a new lover can be quite tasty. A steady lover grows predictable, but someone new – you'll never know what they might do! Or what they're packing in their shorts.

To that point – a few comments on dick size. I've tried to explain this to James, as it's one of his keener fascinations. Does James have a monster dick? No. Did Carlos and Ethan have monster dicks? I'd say yes. And yes, that was a – large – part of their appeals. But getting fucked by a really big dick is like – riding a rollercoaster. You get hyped for it. It's thrilling, it's intense, and a little bit scary. It can feel fun and amazing, but if it isn't done right, it can jostle you about and feel really uncomfortable. James taught me a couple modern terms that he learned from the Internet – "vacation dick" and "boyfriend dick." In this case, they're completely apt. From Urban Dictionary, "vacation dick" is a large dick that might be fun to have for a brief duration, like during a vacation or a one-night stand. "Boyfriend dick" is a nice but moderately-sized dick that is enjoyable and won't wear you out from long-term usage. James has the ideal boyfriend (or husband) dick for me. To coin my own metaphor, I'd refer to "vacation dick" as "rollercoaster dick," whereas "boyfriend dick" is more like "sports car dick." A sports car dick is a smooth ride that's dependable. It's ideal for your daily enjoyment, as you can coast comfortably along beachside highways with the top down, or you can throttle it up a notch as needed. Do I like roller coasters? Of course! Can I go the rest of my life without riding one? Definitely. Would I give up my sports car to ride a rollercoaster every day? No way. So in conclusion, I'm completely satisfied with my sports car parked at home. And while I may dream about roller coasters on occasion, I won't be seeking one anytime soon!

In related news, James bought me a new toy this year! It's a large rubber dildo he initially tried to name "Ethan." Ha. Ha. I warned him never to call it that, or I'd shove "Ethan" up his butt. Occasionally, James brings out the dildo and wants to use it on me. I usually let him, and after a few minutes, James will ditch the toy and service me himself. He seems to enjoy using it, and he's usually pretty riled up by the time he gets his turn. I think he's more interested in the dildo than I am – though I'll admit, I have used it a few times on my own when James is away.

Fourth, James and I both learned some new techniques for the bedroom. Admittedly, things had been getting routine between James and me, so spicing things up was a welcome change. In addition to toys, we now include face fucking (from Julian and Ethan), face sitting or "queening" (from Emilio), sex while I'm lifted off the ground (from Carlos), and improved hand play (from Dio). He's even eaten my asshole once or twice, and I've shown him how I can place a condom using only my mouth. We've also gotten a book on sexual positions, though only a handful of those are winners.

I now should address the burning question that's in all the readers' minds, I'm sure. Would I be open to another erotic adventure? Honestly, the thought makes me uneasy, and as we learned, the joys come with many risks. We have no current plans to open our marriage again on either end. James has joked about bringing another woman for a threesome, but he's insisted he isn't serious. We've discussed once or twice, hypothetically, what it might look like if we tried our experiment again. These talks took place on the phone while James was out of town for work, and I'm pretty sure he was masturbating at the thought of it.

We started by saying it wouldn't be while I was away from him again. The distance was unbearable and made us feel more – distant, emotionally. I understand what James was going for – he didn't want to be the one pulling the strings, as he wanted my choices to be mostly my own. But I think if we ever try this again, he and I would need to plan things together and debrief immediately after each affair.

And where would we find the men? James suggested the internet, after a careful vetting process. We can make sure they're clean, sane, and willing to follow whatever parameters we set. James also suggested vetting their dick sizes, but I assured him that item is lower on my list! However, he also pointed out that finding men on the internet reduces the spontaneity of meeting a person in public, getting wooed, and taking a chance with getting frisky, so that idea fizzled and burned.

He then suggested meeting men in bars, which I refused to do, or clubs, which was only slightly more appealing. We realized that when it comes to something casual, vacation sex – especially resort sex – has some advantages. You see, when you're on vacation, people are down to have fun and understand that there are no strings attached. You're often relaxed, and the flirtation can be fueled by liquor, as well as the willingness to take risks. You also know a few things about the person right off the bat, including that they're put-together enough to organize a nice vacation, and they have a decent, nearby room to use if things go well. They needn't come to your private residence, which can be dangerous, and you needn't to go to their private residence, which can be even more dangerous. And when the vacation is over, they're gone, presumably hundreds or thousands of miles away. No stalkers, no late-night requests for booty calls, just wham, bam, thank you, ma'am (or sir).

The final idea we discussed was having James meet a potential suitor in person with me. For example, if I met someone attractive at work or at the gym, I could invite them out to meet my husband for approval before we "did the deed." Likewise, James and I could go out together, locally or on vacation, and solicit someone who might be interested in sleeping with me with James's permission. James was opposed – he said this felt too close to cuckoldry, and he had no desire to face the man about to fuck his wife, to compare himself in person, or to be belittled. Besides, he reasoned, if he were around, why wouldn't I just sleep with him? That conversation stalled fast, and the fantasies died around there.

So, in conclusion, I don't foresee more stories coming out like this one. James and I are happy, and the memories and fantasies appear to be enough. But who knows – the original idea grew like a weed, and the seed of a new one has not yet died away. I still may ride a rollercoaster again. And if I do, I'll be glad to share the experience.

With warmest regards,

Samantha

Printed in Dunstable, United Kingdom

81825996R00112